Yvy DeLuca is a writer, performer and activist. Yvy is the author of *Tainted Beauty – The Memoir of an Authentic Creation*, telling the story of her experiences as a South Asian transgender woman. She also performs as *The BollyWitch*, blending Bollywood culture and witchcraft to create performance art. She currently resides in Salford, with her husband, Jack, and their two cats, Nyssa and Pirlo.

For Zohra, the strongest woman I will ever know.

Yvy DeLuca

YVOLVED

The Memoir of a Tainted Beauty

love,
Ydelien 97x

AUSTIN MACAULEY PUBLISHERS™

LONDON ∗ CAMBRIDGE ∗ NEW YORK ∗ SHARJAH

A CIP catalogue record for this title is available from the British Library.

ISBN 9781398451537 (Paperback)
ISBN 9781398451544 (ePub e-book)

www.austinmacauley.com

First Published 2023
Austin Macauley Publishers Ltd®
1 Canada Square
Canary Wharf
London
E14 5AA

Prologue

Hiyas! For those who know me from reading my first book, welcome back! It's great to have your hands all over me again! For those who have no idea who I am or what I'm about, let me be the first to say…rude!

No, wait, I'm only teasing. If you don't know who I am, my name is Yvy (that's pronounced 'ee-vee'; trust me, it helps if I explain it to you in the long run). A little summary about me. I'm Indian. I'm trans. I'm fabulous. Now, for the next number of pages, you're going to learn a little something about me, about life and maybe even something about yourself. It may seem that I've got my life together, given that I can so openly say that I am a trans woman of colour, but that's not the case. It's taken a lot for me to get to where I am. So much so that I couldn't fit it all into my first memoir.

And so here we are. Once again, I'm not here to tell you how to live your life. I'm simply here to speak a truth that we as Desi Queer people seldom get the opportunity to do so. We all have a story to tell, so when life gives you an opportunity to tell it, you should. The story continues…

Chapter One
Blackburn, 1999

I lay in bed, knowing that today was the day I was going to do something so drastic, so final. I looked at the mini alarm clock that Feroza claimed through collecting an abundance of Benson & Hedges vouchers, and saw that it was just past 8:00 am. I didn't want to go through with it. I was starting to have second thoughts. *Should I go through with it? Will it be worth it?* I mean, up until now I had endured it all, but when does the time come when enough is enough and you have to take back control? That time was now.

I willed myself out of bed, quietly rolling out of my bottom bunk so as not to wake my brother, Fareed. I always tried to avoid waking him up on the off chance that he awakened in a bad mood. As I lifted off the bed, the metal coils retracted under the thin mattress, causing the whole bed to shriek like rusty wind chimes that had been disturbed by a sharp breeze. I looked up and saw his face, firmly planted in a pillow stained with spit. Then again, I'm one to talk. I may have had nice sheets but the pillows look like they'd gone through a decade in a skip. The curtains were still drawn, blocking out the morning light, but I knew my way around our bedroom like a carefully planned maze. Every obstacle, every creaky floorboard under the royal blue carpet was imprinted in my brain. Before long, I was out of the bedroom, Fareed still sound asleep. I looked out the window just outside our bedroom door and saw that it was a beautiful day. A Saturday. The day I was waiting to finally come. I had made my decision and my decision was final. *I'm going through with it.*

Standing in the bathroom, I barely recognised myself. I was so sick of being taunted, harassed, humiliated. I mean, what the fuck is so fascinating about me that generates so much attention? Are the people at Pleckgate High School so intrigued by me that they don't know how to act around me? Or is it that they simply don't like me? The freak. The khusra. The gay. I fucking hate that expression. *The* gay. Like I'm the only one in the whole damn school. They know fuck all about me. What's infuriating is that girls can walk around with their skirts rolled up, with glossy lipstick and perfect hair, and the boys don't say shit to them. It's as if beauty and popularity is all that fucking matters. But dare to act like yourself, and you're done for. I'm tired of being myself. I'm tired of being tired. I want all of this to be over. I'm going to do it today.

I was going to ask Mum to help me do it, but decided not to this time. She helped in the past but this time I felt like I had to do it on my own. This was my choice. I mean, if this is really what I wanted to do, I didn't want this moment to be tainted with other people trying to talk me out of it. I had already made my mind up and in all honesty, I was beyond caring what anybody thought.

After getting dressed and saying my goodbyes to Mum, I left the house and started my journey. Walking down Shear Bank Road, the steep, declining hill made my pace unsteady. I listened to the rustling of the looming trees that shielded the sun from touching the grey pavement as I made my way into town. I always preferred Shear Bank to Shear Brow because of its privacy, its emptiness. Shear Brow was on the other side of the street that I lived on in Blackburn, but was much more exposed and busier with traffic. They both led into town, but although walking down Shear Bank took slightly longer; I didn't care. It gave me a little bit more time to myself, to collect my rattling thoughts and take in the quiet. Once I made it to Preston New Road, all the quiet I was enjoying soon vanished. Car after car drove along the busy road and soon enough, I was in town and standing at my intended location. *This is it.*

By now you're probably thinking 'what the fuck is she going on about?' First of all, thank you for using the correct pronouns (and never be afraid to ask respectfully if you're ever unsure). Secondly, this was a very big day for me. To put things into context, it was the 1990s and I was sporting the signature curtain hairstyle that most teenage males were rocking at the time. My thick, Indian hair never rested on my head the way I wanted it to, and so, before I transitioned into the beautiful woman I am today (and learnt about the miracle of GHD straightening irons), I had to rely on a nocturnal routine of sleeping on my hair in a desperate attempt to keep my thick waves from being so prominent.

All I wanted was to have beautiful hair. I mean, I had dreamt of it ever since I was a child, when I would put a jumper on my head like a perfectly styled lace front wig. Although my attempt to straighten my hair when sleeping didn't quite have the desired outcome, it was enough to get me through most of the school day before the waves and kinks started showing. That is, unless it was rainy or windy outside. I wish that was the only reason why I had decided to cut my hair off, but there was a lot more to it. I suppose for many of us, our hair is a huge part of us. Whether you have long hair or don't have much at all, it's still one of the first things people notice. Some of us, myself included, see our hair as an extension of ourselves while others don't really think much about it. The funny thing is, the people who say they don't care about their hair often don't want to make any changes. That in itself tells you that a lot more people see their hair as a part of their personal reflection than they even realise.

I stared across the street at the barbers, Passerini's. I had never entered Passerini's before in my life. I always had my mum, Zohra, cut my hair. I just couldn't face it. I imagined it being a fortress of tough men looking at walls covered in bare-breasted women and roasting every newbie that sat in their chairs. In short, it was a man's world. For as long as I could remember, I always gravitated to anything feminine. I didn't know I was transgender at the time, but I knew for sure that I wasn't a man. I didn't want to associate myself with being a man.

However, school was becoming unbearable. All the taunts about my hair were getting out of hand. Funny, that all the taunts and laughs were coming from other Asian kids. I mean, can I not even fit in with my own culture? Why was having curtains such an issue when there was about a hundred other people in Pleckgate with the same haircut as me? I just didn't understand. I knew I had to go in Passerini's and face my fear. *Just go in and get your hair cut. Look like everybody else. It's easier that way.*

I pushed the door open and entered the waiting area. It wasn't a large room, and had a few seats lining the walls. The walls were dull and had old posters of what looked like hairstyles from *Happy Days*. Against the window were two arcade games. I peered through the open entrance to see a few barber chairs and suddenly I heard a booming voice coming from inside.

''Ave a seat, son. Be with you in a sec.'

Oh God! Already I could feel my skin peeling off and my skeleton trying to escape. *He just called me 'son'.* I sat down, listening to the intro music to Mortal Kombat blaring from the arcade machine. I watched as Sub-Zero kicked the crap out of Liu Kang and then sever his head and spinal cord from his body. *Oddly comforting.*

'Alright, son! Your turn!'

I had to bring myself back from the Netherrealm and face reality. I walked into the barber's area and found, to my horror, that I was dead on with how I imagined it would be. It was as if I had somehow walked into my imagination with the dense, macabre soundtrack of Mortal Kombat adding to the terror that was a man's world.

'Get in the chair, lad.'

I looked at the barber and the three other men stood across the room. I didn't know how to act. *Should I be manly or should I just be myself?*

'Hello!' I said with a wimpy wave. The men all looked at me and then looked at each other. *Oops, bad move. Butch it up!*

'What's it gonna be then, son?'

'Errrm.' I didn't know what to say. Sitting on the faux leather chair, the barber threw a white sheet around my neck and awaited my instruction.

'Short back n' sides, is it?' he asked impatiently.

'I guess so.'

'You sure, lad?'

I wasn't sure if I had a choice. The way this guy just assumed a short back and side haircut was what I wanted, I assumed that was pretty much the only haircut he was able to accomplish, other than possibly the greasy Fonz hairdo that was plastered on the wall in the waiting room.

'Yeah, but not too short.'

'I'll give you a number two, then.'

'Umm, okay.' I just pretended I knew what a number two haircut was. Maybe the hairstyles he did were numbered, like when you order off a Chinese takeaway menu.

I looked around the room and saw an array of topless photos of newspaper models, with a few smaller pictures of Max Power girls bent over cars with their unusually large breasts resting on the hoods. I didn't know where to place my eyes. I didn't like looking at women in this setting. I knew that all the men were objectifying them. I never thought at the time that it could be seen as empowering for a woman to be so positive about her body, showing it off in ways that she chooses. Instead, I felt more protective of these women on the walls. I looked at each one and saw that they were plastered on the wall for nothing more than to be ogled by a bunch of sweaty men who couldn't care less about who the women were or what she was all about. It was purely about tits.

I looked in the mirror in front of me to try and keep my eyes focused. Thankfully, the mirror reflected the waiting room. I could see the side of the arcade machine peeking out from the door frame. As the barber grabbed a chunk of my hair and started cutting and razoring, I felt shivers going down my spine. With every snip, I felt a part of me fall away. I knew I was making a mistake by coming here, but I had to prove to the world that I could do it. I should just be the boy I keep being told I'm supposed to be. *I am a boy. I must be. I have to be.*

'All done, lad.'

I looked in the mirror and I wanted to scream. I saw a skinny Asian boy staring at me. His skin was blotchy with spots. His ears were small and nose slightly large. His hair was completely shaved at the sides and a patch of hair sat on the top of his head like a top hat. *Is that really me?* I stood up as the barber took the white sheet off of my shoulders and paid him the three quid it cost to take away the last remaining external resemblance of the person I related to and made my way out. As I walked past the arcade machine, a low booming voice sounded.

FLAWLESS VICTORY.

***

I would say I'm a very complex person. Then again, who the Hell isn't? We all have those moments in our lives that for some reason stick in our minds. Even something small like getting your hair cut can somehow embed itself into your brain and surface the moment you are ready to understand what you're supposed to learn from it. Over the years I learnt to adapt and understand what it meant to be me, but I still had so much more to learn. For a while I thought I didn't need to learn anything because I was in a better place than I had been only a few years before. That's the tricky thing with the old noggin, it can proper mess you up when you least seimaerdemosemmig—sorry, Pirlo just put his big cat paws on my keyboard. What I meant to say was, it can proper mess you up when you least expect it.

With that said, nobody is expected to have to deal with every single little memory that creeps up. Not every thought has to have a lesson to learn. Most of the time, a memory can simply be a memory. Often a memory can leave you feeling a certain way, whether it be happy or sad, but if that feeling doesn't leave you and starts to carry into other areas of your life, that's when you should pay a bit more attention as to why that particular moment in your life still resonates.

Sitting in that barber's chair, I felt exposed. I was a fraud who had entered a masculine world. A world I had no place trespassing in. I mean, that's how it felt at school every time I did something remotely masculine. My all-time fear in high school was P.E. For me, P.E was the only subject in school that set the binary boundaries so ferociously that it felt as though it had nothing to do with exercise or getting healthy, and everything to do with dictating what a boy should be doing and what a girl should be doing. Boys play football, now do it! That's how it felt to me. I was forced to participate in a sport I hated, not because I hated football, but because of what I was made to believe it meant. I'd see the girls doing P.E and wished I could be with them. Instead, I was made to stand on a field and attempt to kick a ball around without embarrassing myself. Of course, I failed miserably, and looking back I bet I looked like the most femme queer trying to kick a ball around without dirtying my white polo t-shirt and shorts. When I think of it that way, it does sound kind of cute!

When I got home from Passerini's, I went upstairs to Feroza's room. My big sister's bedroom was where I spent a lot of my time when I was at home before Mum gave me the front room downstairs and I stopped sharing a bedroom with Fareed. The three of us were all so different from each other. But I got on with Feroza the most. I walked in and saw Feroza's face as she checked out my new hair style.

'Bloody hell, Sal,' she said. 'I can't believe you really did it!'

Neither could I to be honest. The moment I heard the buzzing of the clippers as they made contact with my scalp, I had a flash of the moment when I made the decision to cut my hair. I was sat in Maths class, bored out of my skull. Nilufar, an Asian girl I sat next to, was a nice enough person but I didn't really have much to do with her in school. I didn't have much to do with anybody really. She was petite, with a short, black bob. She rarely had anything interesting to talk about and always seemed to be slightly awkward around me, as if she had something important to say to me but never actually said it.

'What's the formula for this again?' She asked.

'I have no idea; I'm as lost as you are.'

Nilu let out a giggle, which then made me laugh. We got on well during class, but never really spoke at any other time at Pleckgate. Mr Garrett, our Maths teacher, looked up from his textbook to find us giggling. He gave us a stern gaze and went back to addressing the class. Nilu and I started whispering to each other and couldn't help but laugh again. This time, we couldn't keep the volume to a mere giggle and I let out an uncontrollable high-pitched sound in a failed attempt at holding back my hysterics.

'SALEEM!' Mr Garrett boomed, sending a shockwave through me. 'See me after class. You as well, Nilufar.'

The whole class was looking at us with judgemental glares. You'd think they would've been happy that someone had caused a fuss in class to steer it away from having to learn equations, but instead the vibe I was getting from everyone was one of annoyance. It felt like because it was me, they were pissed off. I've seen plenty of other students cause a scene in class and the rest would find it hilarious, but not when I did it, no, when I do it, they don't like it. They already think I'm a freak, so who wants to listen to one in class? That's how it always felt.

When class was done, Nilu and I stayed back while the rest of the students left for lunch. I was so hungry, my stomach tied in knots. I wasn't too bothered about what Mr Garrett had to say. He was creepy and unsettling in his own way, which made it hard to take him seriously.

'I'm not going to tolerate this behaviour again,' he said, his face stern and unhinged.

'We won't,' I said, trying to keep the conversation to a minimum so I could get the hell out of class and stuff myself with chips and beans.

'Good. It's not fair on the others, Nilufar, and you shouldn't be holding up the class.'

'I'm Nilufar,' Nilu spoke up. I looked up, realising that Mr Garrett was in fact addressing me as Nilufar. *The prick doesn't even know who I am.*

'Oh, well, you both look so similar with your girly hair. Now, I'll see you both on Thursday.'

I was in shock. Did Mr Garrett actually say that I had girly hair? That means he's seen me that way all this time. *Girly Boy.* If this were ten years later, I would have been thrilled for someone to mistake me for a girl. But in that moment, it hit me in my sixteen-year-old face like a sudden punch. It's one thing being called all sorts from my fellow students, but when my teacher actually called me a girl to my face for having "girly hair", well, that was the last straw.

What will it take for people to leave me alone? I was tired of being judged by how I looked. Plenty of white boys in school had curtains. Why was it such an issue for me to have the same hairstyle? Am I not worthy of having slightly longer hair? I loved having longer hair. Even though I was still secretly putting my long-sleeved tops on my head in my bedroom when Fareed was out and pretending to have flowing locks of hair, I liked that a tiny part of that feeling stayed with me. I could look at my hair and imagine it growing longer and longer, flowing all around me. I'd imagine braiding it into a beautiful Indian hairstyle. However, the moment I stepped into school, the students were savage with their taunts. It just never let up.

The moment Mr Garett called my hair girly, I'd had enough. One thing I always did in life when things were going badly was pull away. I became invisible, or at least I wanted to be invisible. To go unnoticed. As I made my way out of school for the long walk up Pleckgate Road and home for lunch, I pushed past all the students in my way. I saw the gang of Asian boys standing near the front of the school. They all turned towards me after one of them alerted the rest of my approach. I walked past, holding tightly on to my rucksack, trying not to make eye contact.

'Eh, khusra! Nice hair. GIRL!'

They all burst into vicious laughter as they continued the joke. My cheeks were burning red as I pushed for the exit.

'Khusra! Khusra!'

I stopped in my tracks. My head slowly raised until I was staring at the reflection behind me in the glass on the school entrance door. My burgundy rucksack slowly slid off my shoulder and I unzipped the top compartment. The boys were still behind me, shouting their inane taunts. Suddenly, I turned, pulling out two steel blades. I looked at them all straight in the eyes and leapt into the air. My legs were bent with precision and as I descended towards the ground, I flipped the blades to reveal a set of razor sharp fans. *MORTAL KOMBAT!*

One by one, I tore those motherfuckers up limb from limb, dodging every worthless punch and kick they attempted to make. With each swift move, I swung my fans in their direction like a boomerang, watching their blood splatter across the school walls and their heads roll in the air. The last boy, the one who alerted the rest to my presence, was the only one standing. He stood there, whimpering, staring at me with fear. I walked towards him and as I looked to my left and caught a glimpse of myself in the school reception desk window, I saw a beautiful woman, dressed in royal blue, and long, long waves of hair. I walked towards the last bully, raised my steel fan to strike at his worthless fucking throat and—

Well, you can imagine what happened next, yep, that's right, fuck all. I didn't do shit about nothing and carried on walking until I was through the school doors. It felt rubbish being noticed like that. Something had to be done. I watched as the barber cut my hair, knowing that I was doing it for all the wrong reasons. To this day, it's a memory that has stayed with me. But the question I ask myself now is, what do I do with the feelings that come with that memory? Is it really about my hair, or was it about something more than that?

I never realised it at the time, but that moment in the barber's chair set in motion a whole new path that went undiscovered for a very long time. A path that could have given me a strong sense of self. A path that had I embarked upon, I may have been even more secure in myself once I began my journey of transition years later.

Right now, you're probably wondering what that means. Let me put it to you this way, in life we have those moments when we know what we need to do without question. For me, it was the moment when I knew I was transgender. From that moment, I knew that I had to transition because it was the only choice. But then we have the flip-side, the subconscious, the moments when we realise something even deeper. So deep that the realisation of what you need to do can get lost in what you are dealing with at the forefront. For me, that lost realisation was building the foundation that was me, Yvy. Sitting in the barber's chair, I saw a part of Yvy literally get torn away. I was watching a part of myself that I actually liked because it was an extension of who I was inside falling away because of the fuckwits at school.

It was at that point that my journey to the core of who Yvy was derailed and I temporarily lost my way. It wasn't until many years later that I finally got back on track, but by that time I couldn't help but wonder: am I too late to find Yvy?

I See You;
Do You See Me?

Chapter Two
Manchester, 2006

It was creeping towards midnight and I was nowhere near sleep for the third night in a row. Moving to Chorlton after living in Blackburn with Mum and my two siblings was a huge adjustment. For one, no matter what time it was, there was always someone in the house. Even when sitting in my room alone, I heard Mum cooking in the kitchen, or Feroza playing a CD in her bedroom and feeling the bass from her subwoofer vibrating through the walls, or Fareed going in and out of the house with his mates. All the while, I sat in my bedroom downstairs, comfortably listening to the world around me.

It was a huge step to move away, but one I had to do. I was so tired of commuting to work and hiding my transition from everyone. The pain of getting ready in Blackburn and skulking in the shadows all the way to the train station to avoid being seen was getting harder and harder. It was like I held my breath every time I travelled on the train to Manchester, buried within my long, hooded coat, finally exhaling the moment I stepped into work. *This is getting really old!*

I sat in my tiny attic flat, alone, with nothing to do. Looking outside, I saw that the flat across the street were having yet another party. People were dancing, and the music travelled softly through the air and into my living room. I wasn't annoyed though, I actually liked hearing the bustle outside at night. Living on the corner just off the main road, it was never silent. Whether it was the night bus, people going to bars, or dragging themselves home after a night out, there was always something. You get used to it after a while and it soon became a comfort to me. I felt less alone in the world. Still, I had to do something to occupy myself tonight.

Fuck it.

I picked up my cordless landline, punched in some numbers and let it ring. After an automated voice boomed through the speaker, I punched in some more numbers, paused for the beep and put the phone down. *There! That should do the trick.*

I was getting peckish, but what should I eat at five to midnight? I looked through the cupboards in the kitchen and found a jar of hot dogs and two onions. *Perfect.* I fried up the onions, boiled the hot dogs and stuffed them in some buns and got comfy on the sofa. It was a hot night, and even with the window wide open, I felt the stuffiness in the room. A perk of living alone when you're trans is that you're free to not give a shit about appearances. The tucking panties were nowhere to be seen and I could lounge around in a baggy t-shirt and some shorts without a care in the world.

I had another rough day at work. It seemed these days that I didn't need to have anything bad happen to me to have a bad day. Just waking up, putting on a full face of make-up and having to smile my way through the day was getting harder and harder to do. I was still on the waiting list to be seen at Charing Cross and I was not going to wait for hormones to start my transition. I wanted to hit the ground running from the moment I realised I was trans, which was why I couldn't hold off until I moved to Manchester and decided to start transitioning while living in Blackburn. Hiding it from my family was so difficult, but I knew that once I moved to Manchester, things would be better.

I finished a long day at work and walked from Deansgate to Piccadilly Gardens to catch the 86 bus to Chorlton. It was crowded, so I put my earphones in and played some Amerie. Soon enough, the blaring intro to '1 Thing' filled my head. As I got onto the bus I went straight to the upper deck and sat near the front. I always avoided the back of buses, which is usually occupied by high schoolers or rowdy people with no sense of personal space.

I was looking out the window when a man sat beside me. I shuffled a little, making sure I wasn't taking up too much room. I could see that he said thank you through the beat of 'Touch' flowing through my ears. The bus took off and the streets soon starting rushing along the windows. It was a late shift so it was already getting dark by the time I finished work, but it didn't matter to me. Darkness and artificial light were my best friends when it came to wearing that much make-up. I was already miles away in my head when the man beside me tapped me on the thigh. I looked over and could see that he was motioning me to take out my earphones.

'You from Manchester?' He asked with a grin on his face.

I wasn't sure if he was just making polite conversation or if this was going in a direction that I was in no mood for.

'No, I'm not, I've only just moved to Chorlton.'

'Oh, whereabouts in Chorlton?'

'Just Chorlton.'

'You Asian women are so beautiful.'

He put his hand back on my thigh and within a split second I could already feel his hand moving up. I took his hand away immediately, but not too rudely as to cause a scene.

'I can show you around Chorlton, you know.'

'I know my way around, thanks.'

I looked out the window and could see that the stop just outside the glowing neon pink lights for Kashmir King takeaway on Upper Chorlton Road was coming up. I pressed the stop request and moved away from him. I prayed that he wouldn't get off the bus, and thankfully saw it pull away with him still on it. I was nowhere near the four banks which was my usual stop, but I didn't want that man to know that.

I knew I should have reacted more harshly to his uninvited bullshit, but a part of me felt like if I did, it would only attract attention to the Indian tranny on the bus. I wasn't prepared to risk it. I could already feel the 5 o'clock shadow pushing its way through my caked-on foundation and all I wanted to do was get home so I could remove it all. Spending all day pretending that this person was me when in fact I was so much more was weighing down on my heart. I knew that I had to do it. I knew that transitioning was going to be fucking tough. But my flat had become such a safe haven for me that I saw the outside world as a series of hazards I had to avoid on a daily basis until I was able to shut the front door behind me and feel safe again in my home.

Although it took me longer to get home, I eventually made it to my safe haven, but by midnight I was still reeling from the day. Flicking through the TV channels, I found the perfect accompaniment to my hot dogs. *Blade.* Oh, how I absolutely adored this movie. It fed a part of me that was dark and macabre, a side that never got the chance to come out and play.

As the movie began, I watched as Traci Lords led her blonde-haired date into the slaughterhouse. When the security guard pulled the cold, steel door open, the music kicked in like a nightmare. I had a hot dog in one hand, the TV remote in the other, and I turned the volume up as the Pump Panel Remix of New Order's 'Confusion' filled my tiny living room. I danced around, feeling the music go through me, and I could see myself in the club. I was amongst the crowd of ravers, jumping up to the rusty pipes and moving in slow motion. I was with them; I was lost in the music. I could feel my—

'RING, RING. RING, RING.'

I stopped jumping around and caught my breath when I heard the phone ringing through the music. I quickly pressed mute on the TV and put my hot dog down. Taking one quick swig of my ice cold Vimto, I answered the phone.

'Please wait for the beep, then begin.' The automated message relayed in a positive tone. I sat back on the sofa and waited for the beep.

'Hi, my name is Yoanna,' I said in a seductive tone. 'How are you doing tonight?'

'Urrrm, alright thanks,' the gentleman said, nervously.

'Tell me what you're doing?'

'Urr, I don't know, just, like—'

'Are you in the mood to play?' I can tell this one needed warming up.

'Yeah.'

'Mmmm, me too. I want to know what you like. You want me to be a bad girl?'

'Not really.'

Oh, well, that avenue is no good then! New direction, Yoanna, I mean, Yvy.

'Oh, I won't be, honey. I'm a good girl.'

'You're a good girl?'

What did I just say, you dickhead? Ugh, this guy's not going to be the one tonight.

'Of course. What are you doing right now?'

'I've got my hand on my cock.'

'Yeah? I want you to stroke it. Are you hard?'

'Yeah, baby, I'm so hard.'

Baby alert! Possible money maker. Keep it going!

'Oh yeah, I want my warm lips around your cock, honey. Tell me what you want me to do.'

'I, I don't know.'

'I'm touching myself.'

'Keep doing that then.'

'I'm feeling you inside me. You feel so good.'

'Aww yeah, baby, I want to be insi—'

A quick pause and then he returned. 'Sorry, bye.'

Ah well, made fuck all money on that call.

I wasn't sure why I took up an extra job on a sex line. Actually, scratch that, I know exactly why I took a job on a sex line. It was something fun and impulsive to do. It was a place where I could act out anything I wanted and be somebody that could turn into a fantasy. I wasn't treated like someone's property. I had full control over everything. When that man touched me on the bus, he made me feel unsafe. Here on the phone, I was in control. Nothing happened if I didn't want it to. I liked that feeling. The phone rang again.

'Hi, my name is Yoanna.' For some reason I thought an American accent was sexy and the fact that I got the name from the season two winner of America's Next Top Model made it feel more appropriate to do so.

'You alright, babe?'

'I'm better now hearing from you, honey.'

'I'm throbbin'.'

'Oooh, I bet it's real big. I want to taste it.'

'Ugh, you're shit, you are.' He hung up the phone. *Prick!*

I picked up my hot dog and unmuted the TV. As *Blade* continued, I looked outside and saw the people in the flat across the street in full swing. Everyone was having so much fun. I parted my net curtains and stood in front of the small balcony. The warm air touched me. It ran along my bare legs, my arms and face. My hair began to lift and float gently against the weak breeze. Suddenly, I felt my nerves wake up.

This was the closest I had ever been to feeling so at ease in public, without having to paint a mask on. To feel this uninhibited outside of my safe haven. Standing at the window, I wasn't hiding anything. It felt dangerous. I closed my eyes and let my mind go blank. My eyes were closed for just a few seconds when I opened them again and saw someone looking at me. He was in the flat across the street, staring at me through the window.

My instinct was to quickly hide behind the net curtain, but for some reason I couldn't move. I was compelled to stay there. He smiled and gave me a discreet wave. I returned the gesture and gave him a smile. Just then, the phone rang again. It didn't even register that the automated message didn't play when I answered, which meant that it wasn't a sex line call. Standing at the window, I reached for the phone.

'Hi, I'm Yoanna.'

'Eh! Hello?'

SHIT!

'Hi Mum!'

'What did you say before?'

'Nothing I was just turning the TV down.' I quickly muted the movie.

'Oh, alright. I was just calling to check in on you.'

'I'm okay, just relaxing. Are you okay? You're up late.'

'No, I'm just getting one of my funny feelings in my stomach so I wanted to check up on you. You didn't reply to my text.'

Mum always seemed to know when something was wrong. For as long as I could remember, she would get a funny feeling in her gut and do the rounds messaging me, Fareed and Feroza to check if we were okay. The weird thing was that she was usually spot on. Most of the time it was Fareed who was up to some sort of mischief, out with his mates in his car.

'I promise, Mum, I'm okay. Sorry I didn't message you; I'm watching a film and mustn't have heard it.'

'Alright then, I'll leave you be then. Don't stay up too late.'

'I won't. Goodnight!'

I put the phone down and looked out the window. The guy across the way had gone and the party was still going. I was getting pretty tired and my head was spinning with too many thoughts. *Go to bed, Yvy.* As I reached for the phone again to log out of the sex line, it started ringing. *Do I do one more?* I hadn't made much money tonight. You only made money depending on how many calls you get and how long you keep them on the phone. The longer they stay on, the more you get paid. A lot of people stay logged in for hours making money, but I couldn't be bothered staying up much longer. *Fuck it, one more call and then bed.*

'Hi, I'm Yoanna.' I couldn't be bothered with the American accent. I just spoke like myself.

'Hi.'

'You looking for a good time?'

'I—I dunno really.'

'Well, I'm here to make you feel good.'

'I want to feel good.'

Hearing those words made me uneasy. It was something I had said to myself for years. Hearing the same words said in a completely different situation can still sound so clear.

'I want to make you feel good.'

'How are you going to do that?' The man said.

'By showing you what I'm capable of.' It was as if I was talking to myself.

'That sounds so good.'

'I know.'

Chapter Three

It was my last week working at the bank, and I was pretty excited to be moving on. Since moving to Manchester and starting work there almost a year ago, I had dealt with so much bullshit from colleagues who couldn't (or wouldn't) accept that I was trans. It got to a point where I was collapsing inside because of people treating me like a leper. Having my friend Sheds with me at the bank was the only comfort I had to sustain me. It was weird because we never really interacted much outside of the workplace, yet it felt like we had known each other for years whenever we were together.

I wanted a fresh start. I wanted to walk into a workplace where absolutely no-one knew that I was "the trans one." I wanted to make a connection with people that didn't involve them wanting to know if I had a pussy or a dick. I wanted to feel real instead of being treated like a fascination. Having only lived in Manchester for a short time, I was still finding it difficult to make a connection. Meeting men online was easy, but I didn't see that as a way of making a connection with someone that I could get close to. It was either men who wanted to fuck a pre-op, or people who had no clue I was trans with whom I was unable to take things further in case it got confrontational, possibly even violent. When it came to friends, I had nobody in Manchester that I had a real connection with. When I say a real connection, I mean the kind I had in Blackburn when I met Isabel, Gillian, Leanne and Kayleigh. Although they were all different, one thing they all had in common was how they treated me. They never once questioned my gender, my sexuality, who I fancied or who I really was. Instead, they simply accepted me without question. I never had to put on any pretence with any of them. Even when I was struggling to articulate how I was feeling inside, I never felt like I had to explain myself at all. It was as if on some level they knew I had something to say, but were perfectly fine giving me the time to speak my own truth instead of being intrusive. To me, that's the perfect foundation of a real friendship.

After moving from Blackburn, it was hard to maintain our friendships as we saw less of each other. Manchester had so much to offer, but without any friends there, I found myself alone most of the time. In a way, I liked being alone. Being alone gave me a sense of security. A sanctuary that only I had access to. Not speaking about my journey was a blessing because I was tired of having to explain myself to others, as though I was obliged to do so.

I sat at my desk, staring at the computer screen.

'You, okay?' Sheds asked.

'Yeah, I'm just thinking about some stuff.'

'Like what?'

'Well, I—' Before I could start talking, our manager called us all for a quick catch-up session around the whiteboard. The board had all of our names on, with columns for each product the bank wanted us to push on calls. I was sick of doing sales to a point where I was not remotely motivated to sell upgraded accounts and ISAs. Still, we had to have our weekly catch-up to praise the big sellers, even though our targets were plastered on the damn whiteboard for all to see.

'Right, everyone! How are we feeling today?' One of the other managers said when he decided to take over the catch-up instead of our own manager. We all nodded our heads as he carried on with the meeting.

'I just wanted to catch up and say we've done a good push on the account upgrades, but we still really need to get more GIS moving forward.'

I looked over at Sheds and could see his face about to crack up. Every fucking time this manager mentions general insurance products, or GIS for short, he always pronounced it as *jizz*. For ten minutes, all twelve of my team mates tried our best not to laugh as he stressed the importance of getting more jizz on the board. While the topic of jizz continued, I looked over at the whiteboard and saw all the cartoon caricatures I had drawn of my team mates. A few months earlier, the team decided that we needed to build some morale and made a game we could play that went with all the sales we needed to achieve on a weekly basis. We ended up making a snakes and ladders game and I was asked to draw little caricatures of all my team mates to use on the board. The team loved how they all turned out, so much that they then asked me to draw some Halloween-inspired cartoons. For each team member, I drew them in a different Halloween costume. I was Samara from *The Ring*. Since Sheds had a weightlifter's build, he was perfect as a werewolf. He could definitely pull off being a sexy werewolf.

Sheds looked over at me and could see that I was staring at his werewolf picture. He leaned over and whispered in my ear.

'Checking me out, are ya?' My skin tingled when I felt his breath on me. My eyes closed and I smiled. As I opened them, I saw some of my other team mates looking over at us and whispering to each other. Immediately I straightened up and paid attention to my manager who took over the meeting from all the jizz talk.

'Right team, a big well done to Simon for opening seven savings accounts this week. And Yvy for a whopping twelve account upgrades this week. Brilliant work Yvy.'

After the obligatory applause the meeting was done and we all went back to our desks.

'So?' Sheds said, his warm eyes looking straight at me.

'What?'

'What stuff are you thinking about?'

'Oh!' I didn't realise we were back to the conversation. 'I'm thinking about my next move, you know, once I leave here.'

'In what way?'

'I don't know. I don't know what it's going to be like working in an actual bank.'

I had found a job in Chorlton, which was only a five-minute walk from my attic flat on Oak Avenue. It was a job working with customers face-to-face rather than over the phone. The pay was slightly better and I didn't have to do any sales, but I was still pretty nervous about working with the public in such an up-front way. It would be the first job working with the public directly I'd had since starting my transition. I didn't know if I was ready for this. I sat at work, and thought of everything I had done up until now.

Realising that I was trans and not waiting until I moved from Blackburn to start transitioning. Hiding my secret from Fareed and Feroza. Disguising myself every morning in order to get to Blackburn train station and make my way to Manchester without anyone recognising me. Finally having enough money to move to Chorlton. All in the space of twelve months I had completely flipped my life on itself and now I was on the road to being who I knew to be. One of the rare comforts I had was not having to deal with the general public too much. Because I worked in a call centre, it was easy to chat to people without feeling self-conscious. The people on the other end of the phone had no idea who I was so it didn't matter. It was interacting with people in person that I couldn't stand.

My mind was racing, thinking that maybe leaving my city-centre job to work in a customer-facing role was a bad idea. I mean, yes, there was the whole fresh start aspect of it all that was very appealing, but on the other hand, I was terrified of what might happen. So many scenarios whirled through my head after I had handed my notice in. *What if someone attacks me again? What if they follow me home? What if nobody helps me this time?* Then, the incident with the guy who attacked me at work played in my head. I couldn't stop my mind from going there.

Before I knew it, I was reliving that moment when I finished work for the night and that arsehole followed me to the toilets to attack me. That moment left such a scar on my soul. Why was I such an issue to him that he felt the need to try and hurt me? Was it because he liked me and felt disgusted with himself after he found out I was trans? Was it purely because he was a transphobic cunt? I never understood why anyone would want to terrify a person in such a way that makes them genuinely fear for their life.

At this point you might be thinking 'Yeeesh, Yvy! You're coming on a bit strong about a new job, aren't you?' That might be true, but one of the worst feelings a trans person feels on a daily basis is the fear that someone will try to destroy them. That constant fear that you might encounter that one person who just doesn't accept your existence and decides to take matters into their own hands. It's a real fear, and unfortunately, a real fact.

After that incident happened, my whole outlook on dealing with people who didn't know me changed. My walls were up securely and I wasn't interested in making any new connections. That makes things difficult when you're going into a job that deals with the public. Being so closed off meant I was in a constant state of nervous anxiety every time I met someone new. I hated that prick from work for making me feel this way. Shortly after I told Sheds about what happened, he told me that he sorted him out, whatever that meant. To this day, Shed's never told me exactly what he did, but it's safe to say he did something because the guy never bothered me again.

Sheds and I grew closer after that. I noticed how he was always protective of me. He was caring in a loving way. Every time I was feeling down, he could always tell. It's as though he was in tune with me and I loved him for that. Sheds was Pakistani, so understood everything about my journey when it came to

Muslim culture and the shit I've had to endure. Even though he didn't identify as queer, he knew how I was feeling in a way that meant he knew how to support me without saying a word.

'Do you think I'm making the right choice?' I asked.

'What, leaving here?'

'Yeah.'

'I think you are.' He said, a blunt response I was thrown by. 'You want a fresh start, don't you?'

'Yeah, I guess, I just don't know if I'm ready to—'

'What are you scared of? You speak to people all the time. Fuck what anyone thinks about you. What do *you* think about you?'

'I just want to get on with it and just do it.'

'So do it. You know you can. Plus, you'll be out of this shit-hole and trying something new. Look, don't let starting a new job scare you off doing what you need to do.'

Sheds was right. Why was I letting myself be afraid of something I've not even started yet? Then it struck me. Before I transitioned, nobody knew that I was trans at the bank, yet I still had the courage to walk into work as Yvy and face everything that was thrown at me. The snide looks, the complaints, the attack, all of it. It wasn't me who was scared, it was everybody else. They were scared of what they didn't understand and took it out on me as the only open trans woman in the workplace. Why did I not see that sooner?

***

When I found out that there was a job going as a Customer Service Advisor at a bank in Chorlton, I thought it was the perfect job for me. I was already working for another reputable bank so had plenty of experience. Plus, living in Chorlton was perfect because everything I needed was on my doorstep. Supermarkets, antique shops, GP, takeaways, I rarely needed to go into the city centre for anything other than work. If I worked in Chorlton too, I would be able to live almost without ever having the need to go anywhere else. To me, that meant containing any possible risks. I would be close to home and on familiar turf. It didn't take long after I applied for the role for me to be offered a job interview.

I arrived at the bank in good time. I didn't have far to come, just a two-minute walk from my flat. As I entered, I saw the layout of my possible future workplace. To the right were two rooms for mortgage advisors. Towards the far end were the cashiers and to the left of the room were three small desks with staff sitting and chatting with customers. It was early, so the bank was pretty quiet. I waited until I saw one of the advisors was free and told them I was here for an interview. Before long, the bank manager came to greet me and took me through to the staff area at the back.

'Thanks for coming, Ivy.'

'Yvy, it's pronounced ee-vee.'

'Oh, I'm sorry,' he said. I wasn't giving him a hard time about the name thing. People mispronounced my name constantly so it became second nature to correct every person who said it wrong.

'That's okay. Thanks for seeing me.'

'I just wanted to talk to you about the role and ask you some questions.'

'Yeah, that's fine.' From first impressions, he seemed like a nice guy. Tall, skinny build and very obvious that he loved his job. He was the type that I would find particularly attractive, but I could see he was wearing a wedding band and imagined him living the cliched life of a big house with a loving family that sat happily together for every meal. Then again, that idea came from the weird notion that most South Asian families believe that working for a bank or a fancy corporation was somehow posh or prestigious. I recalled one of my aunties thinking it was great that I worked for a bank, like it was some sort of status symbol to prove that I had made it. *Ridiculous.*

After a few competency-based questions, he let me know that the interview was done and that I should expect a call soon if I was successful.

'That's great, thank you again for seeing me.'

'You're very welcome,' he replied. 'We'll let you know in the next couple of days. If you are successful, you'll need you to bring some ID in for us to get things moving.'

'ID?' I asked like an idiot. Of course, I bloody knew what he meant by ID.

'Yes, something photographic like a passport or driving licence. We'll also need proof of address, so utility or council tax bill will do.'

'Great, okay. Erm, I don't have a passport or a driving licence so would I need something—'

'A birth certificate will be sufficient if needs be.'

'No problem.'

That evening, I sat in the flat, stirring my brain into oblivion with constant heavy thoughts. I didn't even know if I had the job and already, I was stressing. The moment I was told I needed to present a form of ID, my heart sank uncontrollably. It never dawned on me until then that I would have to give proof of identification, which is stupid given that I've had to give proof of ID at every job I've had. But this was different. This was the first time I had applied for a job as Yvy, not as Sal. Being Saleem was easy on paper because everything matched.

This time, I was going to have to give them my birth certificate with my dead name and incorrect sex plastered on it. I'd have to give them my change of name deed and explain it all. Before I had the chance to see if I could have a fresh start, I would have to begin with the one thing I wanted the fresh start from. No matter what, I'm going to have to explain myself. That feeling filled me with rage. I needed to get my mind off it before my head exploded.

I was in no mood to chat to men on the sex line. I was getting tired of doing it anyway. I never made much money from it and I thought that it would in some way let me chat with people who wanted me for the woman I am, but in all honesty, I was so fucking horny all the time and needed an outlet that didn't involve having to touch myself. At the beginning it sort of worked. Talking with men who wanted to be with me, who were turned on by me, who wanted to fuck me was pretty hot.

But the novelty soon wore off and I grew tired of putting the desires of men before my own. They had no fucking interest in my pleasure at all. All they wanted was a quick wank with someone over the phone. I had the odd person who called to chat about their day, which were the calls I liked the most because at least I made some money keeping them on the phone. But it wasn't like I could actually talk to them about my day, hell, they didn't even know my real name.

What's ironic was that I thought it would be a great way to connect with people who didn't know me, but it ended up making me feel even more disconnected than sitting at home alone. At least when you're alone in the house, there's a reason nobody is listening to you. I was on an early Friday shift the next day and I didn't want to stay up late, so decided to have an early night and escape my thoughts.

The next day the manager from the bank called and told me I had got the job.

I didn't have to give too much notice at my current workplace, and my last week soon came around. I thought that a weekend trip to Blackburn to see Mum, Fareed and Feroza would do me some good before I started my new job, and I was looking forward to some down time. Even though I knew Sheds was right and I was doing the best thing by starting a new job, I still couldn't shake off the anxiety. What I needed to do was calm the fuck down. I needed a distraction. I didn't realise it, but my thoughts caused me to stare blankly at my computer screen, motionless.

Sheds noticed and did something I wasn't expecting. He leaned in and put his hand on my leg. At first, I didn't register his gesture. I wore my favourite denim flare skirt that buttoned from the centre all the way down. I always left the bottom half of the skirt open and paired it with my faux crocodile skin boots and fishnets. As Sheds moved his hand up my leg, the denim slipped off my knee and I felt his touch through the small holes of my tights.

I looked over at him, at first to ask what he was doing, but instead I caught his gaze and I felt warm. He was looking at me, smiling, not saying a word. It felt like we were looking at each other for ages, but it only took a few seconds before a person on our team, Mary, decided to comment on what she was seeing.

'Oooooh Yvy, I was right about you two!' Sheds and I looked at her and decided not to respond. Mary didn't see his hand on my leg, but she was still jealous of my relationship with Sheds. Mary was a lovely person, but had a tendency to get clingy with men she fixated on or attempted to date in the office. Only recently she had been out on a date with Sheds, which I found odd as I never thought Mary was his type, but it wasn't my place to get involved.

Sheds told me about the date, and I was encouraging which seemed to get his back up. His behaviour started changing around me, being standoffish and blunt when I asked him a work-related question. One thing about me that Sheds knew was that I never pried into his life, even if he was in a bad mood. If he wanted to talk to me about anything, he knew he could, but I would never push him to talk about anything he didn't want to.

When he went on his date with Mary, they went to watch *The History of Violence*. I was leaving work after a late shift when I saw them both outside and gave them a polite 'enjoy the movie' gesture before heading home. The next day, I asked Sheds how the movie was and both him and Mary started jittering like idiots. It was like I had asked Mary if she sucked him off in the theatre, the way they were both acting all weird. I quickly lost interest and decided not to bother trying to understand whatever it was they had between them.

From how Sheds quickly cut Mary off, it didn't look like there was much between them, but ever since their movie date, I always noticed how Mary was almost uncomfortable with my friendship with Sheds.

'You going out for drinks after work, Yvy?' Mary asked.

'I'm going to Blackburn after work, hun.'

'Awww I thought you'd be out tonight for drinks with us.' I knew the team had planned a night out tonight, but I wasn't interested in going. It was never my scene to go to yet another stale, old, white man type pub and spend the entire evening talking about bloody work. Isn't the whole point of going out, to escape talking about work? Every time we had a night out, I grew so tired of the endless bullshittery and arse-kissing that I'd throw a bomb in the conversation and asked a completely random, non-work-related question that caused the conversation about how many sales each team had done to come to an abrupt end. I think my favourite question was when I asked if anyone ever tried anal. Surprisingly, a few people actually answered the question.

'No Mary, I'm not out tonight.'

'Shame Yvy. I love your little questions you ask us. So funny!'

I stared for a moment, followed by a slow blink and carried on with the rest of my shift.

It was creeping towards 9:00 pm and my last day was almost done. The call centre floor was pretty much empty, just a few of us working the late shift. Sheds was also on a late so it made my last shift bearable. I couldn't wait to finish. The phone lines were quiet for a Friday, which gave Sheds and I a bit of time to talk.

'So, what was that earlier with Mary?' I asked directly. 'Do you two still have a thing or what?'

'Nah, I'm not going there again.'

'Why? Date not go well?' I said jokingly.

'Do you think if—' He stopped himself mid-sentence.

'What?'

'Nah, it's nothing.'

'No, go on, what were you going to say?'

'Do you think that if you were—'

BEEP! The sound in my ear from the incoming message of a work call pierced through the conversation. ACCOUNT CALL. BEEP!

'Good evening, you're through to Yvy. Can I take your name and account number, please?'

It was quarter to nine and I hoped my last call would be an easy one. Instead, I had my last vile, shouty customer who insisted I spoke with them for as long as needed, despite the fact that we closed in fifteen minutes. My train to Blackburn was shortly after 9:00 pm and I was in no mood to wait an hour for the next train. As the end of my last shift grew closer, I was nowhere near the end of the damn call. I felt myself growing more impatient to a point where I was tempted to just disconnect the call.

By the time I was done, it was well after nine and I had missed my train. Sheds had already left, giving me a quick wave when I was on the phone, leaving me alone in the office. I packed up my stuff and left the building once I wrapped up my last call. Making my way down the stairs and into the reception area, I looked around for the last time. I looked over at the toilets where I used to get changed every morning after travelling from Blackburn in disguise and then having to put on my heels, breast fillets and lippy before walking into the office.

I saw the place where I was viciously attacked by a colleague. I saw the cafe area where Sheds and I ate lunch every day. I was glad to see the back of this place, but was also grateful that I got through it all feeling somewhat stronger and determined to move forward.

I stepped outside and the bitter air stung my cheeks. I walked past work and around the corner to make my way to Salford Central Station. I had plenty of time to kill, but thankfully I had my Tess Gerritsen book with me so I knew that would be a fine way to pass the time before my train arrived. As I made my way onward, I saw a figure standing nearby. I saw that it was Sheds. I thought he had left well before now.

'What are you still doing here?' I asked.

'You've missed your train.'

'Yeah. That's okay, I'll just wait for the next one.'

'I can take you home, if you need.'

'To Blackburn? How are you going to do that?'

'I'll drive you.'

'I've never seen you drive to work before!'

'Shut up and let me help, will ya! I've got my car today.'

'Alright then, thanks!'

The roads were black, lit with glowing lights rushing past the car windows. Sheds turned the radio on so we didn't need conversation. The atmosphere was dense. I wasn't sure what was going on and Sheds looked like he had something to get off his chest, but for some reason he was keeping quiet. The last time it felt awkward like this was when he went out with Mary, and even then, I wasn't sure why things got weird.

Sheds seldom spoke about his feelings, and I rarely asked. It wasn't because I didn't care. I could see so clearly that Sheds enjoyed being around me, because I didn't ask him questions he didn't want to answer. He liked that he could relax around me. He'd talk about his feelings when he was down, but the conversations were usually short and he quickly moved on to something else.

This was different though. Sitting in the car, he couldn't think of anything else to say. He had nothing but what he wanted to say on his mind, but the words just wouldn't come out. I was growing tired of the weirdness and I was way too straightforward to have to deal with unnecessary tension. I turned off the radio and looked at him as he drove.

'Are you okay?'

'Yeah, why?' He said with a surprised tone.

'I don't know. I can tell something's up and if you're driving me to Blackburn, I don't want the entire journey to be in silence. So go on, then.'

Sheds paused, looking into the dark night, then a smile started forming on his face.

'Don't fuck around, do you?'

'Depends on who wants to fuck around.' Sheds glanced over at me, surprised.

'I don't know what's wrong. I'm just feeling shit.'

'What's on your mind.'

'Do you ever think about us?'

'Do you?'

Sheds pulled up into an empty gravel car park and turned the engine off. I could tell he really wanted to tell me something, but was afraid. I never felt scared around Sheds.

'I always thought about us, you know, together,' he said, looking down.

'Can I be honest? I know there's something between us, but I don't know what we can ever do about it. I know that you like me, and I like you too, but I can't be with you. Not the way I want to be.'

'I get it. You're going to have your surgery soon though?'

I knew where he was going with this. I knew he was holding onto some vain hope that once I had my gender surgery, it would somehow solve the issue and he could be with me. But that wasn't enough for me. I didn't want to feel that way about Sheds. He's a decent guy, but I'm not going to be treated as a fantasy that can be created for him.

I knew that if this went further, I'd have to stay in a holding pattern until I was perfect enough for him to finally have me. That felt so disrespectful. I'm not going to cater to someone's shame for being attracted to a trans woman and I'm certainly not going to entertain the notion that the future of my vagina, or Missy as I like to call her, was for someone else's gain.

'I like you. I really do. I wish I could be with you the way I'd love to, Sheds. You and me. I love what we have.'

Before I could say anymore, Sheds leant in and kissed me. It was the first time we'd kissed. I kissed him in return and he pulled the seat back. I had no control over myself, and feeling Sheds' hands on me felt so good. I pulled his arm over to motion him to climb onto the passenger side. The seat was almost horizontal, and I turned my body around. Sheds admired the curve of my back as my denim skirt hugged tightly to my hips. He climbed over and positioned himself on top of me, his bristly chin sinking into my neck. The feeling of his short, coarse hairs tickling my shoulder set my nerves ablaze.

All I wanted in that moment was to fuck his brains out. But I knew I couldn't. His kisses were soft and warm. He was so hard and pressed against me in a way that made me fully aware of just how much he had grown. As his kisses deepened, I let out a gentle moan that turned him on. Sheds began moving his hips against me, slowly building up his speed and holding onto me. Then it dawned on me what was happening. *Are we dry-humping? Am I actually getting dry-humped right now?*

After a few minutes, we called it a night and drove the rest of the way in awkward silence. By the time we arrived in Blackburn, we said our goodbyes and he drove back to Manchester. I opened the front door and Mum was sitting in the living room with Feroza.

'You're a bit late tonight. Did you get the train?' Mum asked.

'No, I missed it. Someone from work drove me instead. Sheds.'

'That's nice that he gave you a ride.'

Chapter Four

Starting a new job is always daunting, but this time was different. I felt a mixture of excitement and dread at the thought of meeting people for the first time who knew nothing about my past or about my transition. *What if they take one look at me and can tell straight off?* Worrying about being figured out was playing over and over in my mind.

I sat in the back area, waiting for my new manager to come and talk me through my first day. The back room was long and narrow. A small kitchen took up one corner opposite the door. On the other side were small sofas and stacked up chairs. A whiteboard stood opposite them, with pale blue scribbles all over it. There were no windows, just the intrusive fluorescent lights above shining harshly on my skin. Already I could feel my make-up sweating.

I decided to dress smartly for my first day. I ransacked my closet looking for the perfect ensemble and eventually decided on my favourite low-cut top with short sleeves, black lace Morgan skirt with baby pink underlay and a pair of dusty pink heels. I tied my hair back into a neat ponytail and wore a pair of black chandelier earrings. I popped open my compact mirror and patted away the excess shine as I waited in the back room. The lighting was unfairly accentuating the dark foundation around my chin and neck. *Hate crime.*

The soft bumps from shaving my face in the morning were slightly visible. Adding extra powder foundation to conceal it only created a mess and I had to powder my whole face to even it all out. When I was applying some more Rimmel Coffee Shimmer to my lips, I quickly realised that there wasn't anything wrong with my make-up. Any make-up looks like shit when under harsh lights.

The manager walked in and I quickly put my mirror away, stood up and straightened the hem of my skirt.

'Hi Yvy, sorry you had to wait,' he said.

'That's okay.'

'So today will be a pretty quiet day for you. I'll have you sit with one of the cashiers first to observe what they do and then after lunch, we'll get all the paperwork sorted.'

'Paperwork?'

'Yes, the proof of ID and your contract to sign.'

'Oh, right, yes.' My heart was pounding in my chest. I had put off giving my ID for weeks. I was asked to bring the information in before my start date, but kept making excuses why I wasn't available. Every time I went around the corner to Morrisons, I kept thinking that the manager would spot me and chase me down the street.

'Follow me and I'll take you to the cashier desks. Actually, I'll take your ID from you now and get them photocopied. I have a meeting this afternoon so I'll get it sorted now.'

My insides started spinning. I felt like Nomi Malone when she got the job in *Showgirls* and that woman was asking her all sorts of questions about her past. I was waiting for the manager to start giving me the third degree about the importance of eating brown rice and vegetables.

I reached for the plastic wallet in my bag that contained my ID. Inside it was my birth certificate, change of name deed and one of my credit cards bills. I pulled them out and handed them over to him.

'I don't have a passport or driving license so—'

'Oh yes, I remember you mentioning. Did you bring another form of identification?'

'My birth certificate.'

'That's fine, thanks.'

Before I could say anything else, he took the documents and turned to leave the staff area. As we walked onto the bank floor, I saw that it was full of customers. Some depositing money at the cashier desks, some in the small appointment offices, others waiting to be seen by the customer service advisors by the window. To my right were three cashier desks, all occupied by staff.

'Yvy, this is Mandy. You'll sit with her this morning and observe. I'll check in with you after lunch. If you have any questions, you can ask Mandy or come find me.'

'No worries, thanks.'

The manager went through the security door and towards the photocopiers by the service desks. I watched as he chatted with customers along the way, holding my ID in his hand.

'Hiya, sorry, is it Yvy?'

'Hi, yeah it is.'

'I know it looks pretty busy, but this is actually a quiet day.'

'Yeah?'

'Yeah, we usually get the older customers coming in first thing, but that's not too bad, and then it usually picks up like this around 10 and dies down after 2.'

The rest of the morning went by quickly. Mandy showed me how to deposit cash, make payments, use the till area and where the panic buttons were. Before long, it was lunch time and I was absolutely starving. It's weird how sitting down for hours can make you so hungry. I sat downstairs and ate the coronation chicken sandwich I had brought from home.

'You going out for your lunch?' I asked Mandy when she walked in to the staff room.

'Yeah, most of us go out to get some air. This fucking place!' She rolled her eyes which I took as an indication that she meant to get out of work rather than to merely breathe in the not-so-fresh air of the busy Chorlton streets. After a few more staff came in to grab their coats and rush out, I was alone again with my sandwich and Tess Gerritsen. I didn't get much chance to read when the manager soon walked in.

'Hiya Tim.'

'You alright, Yvy. How was this morning?'

'Good, thanks. It was interesting watching what queries you get from customers. It's quite similar to what I used to do so I know it'll come to me easy.'

I knew the moment the words came out of my mouth that I came across a bit kiss-arsey. Of course, he knew I would learn how to do the job, otherwise he wouldn't have fucking offered it to me.

'Well, you won't be doing the cashier role, but it's always good to see what we all do. At times we pitch in if needs be.'

'Yeah, that makes sense.'

'Here's your ID. I just wanted to let you know—' *Oh God, he knows.* 'We won't be able to accept a credit card statement for proof of address. Can you bring in a utility or council tax bill?' He asked.

'Yes, of course.' I was instantly relieved. 'I only live up the street. I can pop home and get it.'

'You can bring it tomorrow, it's not a problem.'

Tim handed me my documents and I quickly put them back in my bag. I turned to Tim and saw his face. He looked confused and slightly uncomfortable. I knew what was about to happen. I felt the room slow down as his face grew ever more uncomfortable, like a young child wanting to confess but is too afraid to say in case he got in trouble. Seconds ticked slower than usual, yet it wasn't enough time to prepare myself. Nothing prepares you for such an inevitable intrusion.

'Can I ask you about your birth certificate?' Tim asked.

'Yeah.'

'I noticed your, erm, name was changed.'

'Yes, I changed it by deed poll. I'm transgender.' I didn't want to mince my words. There was no need. *Just tell it like it is, Yvy.*

'Oh, right. So, you used to be a man, then?' I hated hearing him say that. 'Sorry, that came out wrong.'

'That's alright.' It wasn't alright. I was angry.

'Well, thank you for letting me know. I think it's best we keep your situation to ourselves.'

***

The kitchen in my flat was tiny. Then again, what did I expect? I knew when I went to view the place that it was an attic flat in a converted house. Still, it instantly felt like home the moment I walked up the steep stairs that led to the attic. The kitchen occupied one wall in the living room. Three cupboards were above the worktops, and three below. I didn't have enough room for a big fridge-freezer, I only had one of those small fridges that fit under the worktop that housed a small freezer compartment. The living room itself was small but cosy. I always felt at home here.

I made it a goal to personalise my home in my own way. After a rubbish week at my new job, I wanted to get my mind off things. Since moving to Chorlton, I spent my first few months repeating a standard routine of working and coming home. No interactions with anybody, no visitors, just me. I didn't see that as a downside though, in fact, it was nice to exist as just me rather than having other people around me. I never tired of the feeling when I walked into my flat after a long shift and heard the sweet silence I longed for all day. No voices around me asking questions. No inane conversations to listen to or participate in. *Just me.*

A quiet, solitary life was something I always wished for. Ever since I was a child, the one thing I yearned for was to be left alone. Going through so much turmoil, I couldn't put into words what I was feeling. The people closest to me were around me, but the fear of losing the ones you love takes over every cell in your body when the world is telling you that the very thoughts you are having could send you to Hell. I couldn't speak to Mum about all the things that were swirling around in my head.

Fear is a powerful thing if you allow it to be. The safest I ever felt was when I was alone in my room, creating art and watching TV. My favourite thing to do was to draw and paint whilst watching *Buffy* or *Charmed*. I could close the world out and focus on creating something else.

Moving to Chorlton, I lost sight of my creativity. A shame really, because creating things was a huge part of my childhood. I wanted to bring some of that back into my flat. I had my own space and the freedom to do whatever I wanted. So what if my kitchen was small, or that I lived in an attic? At the end of the day, this was my home. *My sanctuary.*

I stood in the middle of the living room, checking all the corners to make sure the old bed sheets I laid on the floor were covering the carpet. I decided to paint the walls to get rid of the off-white colour that made the room look so dreary. I had already collected some antique-style furnishings to go in the living room. An old table lamp, glass perfume bottles, ceramic umbrella stands filled with dry flowers, but there wasn't much on the walls. The ceiling was low and sloped on the right-hand side, which gave limited space to hang up any pictures or put up any shelves.

Still, it didn't mean I couldn't do something nice to the walls. I dipped the roller in the light pink paint and started applying the rich colour onto the walls. With each roll, I saw the colour getting brighter and richer. It was calming to see the once-drab room suddenly burst into a beautiful new shade. After I finished the left wall, I moved onto the ceiling beams. I didn't want to paint the whole room pink, I thought it would look better if I painted the room in strips. The ceiling was divided by two beams covered in wallpaper, so I decided to only paint the beams. Once that was done, the right wall was painted pink. I finished off by going over the remaining walls with a bright fresh coat of white to get rid of the dismal, stained paint that remained exposed.

As the brilliant white touched the walls, it made the colours I added even more prominent. It felt good to rid the walls of its past. Every morning, I painted a face on to rid the world of the one beneath it. The face that was the past staring at me. A past I could not escape yet. A past that was very much present. I couldn't do anything else other than what I was already doing. After speaking with my GP in Chorlton, I began the process of being referred to Charing Cross, but I hadn't quite got to that point yet. All I could do in the meantime was deal with each day in the hope that I would come across a day when I was able to finally paint over everything I wanted to leave behind and start fresh.

Monday soon came around, and with it my second week at the bank. My first week was filled with the usual stuff that came with starting a new job. Observing people when they worked, online courses to complete, the usual. I was still struggling with what Tim said to me. *I think it's best we keep your situation to ourselves.* What did he mean by that? I'm more or less certain that he didn't mean it in a bad way, but hearing those words felt insulting.

It made me feel like I was being told to keep my mouth shut about being trans. Or was he warning me to keep quiet because he knew that certain staff were transphobic? Or maybe he just meant not to mention it now and we could possibly discuss it later? Ugh, I hated not knowing what to think. I thought I had dealt with these feelings at the last bank I worked at and that I was better equipped to handle these sorts of situations. I walked into work, determined to put last week behind me.

'Hi Tim!' I said enthusiastically.

'Hello Yvy, have a nice weekend?' He asked. I couldn't help but notice that he gave me a quick once over as he scanned me from head to toe with his eyes. I chose to wear my grey blanket skirt with a pair of black boots and a black turtleneck with long ladder sleeves.

'I did, thanks. I spent the weekend painting the living room.'

'That sounds nice.'

'You?'

'Oh, the usual family stuff.' I had no idea what usual family stuff was, but judging by his demeanour, I assumed it was something dull, possibly involving quality time with an equally dull family.

'So today, Yvy, you'll be sitting with Amy, one of our advisors.'

'Yep, that's fine.'

Amy walked over to introduce herself. She was petite, with short blonde hair that looked weak and thin. She wore a short-sleeved blouse and pencil skirt, along with a pair of scuffed black court shoes. I briefly met her when I started last week, but didn't get much chance to talk or get to know her. From what I saw around the bank, she seemed pretty laidback.

'Hiya, Amy,' I said. She gave me a subtle gesture that acknowledged my greeting and took a seat at her desk. Tim pulled a chair next to hers and motioned that I should take a seat. As Tim left, Amy and I started chatting.

'How are you finding it?' She asked.

'Not bad. I've worked at a bank in town for a bit, so it's all similar to what I've done before.'

'Yeah, this job's a piece of piss once you get the hang of things.'

As the customers started coming in, most went over to the cashier line, while others waited to see an advisor by one of the meeting rooms.

'I've only got one appointment this morning so you can sit through that one. It's an easy savings account appointment so it won't take long. This afternoon, I think I have an account upgrade and a possible mortgage one, and then after that I have an account dispute. So at least you can see a different range of stuff.'

'Cool.'

The morning went on and I sat as Amy dealt with her first customer. She introduced me as a new member of staff and I remained silent as they both went on with the appointment. I looked around the room and saw more and more people coming in. It was getting louder and I could see that Amy was getting frustrated with the lady she was speaking to. The customer wasn't saying anything wrong; she was an old lady who looked distraught about something.

Usually, when I dealt with people like that over the phone, I let them get what's bothering them off their chest without interrupting. Most likely it's their own frustrations they want to let out, and once they do, they tend to calm down. This lady seemed to be just like that, only Amy wasn't allowing her to speak. She was getting antagonistic with her, unnecessarily. Eventually, the old lady backed down and the appointment was over.

'I'll be back in a sec.' Amy stood up abruptly and went through the security door to the staff room. *Toilet break, probably.* Tim noticed I was by myself and came over, putting his hand on my shoulder in an unfamiliar way.

'You alright, Yvy? How's it going with Amy?'

'Yeah, fine. We've only had one customer. I think she's nipped to the loo.'

'Excellent. Well, let me know if you need anything.' Before walking off, Tim gave me a gentle squeeze on the shoulder. 'Oh, I wanted to talk to you about work attire.'

'Right.'

'We'll need to order you a uniform so you'll need to fill in a form for me to send off. Doesn't take long for a uniform to arrive, about a week.'

'That's fine.'

'In the meantime, you'll need to wear something more appropriate.'

'Appropriate?' I was confused by his statement.

'Yes, I think *this* isn't too suitable. A bit too experimental.'

Experimental? What the fuck is experimental about a fucking turtleneck? Amy returned and Tim flashed a quick smile before excusing himself. As she sat, I could see that Amy was a bit wired. Before she left, she seemed down, almost drained. Now, she was on edge, as if she had become fully aware of her surroundings and felt as though everyone was watching her.

'Tim just said what I'm wearing is 'experimental'. What does that even mean?' I said jokingly.

'It means he's a cunt,' she said without hesitation.

I could tell by how she was acting that she had taken something when she went to the loo. *Fuck it, Yvy. It's not your problem.*

By lunchtime, I was ready to go home. There was something about this place I just didn't like. I'd only been here a week and already I was sick of it. *It's only been a week, Yvy. Stick it out.* I bit into my sandwich and stared at the whiteboard in the staff room. Staff members came in to grab their coats and quickly scuttled out. I didn't pay any of them much notice.

'You not going out too?'

I didn't register the strong Liverpool accent talking to me from across the room.

'You eating lunch by yourself?' He said, trying to get my attention. I looked over and saw that one of the guys from the cashier desks was looking straight at me.

'Sorry. Yeah I am.'

'Mind if I join you?

'No, please.'

He sat at the sofa opposite me and opened his bag to grab his lunch.

'I'm Bradley. Haven't had a chance to properly say hi. Always manic in here.'

'Yeah, seems it.'

'How you finding it, anyway?

'Not bad, getting used to it.'

'You live around here?'

A slightly forward question to ask, but I went along with it. After all, he wasn't some creep on a bus asking me where I lived.

'Yeah, I live close to here.'

'Right, I'm in Hulme. Been working here for about a year now.'

'Where's Hulme?'

'You don't know where Hulme is?'

'No, I don't really know Manchester much, except Chorlton and a bit of city centre. I moved here from Blackburn so I don't know my way around that much.'

'Ah, right! Well, if you ever want a night out or if you need any help getting around, let me know.'

'Thanks.'

Amy and a few others walked in from their lunch outing. Hanging their coats up, they noticed Bradley and I talking and felt the need to join in the conversation. By the afternoon, I was back on the floor with Amy, sitting opposite her last booked appointment.

'So, you gonna sort me money out, or what?' The customer said intimidatingly.

'A cheque can take a few days to clear in your account, I'm afraid,' Amy said calmly, the woman glanced at me, then directed herself at Amy again.

'D'ya think I'm thick or summat?'

'No, I don't, but I can't help you if the funds aren't available.'

'You think you're clever talking to me like that, like a piece a shit?'

I looked over at Amy but she seemed unbothered. In actuality, she seemed pretty out of it. I could tell this was angering the customer even more.

'I'm sorry but—'

'If you say sorry again, I'll kick your fucking teeth in.'

I felt unsafe. I was shocked that Amy continued to do nothing. She didn't ask the lady to calm down or stop swearing. She simply took the abuse from her. A few more minutes of chat went by before Amy got up to photocopy some paperwork, leaving me sitting in front of this abusive woman. At first, we were silent. I didn't have anything to say to her, but our eyes kept catching. With every catch, I could tell she wanted to say something to me. I felt my skin warming, my make-up feeling heavy on my face.

'You work here, do ya?' She asked.

'I'm new.'

'You don't wanna fucking work here with the likes of these.'

I remained silent; I was in no mood to add to the tension that had already arisen.

'Are you a tranny, can I ask?'

My skin froze onto my bones. I felt every nerve in my body spark, causing my cheeks to flush until it hurt. I looked up at the woman, staring right at my face with an intrusive glare. Her eyes violated me, seeping underneath my skin and causing my heart to splinter in sharp shards inside my chest.

'What?' I said with a whisper. I barely heard myself speak. I used every ounce of strength to get that one word out, yet it disappeared like smoke from a candle, barely noticeable. Amy returned and sat down on her chair, placing the paperwork she had sorted on the table.

'You look like a tranny. Are you?'

Amy looked at me and then back at the customer.

'There's no need to speak to her in that way.'

'I'm just asking. Was I being fucking rude to ya?'

'Please, can you calm down?' Amy asked.

'Was I being rude or was I just asking ya a fucking question?'

The woman leant forward. I flinched. I couldn't look at her in the eyes. I couldn't do anything other than stare down at my hands. *Don't cry, Yvy. Don't fucking cry.* I didn't realise that I was holding my breath until I started feeling dizzy.

'You need to stop or you'll have to leave,' Amy warned her.

'Whatever.' The lady grabbed her papers from the desk and left.

For a few seconds after the woman vacated, I was frozen to my chair. I was humiliated. *Why did such few words hurt so deeply? Why did they have such power over me? Why am I not stronger?* The questions cut just as deep as the words themselves. I couldn't breathe. I wanted to get up but the more I willed my muscles to awaken, the heavier they became.

'Are you alright, Yvy?' Amy touched my arm. I jumped as my senses kicked in again. 'Don't know why she was saying all that. Fucking idiot.'

'I don't know. I need a break, sorry, I need to just take a—'

'No, totally,' Amy said, knowing that I needed to take a moment. 'Yeah, go make a brew or a drink.'

I sat in the staff room, shaken. It was the first time I had ever been confronted in that way since I was attacked at my last job. I couldn't understand how I could let someone I didn't even know or care about bring me down like that again. *Fucking weak bitch.* I went to the toilet and locked the door behind me. Sitting on the toilet lid, I put my knuckles to my temples and squeezed. My cheeks were warm and my hair dropped to cover my face as I hunched my shoulders down. I stared at the white tiles on the floor, feeling a tear run down from my eye and drip onto the surface.

Fucking look at yourself.

I heard his voice in my head. The voice that filled me with fear. The voice of the man who attacked me. Suddenly, I was reliving what had happened to me at my last job. I saw myself back in that accessible toilet room I used so many times to get changed in. I felt his grip on me as he pushed me in and locked the door behind him. I released my knuckles from my temples and stood up. *Don't relive this, Yvy. Don't relive this.* My mind was racing, the memory of what happened to me came rushing back. I could feel every touch, every hurt.

You are disgusting.

'No, I'm not.'

I leant against the wall. I could feel myself reliving the moment I crashed onto the ground as he threw me from his grip. I felt him grab me and force me to look at myself in the mirror. Somehow, I made my way to the sink, standing in front of another mirror. I looked up and saw that my make-up was running. *You are disgusting.* The words of a mad man who chose to terrorise me were screaming in my head.

You are disgusting!

Are you a tranny?

LOOK AT YOU!

YOU LOOK LIKE A TRANNY!

The tears were streaming. I couldn't help but look in the mirror, hearing his voice in my head scream louder and louder. My breath was sharp, I couldn't keep up. Every inhalation made my heart splinter even more. *STOP THIS!* I hit the glass as hard as I could. With every hit, the mirror began to break. Pieces of glass fell into the sink, then the blood. I looked down and saw my hand bleeding. As it bled, I quickly turned on the cold tap to stop it from continuing. Within seconds, I heard a knock at the door.

'Yvy, are you okay?'

'Yes, I'm fine,' I said as I turned to the door to respond. I could tell it was Amy on the other side. I looked back and saw the mirror, unbroken. I glanced down at the sink and saw no shards of glass. I lifted my hand and saw no blood.

'I'm fine.'

That night, I lay in bed at 2 am, no closer to sleep. *Another restless night.* All I could think about was what had happened. Trying to make sense of it all was impossible. I couldn't understand why my mind and body reacted that way. All I knew was I couldn't set foot in that place again. I felt defeated. I felt weak. *You are weak.* The air was blowing a cool breeze through my bedroom. The lights from passing cars ran across the walls. I watched as each light started as a concentrated beam and slowly faded as it travelled along the ceiling and disappearing on the sloped attic wall. *This was just an isolated incident, Yvy. It's not going to happen again.*

I tried to convince myself that that was the truth, but I knew better. I knew that not a day would go by without someone or something to remind me that I was a tranny, a cross-dresser, a he/she, an It, the disgusting monster. I'll always have that reminder. Even after I gave Tim my identification, the first thing he felt the need to mention was to keep my identity to myself. *Yeah, don't tell anyone, Yvy. I'm a shameful secret. An embarrassment.* My head sank into my pillow, watching the lights pass by.

I just want to be me.

Chapter Five

Making a connection with the world you live in can seem impossible at times. I'm not talking about love or friendship; I'm talking about that profound connection with the world that lets you know that you were meant to be here. A connection that surpasses all relationships, friendships, love, sex, fear, anything you have ever encountered. A connection that fills you with self-worth. A connection that you feel in every cell in your body the moment you open your eyes in the morning.

Most people are born with their connection to the world beaming out like a strong Wi-Fi signal. *HERE I AM! THIS IS ME!* Those signals are mostly afforded to cis, straight, white people. The type that society puts on a pedestal. *The way to be.* Then it seems the further we work through the differences in us, the weaker the signal becomes.

If a person is gay, ooooh sorry, that signal needs to come down a bar. Then the inevitable occurs and that person is teased for being gay. They hurt, feeling hopeless and isolated. But wait, if someone is gay and a person of colour, the signal weakens even more. They can't hide their skin colour, so even if they are able to hide their sexuality, they still have to deal with being abused, looked down on, even violated, just because of the melanin in their skin.

Of course, not all people think this way, but just because you may not reject someone because of their ethnicity or sexual orientation, it doesn't mean that they don't experience it on a daily basis. As the signal weakens, we get to where I was. A queer, trans woman of colour. May as well turn the Wi-Fi off because my connection was so weak it could barely download an episode of *Pose* off a dodgy website. Trans people fight so hard to have a strong connection with the world that we deserve, no, have every right to be a part of.

The thing that weakens our connection is how society chooses to perceive us. If we were treated the same way as a white, cis, straight person, we wouldn't have a problem. It's almost as if we as queer people are a threat to a particular group of delusional, ignorant people that feel the need to let us know that although they see us, they do not acknowledge us as people who deserve to be here.

I was sick of having a weak connection. I was sick of taking the time to straighten my hair, pick the right outfit, pile on make-up, tuck my genitals back tightly, wear gel fillet breasts and walk out the door to face the world, only to be confronted every day with fucking arseholes who had the nerve to call me a tranny to my face. *Of course, she had the nerve.* To her, I was nothing. She genuinely thought she could speak to me like that and expect me to answer her offensive question.

I sat at my folded dining table in the living room, my Cheerios swimming in a pool of cold milk, replaying the scenario in my head over and over. *What could I have done differently? Should I have yelled at her? Should I have just answered the question?* Maybe I should have called Tim over and asked that she be removed. But then, would she have announced my identity to the whole room? I wanted a fresh start, so that wouldn't have been the best thing to do.

The spoon in my hand swirled around the bowl, clinking against the side. I wasn't hungry, in fact I was never hungry in the morning. It was creeping towards 8:00 am and I was due in work in thirty minutes. The more I stirred my spoon, the softer the Cheerios were getting. I took a spoonful and crunched on the remaining dry loops. Sitting in my nightgown, I was nowhere near ready to go in to work. I wasn't sure if I could face going back in today, but what was the alternative? I couldn't hide from the world in an attempt to heal this pain. I couldn't just tell them I wasn't coming in.

I spent the weekend watching *The Lord of the Rings* to get my mind off my troubles. I knew that losing myself in a fantasy world would distract me from all the disquiet I didn't want to give any further attention to. I just about accomplished that very thing until a scene came on that reminded me of something important.

I lay on the sofa with the lights off, snuggled in my duvet as I watched the final battle in *Return of the King* when Eowyn, niece of Théoden, King of Rohan, faced off with the Witch King of Angmar. As the chief of the Nazgûl flew in on his steed during the battle at Minis Tirith, Eowyn watched in horror as Théoden was fatally wounded. Defending her uncle, she took up her sword and shield in an attempt to take on the Witch King. With every swing of the Witch King's heavy mace, Eowyn found herself closer to being defeated. Finally, the mace made contact with Eowyn's wooden shield, shattering it into pieces. She stumbled back onto a fallen horse, clutching her wounded arm that was once protected. The Witch King approached, and my eyes widened, knowing what was about to happen. I watched as the Witch King stood in front of Eowyn, grabbing her by the throat and speaking deeply. *No man can kill me. Die now.*

Then Merry, a hobbit that Eowyn had brought with her to battle, stabbed the Witch King from behind. Eowyn was released from his mighty grip and found her balance once again. She removed her helmet, revealing her flowing golden hair and looked down at the Witch King. In one breath, she said the final words the Witch King would ever hear.

I am no man.

Eowyn plunged her sword into the Witch King's face and watched as he fell to pieces and crashed to the ground. As I watched the Nazgûl crumble into nothing, it made me think about what it took for Eowyn to finally stand up and be counted. She had been told that the battlefield was no place for a woman, yet she had proven herself worthy of just that. No person on the planet can make it through life alone, but that does not take away a person's strength, a person's perseverance and courage.

Eowyn defied the words of men and stood strong in her convictions. It took almost being defeated to say those words that spoke volumes to me. I wanted so much to be like Eowyn. I wanted to stand up and take control of what I felt was spiralling out of control. Sometimes, that doesn't always mean proving how strong you are. At times, the best thing a person can do is take a step back, heal, and give yourself a moment to focus. Even if wounded, you need to let yourself feel the pain before continuing. That's exactly how I was feeling.

I knew that I wasn't a weak bitch. I knew I was capable of great things. What I needed in this moment was a break to heal. I knew that if I walked back into work today, I would feel nothing but fear. With every customer I encountered and every hello from a colleague, I felt as though any moment someone was going to remind me that I was the freak of the workplace. If I walked into work, my mind would take me to an irrational place that wasn't healthy. An angry person was not something I wanted to become. There's no need to take on another person's bad energy and claim it as my own. I had to take a step back before my irrational side tried to convince me to do that.

No, I had to think about myself. I had plenty of time to step onto the battlefield again. There was no rush. I picked up my phone and dialled Tim's number. *Just call in sick and take a few days off.* As the phone rang, I knew that if I said I was sick I wouldn't get paid. I hadn't been working there long enough to get paid sick leave, but a few days won't hurt. *Maybe a week?* No wait, that might be too much time off. Then again, what's the point only having a couple of days off? What am I going to accomplish with only having two days off work, other than having a period of sickness on my third week of a new job and less money in my wages when I got paid? *Maybe this isn't such a good idea.*

'Hello?' Tim said as he answered the phone.

'Hi Tim, it's Yvy.'

'Oh, hi Yvy, you alright?'

The moment he asked me if I was alright, I lost it. I wasn't alright. I was going through so much and I had no way of talking about it to anyone. The closest person I could have spoken to was my mum, but I didn't want to admit to her what was happening. I didn't want to let her know how much I was struggling, to see me crumble. No, I had to handle it myself. My voice cracked as the tears ran down my face.

'No, I'm not, Tim.'

'What's happened?'

Suddenly, the words just came out without any hesitation.

'My sister passed away last night.' *Did I just say that Feroza died? No wait, I didn't! I just said my sister, I didn't give a name! Make one up, Yvy! Make one up!*

'Oh Yvy, I'm so sorry. Your sister?'

'Yeah, my sister Nazgûl.' *Tim will never believe that!*

'I'm so sorry, Yvy. Don't worry about work.'

'I can't afford to be off, I just wanted to tell you before I came in.'

'Don't worry about coming in, Yvy. You won't lose any pay, I'll make sure. Just take a couple of weeks to take care of yourself and let me know if you need anything at all.'

'Thanks Tim.'

I put the phone down and sat back in my chair. *I just killed off my fictional sister, Nazgûl.*

✳✳✳

What sounds like the logical thing after taking a fortnight to grieve the passing of a fake sibling mostly known for hunting down hairy-footed hobbits would be that I returned to the bank clear and rejuvenated. However, that couldn't be farther away from the truth. In fact, I never returned to the bank. I couldn't face the thought of people asking me how I was or asking questions about Nazgûl. I mean, what if someone else at work had also seen *Lord of the Rings*? It was hardly out of the realm of possibility. No, the best thing was to never return, and I didn't.

That then meant I had another issue to deal with. I had no job. Spending the last two weeks off work did me a world of good. I felt lighter and ready to get back on track. Once again I needed a fresh start, but this time I came at the whole work situation differently. What irked me so much when starting my job at the bank in Chorlton was having to give my ID to the manager. From that very moment, I was on edge. Watching Tim stare at my birth certificate and ask the question he already knew the answer to was so gut-wrenching. I didn't want to experience that again. I was pretty sure he didn't mean anything by it, but that didn't make the situation any less out of my control, and I realised I was always going to have to explain myself before I could get a foot in the door.

Before anybody could get to know me, they'd immediately see me as the trans one. Why couldn't I just be Yvy? I doubt Tim told anybody at work that I was trans, but he still knew. Every time I walked into work, I couldn't help but wonder if his indiscreet stares or his monosyllabic tone had anything to do with him trying to figure me out. Needless to say, I never felt comfortable around Tim.

But what to do? Even if I do find another job, I'm still going to be faced with the same issue. At some point, they're going to ask for a form of identification.

Knock, knock, knock!

I heard a loud pounding on my front door. *Who the hell is that?* I never had anyone knock on my front door, especially from the inside of the house. Usually when someone delivers something they rang the doorbell outside. In the house I lived in, there was the outside door that opened to the porch, then the porch door, and then a flight of stairs that led to the first floor of the house. There were three doors on the first floor. On the left and right were doors which belonged to one flat that occupied the whole floor. I wasn't sure why they needed two doors, and noticed that the tenants only used the door on the right. In the middle of the corridor was a third door, which was mine.

As soon as my door opened, the steep staircase went up to the attic. Nobody ever knocked on that door, so I was surprised to hear someone trying to get my attention. I tied my robe and quickly looked in the mirror before answering the door. I was pleasantly surprised to see that I was looking pretty good, given that I didn't have any make-up on. *Knock, knock, knock!*

As I walked down the stairs, my first thought was that it was my landlord, Mr Kyriacou. He was a couple of days late collecting the rent which wasn't like him. I tried to let him know that I was happy to pay rent through my bank account, but he insisted it be paid in cash. I opened the door and didn't see my landlord. Instead, there was a young woman. She was short, with brown hair that fell to her shoulders.

'Hi, I'm Sarah, I live on the ground floor.'

'Hiya.'

'I don't want to cause any issues, but I heard a lot of noise from your flat last night.'

'My flat?' I was confused. 'You heard noise from me?'

'Yeah, I heard a lot of crashing.'

'I doubt it was me. Even if I was making noise, I don't know how it would register in your flat. I'm in the attic.'

'Oh, sorry! I thought you were on this floor.'

'No, it's the other doors. You got me worried then! I was having to think what I was doing last night to make so much noise!'

'Aww sorry, I didn't mean to worry you. Did you hear it then last night?'

'No, I didn't. Then again, you might hear it a bit more if you're directly beneath them.'

'Yeah, anyway, thanks for letting me know.'

I shut the door behind me and went back upstairs to get changed. I managed to get myself an interview for a car insurance company in city centre and wanted to make sure I got there in good time. Searching for work was easier than I thought, especially when it came to looking for call centre work. I quickly found that there were no problems with actually finding jobs to apply for, as there were so many calls centre jobs around. My only concern was what I was going to do to avoid having to have 'the talk'. Then it hit me. *Yvy this will never work.*

After securing the job at the car insurance company, I began the two-week training course that involved a lot of group activities and fake pleasantries that came with working for a call centre. Soon enough, the moment I was waiting for came up.

'Alright everyone,' the trainer said. 'Before you go for the day, can I remind you to bring in your ID on Monday?'

We all agreed collectively and started towards the training room door to leave for the weekend. I knew this was going to happen again, but this time I had a plan. *Maybe it'll work.* Working in town meant having to get the bus home again. I didn't mind, it was springtime and the days were brighter for longer. I sat on the bus, letting the sudden bursts of the setting sun sting my eyes as it peaked through every passing building. I thought about my plan and the more I thought about it, the more genius it seemed. The plan was simple. Alter my birth certificate by scanning it to my computer and changing the name and sex, then print a copy and tell work that the original has been sent off as part of a passport application. That way, they'll be sure to accept a photocopy as passport applications can take ages. *Perfect plan, Yvy!*

I logged on to my computer and got to work on my birth certificate. It was quite easy to change the details on it as I didn't need to worry about the paper matching the colour of the certificate. I was going with a photocopy version so it wouldn't make any difference if it was in black and white. As I printed off a copy to take with me to work, the nudge notification on my MSN Messenger sounded. I looked and saw that it was Toby.

T: Hi Beautiful.

I didn't know if I should respond. The last time I spoke to Toby, I rejected him. He was a sweet guy and all, but I knew after we slept together that I just wasn't ready to take things any further. I didn't want to be with someone who wanted me for what I was, rather than who I was.

T: How are you?

On the other hand, it was nice to talk with someone who knew I was trans and didn't make a big deal out of it. My mind went back to the first time I met him in his car. At no point did he make me feel uncomfortable or uneasy. He was nice to be around. Yes, I wasn't ready to form a romantic connection with someone, but that didn't mean I had to cut off every person that I became a little close to.

T:???
Y: Hi Toby. I'm gud thanx. How are you?
T: Not bad beautiful. Started a new job.
Y: Yeah? Doing wot?
T: Driving instructor
Y: Cool.
T: Love to see you again. Fancy meeting up nxt week?
Y: Sure. Yeah, I'd like that.

Monday soon came along and another day in training was coming to an end. I sat around the tables that were all pushed together to form one big rectangle which took up the centre of the room. There were twelve new starters in total. I couldn't remember most of their names, and by now it was too late to actually ask what their names were again given that we had been in training together for a week.

The walls were covered with large sheets of recycled white paper, written on with coloured markers from the many exercises we completed during training. To the front of the room was a desk where the trainer left her things but seldom sat behind when training. We wrapped up another day and the trainer addressed the room before we left to go home.

'Thanks for today everyone. Tomorrow we'll go on the floor and do a bit of call listening and then the afternoon we'll start working on the systems. Hopefully, I'll have all your logins ready.'

We all smiled and thanked her for the day. As we all got up to gather our things, she spoke again.

'Oh, can everyone who brought in your ID pass it to me. I'll get them back to you tomorrow.'

As a few of us began an informal queue near her desk, I put myself at the back of the line. I didn't want people seeing my photocopy or hearing my explanation. They might clock my birth certificate and say something. It didn't take long before I was at the front and the others were pretty much out the door.

'Here you go,' I said confidently. *Why would it be an issue?* I handed her my council tax bill and my birth certificate. 'I've photocopied my birth certificate because I sent the original off for my passport. I made sure to make copies because I was applying for jobs.' *Stop over-explaining. You sound nervous.*

'No problem, Yvy. That's fine. Thanks for bringing it in,' she said without hesitation.

I passed her the documents and walked out. Stepping outside onto the street, the sun was still shining brightly. I couldn't believe that had actually worked. *That's it, it's done.* I don't have to worry about it any longer. For the first time in a long while, I felt light. I never really thought about just how much a piece of paper with my old details on was affecting me.

For so long, my birth certificate was used as a way of wholly identifying my very being. A piece of paper I had no involvement in putting together. I was brought into this world and assigned this paper that said who I was, what I was, and given a formal stamp and signature of approval for me to go forth into the world with the apparent confidence that my sense of self-identity was already decided on. This paper was like a ghost that haunted me. It's as if it had more power over how I was to be seen, rather than me actually telling someone who I was. *You can't be a woman; your birth certificate doesn't say you are!* When I presented it to Tim, it felt like a part of me was chipped away. I didn't want to ever feel that way again. I didn't want to have to tell someone about me being trans unless it was on my terms and not because some fucking piece of paper was forcing me to do so.

Walking along Barlow Moor Road, the streets of Chorlton were still busy. I felt the air starting to chill as the sun began its descent and the wind slowly pick up. Turning onto Oak Avenue, I saw the old tailors on the corner that belonged to my landlord, Mr Kyriacou. I hadn't heard from him in a while and he still hadn't picked up the rent. I went over to see if he was still in the shop. Peering in, I couldn't see any lights on and the door was locked. I decided to leave it and walked next door to my flat. As I reached for my keys, a familiar voice came from around the back of the house.

'Hi!'

'Oh, hi Sarah. You alright.'

'Yeah, I'm fine thanks. How are you?'

'Good, thanks. Actually, have you heard from Mr Kyriacou?'

'Who?'

'The landlord who owns the building.'

'Oh right, no I haven't, but then again my girlfriend deals with the rent so'

'Ah, no worries then. So have you settled in then?'

'Yeah, it's lovely around here.'

'Yeah, it's nice being so close to everything.' I searched in my bag for my keys and heard them jingle as I grabbed hold of them.

'Are you up to much tonight?' Sarah asked.

'No, just another quiet one tonight.'

'If you fancy a cuppa or something then come around to ours. Steph is working late so it's just me and the telly.'

'Thanks, I'll see how I get on later.' I knew that was a brush off, but I wasn't sure how else to respond.

'Cool, well, I'll let you get on then,' she said as she walked away.

I reached for the door handle and pushed my key in the lock. I stopped and went around the side of the house where Sarah's front door was.

'Actually,' I said as she was about to enter her flat, 'I will come around, if that's okay.'

'Of course! 8ish alright with you?'

'Yeah, that's fine.'

I knocked on Sarah's door later that evening and was greeted by her smiling face, already in her cosy nightgown. I walked in and saw that the flat had already been unpacked and decorated. They moved in a few weeks ago, but I recalled seeing a lot of boxes going in the flat and assumed it would still be in a state of unpacking. Clearly, they knew where they wanted everything to go because there wasn't a thing out of place. The living room was decorated with an array of green plants and candles. It was so cosy and warm. The furnishings looked worn and used, very much like the furnishings in my flat, although it looked a lot more spacious in Sarah's flat. She didn't have a sloped ceiling cutting the height of the room in half.

After a couple of brews, we had already gotten through the usual conversation topics of where we were from and what we did for a living. It was nice to chat with another woman about, well, anything really. I hadn't had much in the way of female friends since living in Blackburn. I missed hanging out with my girls and being alone in Manchester made it difficult to meet new people. Sarah wasn't interested in whether I was trans or not. In some way I felt more comfortable to tell her that I was because she was a lesbian, but a part of me didn't want to. It had nothing to do with Sarah and everything to do with the fact that I didn't have the energy to discuss it. So instead, I opted for the standard conversation subjects that somehow dodged any aspect of something so real.

'How are you finding your new job?' Sarah asked.

'It's okay. Not too keen on call centre work but I need the money so needs must.'

'Totally.'

'Got some interesting people working there. There's a trans woman in the training group who's really nice.' I didn't know why I said that. To test the waters maybe? Or maybe to talk about myself without having to actually talk about myself. *Who knows?*

'Really?'

'Yeah, she's really nice.'

'I find the whole idea of being trans so strange.'

I was thrown by her comment. I didn't know whether to probe further or end the conversation. Either way, it made me uneasy.

'It's hardly a preferential lifestyle to change sex just because you find it hard to understand who you are. Does she believe she is a woman then?'

'Uh, well yeah, I mean, she is a woman. I don't think it's that she believes she's a woman. Makes it sound like she's wrong to think it.'

'Yeah sorry, that was shitty of me to say. I guess I don't really get it, but I suppose it's not for me to get so—'

'I don't think it's a case of it not being for you. If a person is trans, that's their identity and it should be respected.'

'But how can a trans woman see themselves as a woman? I mean, I'm a woman which means a lot. I menstruate, I can have children, all that stuff. If a person is a transgender, none of that applies so I find it hard to believe they fall under the category of being a woman. That's all I'm saying, really.'

I was done having this conversation. What she was saying really rubbed me the wrong way.

'I best be off.'

I was back in my flat and safe in my little sanctuary. The whole evening was weighing heavy on my heart. Here I was, trying to connect once again with some semblance of the world that didn't involve just me, and I still got bitch-slapped. I wasn't expecting to become best mates with Sarah, but to have at least one person close by that I felt comfortable enough to just be myself without the worry of having to hear bullshit like that would've been a welcomed treat.

All I seemed to do these days was dodge bullet after bullet linked to the fact that I'm trans. I'm almost beginning to feel like it's something to be ashamed of. *Don't go there, Yvy. Don't you fucking dare go there.* A feeling of loneliness was creeping in, which was something I loathed. I never saw myself as lonely. I always saw the difference with being alone and being lonely. Feeling lonely meant I was yearning for someone or something. I didn't like that feeling. I opened my laptop and saw that Toby was online.

Y: Hey ;-)
T: Hi Beautiful. U ok?
Y: Yeah. Gud thanx. You free tonite?
T: Tonite? I can be
Y: I want to see you
T: Yours at 11?

I waited until 11 o'clock for Toby to arrive. Soon enough, I saw his car pull up on Oak Avenue. I opened the living room window and stepped onto the roof of the bay window below as he got out of the car. He looked up and saw me. His beautiful face was even more stunning than I'd remembered. I let him in and we barely made it up the steep staircase in my flat before he spun me around and kissed me. My body fell onto the stairs and Toby pressed himself onto me.

In that moment, I let go of everything that was weighing on my mind and gave in to his touch. We didn't need to speak; we didn't want to. We both knew what we wanted and wasted no time taking it. Tasting his sweet tongue in my mouth brought back a feeling of pure passion that I missed so much. As we made our way to the bedroom, he took his shirt off and began unbuttoning my blouse. My lips travelled down from his chest to his abdomen, relishing the taste of his warm skin. Something unexpected was happening. I no longer felt the same reservations as I did the last time I was with Toby. I felt able to just take this moment as a way of releasing something I had been holding on to for so long. That yearning for a connection. To feel real. To feel something other than the harshness that reality was forcing me to experience. He pulled me up and kissed me ferociously. As he undressed me, I laid on the bed and let him place himself between my legs. He was so hard and it was making me hungry for his touch. I wanted him in my mouth so badly that I took control and told him to lie down. As I worked on him, his moans grew louder and louder. I wanted him to be on the brink of an orgasm, to want to explode more than anything. When I felt him almost reach that moment, I stopped and looked at him straight in the eyes. I smiled, and he knew I was teasing him. Toby turned me on my front and spread my legs. I arched my back as hard as I could and let him enter me. He took me in ways that made my body scream. He felt so incredible inside me. From that moment, our bodies were in rhythm. With every thrust, I could barely control myself. He bit into my neck so hard as he came that I thought he broke the skin. It felt amazing. He felt amazing.

The next morning, Toby had already left when I awoke and I was alone in the flat. I already knew he had left during the night, so it was no surprise to wake up alone. It didn't matter anyway, I had to get up for work. I was feeling positive. I let go of what I was feeling last night and today I was going to walk into work knowing that I was going to be able to get on with my job without the worry of having to explain myself. Finally, things seemed to be on track. The morning went as planned with a few hours of call listening. By lunch time I was looking forward to nipping to M&S for a chicken and stuffing sandwich. As I made my way out, the trainer stopped me.

'Yvy, can I have a word?'

'Of course.'

'I've passed your details to HR but they have asked that as soon as you get your original birth certificate, if you could bring that in.'

My heart sank.

'Is something wrong?'

'No, nothing's wrong. It's just a HR thing. They need to see original copies. The photocopy is fine for now, don't worry. Just when you get the original back, they'll need to copy that instead and then it's job done. Headache I know!'

'Okay,' I said with a forced smile. 'That's fine.'

From that moment on, I knew my time was up. I knew that I was going to have to leave my job. Again. I couldn't bring myself to show them my birth certificate. I just couldn't. It filled me with so much anger that this fucking piece of paper was causing so many problems. The inevitable eventually happened and I stopped going into work. Soon enough, a P45 came for me in the post and I was back to finding another job. I found a job, then left again after facing the same problem, then found another job, and left again.

Jumping from job to job, I stayed for a few weeks and then left before anyone caught on that I was using a fake document to get a job just so I could stop having to explain myself. It took leaving eleven different jobs in a space of a few months before I finally came across one that accepted the photocopy as proof of ID and I was able to work without any issues in the workplace.

What I came to realise was the connection that I was sending out as an external pulse was bouncing across everyone I met and everything I did, but wasn't coming back to me in a way that made me feel like I belonged. Instead, I heard an empty echo that felt cold and lonely. Nobody was interested in who I was, just what I was on paper. As a result, the guard I had up meant the people around never saw who I was because I didn't allow them to.

Fear was setting in and it made living at a distance excruciating. *How is that living?* Can you truly live if you don't allow yourself to be seen? A connection to this world is afforded so easily for some, and yet it was the hardest thing for me to achieve.

It wasn't until years later that I truly understood that in order to give a strong signal into the world, the connection I needed to work on was inside me. I was already working on becoming the authentic creation I knew I was going to become, and nothing in this world came without a price. For me, it meant for a brief period, my connection to the world wavered, but soon enough, that connection was going to pulsate from me in waves.

All is Full of Love

Chapter Six
Blackburn, 2008

I stood and watched the blonde girl dressed like Lara Croft use some sort of rocket launcher to blast through the door of the warehouse. The door instantly went up in flames and she managed to walk right through them in slow motion without even singeing a hair, the amber sparks cascading through the air in a frantic dance. As she entered, two white men dressed in black bomber jackets and balaclavas came out of nowhere to take her on.

The woman reached for a rifle that was strapped to her back and shot one of the men in the stomach. He let out a hilarious shriek and collapsed to the ground, clutching his wound. The second man pulled out a hand gun and starting shooting. The woman balanced a metal bin lid onto her leather lace-up boot and spun around at fantastic speed, lunging her foot forward. Her boot made contact with the lid and it flew towards the gunman, shielding every bullet.

Somehow, the bin lid also had the capability to ricochet the bullets back at the gunman and riddle his body with punctures until he hit the ground in a pool of blood. *Oh, sweet Jesus, when will this shit end?* The woman stood over the two men, victorious. Her white tank top was tied tightly under her heaving bosom. Her cleavage was glistening, her nipples hard and visible through the wet patches of sweat. Her shorts were black denim, cut roughly at the edges and high enough to get a glimpse of her arse cheeks popping out provocatively.

She stood in the warehouse, wiping her mouth with her bare arm and clutching her handgun. She heard a struggle from behind a few rusty barrels. She lifted her handgun in their direction and made her way over. As she moved the barrels, she found a well-muscled man tied loosely to a wooden chair with white rope. *How the hell did he not escape from that shitty rope job?* She walked over to the man who was gagged with a filthy rag and untied his hands and feet. The man remained seated as she took the rag out of his mouth.

'Maybe you can use this on me?' *Fuck's sake, this just gets worse by the second.*

The hostage gave the woman a cheeky smile and she got on her knees, proceeding to unbuckle his belt and unzip his pants. She pulled out his huge penis and began sucking on it in a most compelling fashion. Her hand was wrapped around the base, swirling around like she was trying to open up a jar of raspberry conserve. Towards the shaft, her head was bobbing frantically and slurping unnecessary. *It isn't a cup of Tetley's, love, it's a cock! Just suck the damn thing.* I crossed my arms and let out an exhale of discontent.

After what seemed to be a few seconds of impressive deep-throating, she came up for air and unbuttoned her shorts, slipping them down slowly. The man watched as his meat sabre did that weird bobby-up-and-down thing men do when they flex their wang muscles like some kind of mating call.

BEEP, BEEP!

The door to the sex shop sounded, alerting me to a customer entering. I paused the movie just as the man was leaning forward to eat the woman's arse out as she was bent over a stack of tires. I looked over the counter and saw a customer walk in from the street entrance. I didn't know who he was, but he didn't seem too much to worry about. Working in a sex shop, I didn't get many new faces come in and was used to the usual clientele that visited. The one thing I was glad about with where I worked was that it never made the fact that it was a sex shop feel sordid.

Most of the sex shops in Blackburn that I came across were always boarded up, unkept dives that looked awful from the outside. I only imagined what it was like inside. I always envisioned them being one of those depraved looking places like the ones Nicholas Cage visited in *8mm*. That wasn't the case where I worked. It was on the high street, bright and was female and couple friendly. We didn't just sell porn; we sold all sorts. Lingerie, toys, furniture, the lot.

The gentleman that came in seemed to know exactly what he wanted, walking straight to the sex dolls. The dolls we kept in the shop were boxed up, and I watched as he carefully examined each one. The first he picked up was the Tera Patrick Party Doll, housed in a red box and boasted free standing capability and weighted base. He looked at it intently, making sure he read every word on the box. He eventually put it down and picked up another box, this time the less expensive plastic blow up Granny Shag Doll.

This was less prestigious than Tera Patrick, and a pretty weird looking granny too. It was clear that he didn't like that one and went back to Tera. I stood patiently, busying myself with the daily sales figures. He held onto the box and started walking around the DVDs. At first, I thought he was attempting to discreetly open the box and have a cheeky feel of the silicone breasts on the doll, something that had happened many times before.

Once, I even caught someone who managed to open the box and start wanking over poor Tera's deflated face. Thankfully, I managed to stop him from coming on her by clapping my hands loudly and yelling at him to get the fuck out of the shop. Rest assured he quickly made an exit with his flaccid member wriggling frantically, like a garden worm having a seizure.

I walked into the small staff room next to the till area and watched through the one-way window that looked over the entire left-hand side of the shop. It was a necessity to have this window to catch any wankers (pun intended) in the porn section. I stood watching this guy, holding the box almost respectfully, as he perused the movies and toys. He eventually made his way to the till area and I emerged from the staff room with a smile.

'Hiya, you alright?' I said politely.

'Hello. How are you?

'I'm good, thank you. You?'

'Very well now, thanks.' He placed the box on the counter.

'Good.'

'You worked here long?'

'A little while.'

'Bet it's proper fun!'

'Yeah, it's fun working here.'

I looked this guy over and guessed that he must have been in his mid-twenties. He had messy brown hair and wore clothes that were at least two sizes bigger than his actual build. His hands were rough-looking, giving the impression that he did a hands-on job like a bricklayer or maybe a mechanic. He didn't come across as pervy or weird like the majority of strangers who tried to have a conversation with me here.

'So, is it just this or are you looking for anything else?'

'No, no, just this. I'm so excited. I saw this in here the other day and was waiting 'til payday to come back.'

'That's nice.' *What a stupid response, Yvy.*

After paying for the doll, he left the shop with a smile on his face. It was pretty certain that his smile meant he was about to have a really good time tonight. I went back to the TV monitor and saw that the DVD was still on pause, the hostage's face still rammed in the woman's arse. *That's it, I get the gist.* I turned off the DVD player after ejecting the disc. A lot of the time, I had to watch some of the new titles from big adult production companies when they came in. The DVDs were £15 each, so it wasn't uncommon for a customer to ask for a preview of the movie before buying it.

We weren't permitted to show the movies, so instead we explained what the movies were like. For example, if a movie had high production quality, I could tell the customer that. If it was a more amateur style movie of a woman who looked like she dry shaved her flange with a disposable razor having sex in a manky hotel room, I could also let the customer know that too. To be fair, the amateur stuff usually sold more than the high-quality ones. There's something about a heavily airbrushed vagina that's just a bit unsettling to potential viewers, apparently.

It was always strange having to explain to a customer what a movie was about. You'd think that it was pretty obvious and I in all honesty never really believed that anyone actually watched the movie for the storyline. Some of the DVDs that came in were elaborate three or four disc editions with extras and documentary interviews, or a three-part movie that lasted nearly five hours. Who has that much time for porn? Maybe I was getting a little bit desensitised from it all, but watching porn just didn't do it for me. I'd rather have sex than just watch it.

***

After having my gender surgery in September, it wasn't long before I was back in work. Healing was slow, but I didn't want to spend all my time at home. Despite being surrounded by nothing but sex, one thing that I yearned for was love. Now don't get me wrong, I wasn't some desperate woman who wanted to find a husband and settle down, it was more that I just wanted my heart to feel something. For so many years, I watched as my friends and family had relationships and experienced everything that came with it. Love, passion, heartache, the lot.

I knew that my time would come eventually so I never felt lonely or unloved, but I still felt as though a part of my being was going unused. I had something inside me that wanted to be unleashed. A force that I had every capability to experience. I wanted to care and love. To experience a passion that surpassed sex. Missy was so new to me. I barely had a relationship with my body; therefore, I had no way of knowing how one truly experiences a love that you feel in every part of you.

Have you ever touched yourself and flinched? To feel so disconnected with the skin that covers your muscles, bones and organs. Often when living in Chorlton I felt compelled to touch myself. To reach between my legs and let my fingers slide inside me. To feel the warmth clench around them and pulsate as I touched the ridges that caused my body to shudder.

I wanted more than anything to climax, feeling my body tingle and my aura explode from me like vapours. A euphoric release from everything. The reality was that unlike when I was younger and still searching for answers, masturbation was a means to an end that gave a temporary fix for something I didn't quite understand. As a young teen, masturbating was a dangerous and thrilling act that felt good only for the duration and instantly became a shameful one the moment I ejaculated.

Once I realised I was transgender, the thought of touching the body I presented to the world became a repulsive thought. I couldn't bring myself to place my hands between my own legs. After my surgery, learning how to connect with my body was going to take time. How much time? I was unsure. With that said, I knew that I was at least one step closer to being able to finally experience a life of love.

It hadn't been long since Jason took me to that sex club and I was more confused than ever. I didn't expect someone like Jason, who I had known from his frequent visits to the shop, to turn on me that way. I may not have known him all too long, but he was still a nice guy whenever he came into the shop and our conversations were always polite. I knew that our relationship was progressing the moment he offered to take me out, but I didn't think he wanted to use my vulnerability as a means to please his sexual appetite. I didn't expect to be taken to a sex club and have him try and use me without my consent.

I'll admit that at first, I was intrigued, but the moment he took my control away and forced me on to the platform in front of a room of strangers, I felt him take over and I no longer felt safe. I couldn't have that. No matter how vulnerable

I was feeling, I knew enough to not let him unravel me. I never saw Jason after that night, but it was still bothering me. Not him, but that I was stupid enough to go into something so blindly and almost be destroyed before I even had the chance to experience everything I wanted to experience.

Missy had only just started her journey and had a lot of learning to do. She was a totally new experience that I wanted nothing more than to fall into and become one with. To have her between my legs made my heart swell, so much that I could almost feel it burst. I spent so long working towards having her, and now that she was here, I was going to make sure that I did everything I needed to do to take care of her, no matter how painful or unpleasant.

The one thing I struggled with was patience. Although I understood that post-operative care was extremely necessary and a lifelong commitment, I didn't want to wait too long before I could start building a life that resembled something I could enjoy for the first time. To be seen as a woman full of love.

It was another day at work, and I had already completed my regular morning duties. Restock the toys, hoover the DVD area, sort out the clothing orders. By 11:00 am I completed all my duties and could relax. Working by myself was the best, not having to worry about any of the bullshit I experienced at past jobs in Manchester. Here, I came into work and the only people I dealt with were the public, and there weren't many. The shop was never packed, and although it was on a high street, it was out of the town centre so the foot traffic was much thinner.

By noon I was ready for my king-size Bombay Bad Boy Pot Noodle and a cup of tea. As I put the kettle on, the door sounded and a customer walked in. I peered outside the staff room to see a couple walking towards the counter. They were young, mid-thirties I guessed. They seemed like an odd couple. The gentleman was very buff, with perfectly groomed hair and a shirt that was so tight I could clearly see the buttons holding on for dear life to stay fastened. The lady was the complete opposite, wearing one of those pastel felt jumpsuits with a wet ponytail that pulled her features back. They approached the counter, looking very happy.

'Hello,' the lady said with a smile on her face.

'Hiya.'

'We're looking for some bondage gear.'

'Well, we have plenty. Is there something in particular you're after?'

'Mostly stuff like gags, separation bars, latex wear. That sort of thing.'

I gestured at the wall opposite the till that was covered from floor to ceiling with bondage accessories. At the top right were the riding crops and whips. In the middle hung boxed up Fetish Fantasy Series bondage accessories. There was a bed binding restraints kit, cuff and tether set and a basic blindfold set with whip and handcuffs. The rest of the wall was covered in the more advanced style accessories, made from real leather. The couple glanced over and started laughing in unison.

'Oh! How did we miss that!' the gentleman said, rubbing his chin with glee.

'Yeah, we stock quite a few different things here, but if there's something specific you need, we can order stuff in.'

'Great. We need some stuff today but this all looks perfect,' he replied.

'Oh, I'm Elaine by the way, this is my partner, Dane.'

I always found that when customers came into the shop, the majority would always feel the need to introduce themselves. It was as though they needed to make sure that I saw them as real people and not just another perv wanting to buy a copy of Ben Dover's *Royal Reamers 2* and a bottle of Gun Oil.

'Nice to meet you.'

'Everyone in our little club finds it so funny that we're Dane and Elaine!' she said enthusiastically.

'Do they?' I was in no mood for this. Already I could smell an invitation to whatever they had planned tonight.

'What's a beauty like you doing working here then?' Dane asked.

'I get paid to be here, darling. That's why I'm here.'

I often got asked that question from slimy men who wanted to either try and shame me for working in a sex shop or proposition me. Either way, I always used the same answer. After a bit of conversation about how long the shop had been going and what other items we could order, the topic of conversation moved to the reason for their visit.

'We're attending a party tonight,' Elaine said gleefully. 'We're swingers.'

'Oh, great!' I had to sound interested.

'Yeah, I love seeing her with other women. The downside is most of the time the women that go to parties aren't that hot,' Dane said.

Oh, I see where this is going now.

'Have you ever been to one before?' He added.

'To a swingers party? No, I haven't. I've been to a sex club, but not a swingers party.'

'Oooh, tell us about that!' Elaine was elated at the thought.

'It was a fetish club of sorts, really.' My mind took me back to being with Jason. I saw myself walking into the run-down building with him, intrigued to explore such a deviant, sexual world. I remembered how exciting it felt to be there, witnessing their sexual appetites and being so turned on. I felt safe with Jason, a feeling that unfortunately did not last long.

'It was fun,' I said to them both. 'I'm more of a voyeur.'

'If you ever change your mind and want to try it out, let us know,' Dane said.

'Oh, yes, please do!' Elaine interrupted. 'We would love for you to join us!'

'Thanks! I'll keep that in mind.' I bagged up the items they chose to buy and put it through the till. Suddenly, the phone started ringing. *Thank fuck for that!*

I picked the phone up as Elaine and Dane grabbed their bags and waved goodbye, but not before Dane left his card on the counter with his number and two words. *Call us.*

When I answered the phone, it was Daniel from the Oldham store. I hadn't ever met Daniel before, but I knew him very well from the daily phone calls I received from him. It was clear that he had a crush on me, which I don't blame him to be fair. Not long after I started working here and speaking with him a few times, we decided to send each other pictures so that we could put a face to the voice. I don't know why I thought that meant I should dress up with my gorgeous legs in stockings and a cute top that hugged my figure, but I sent it to him anyway. Safe to say he bloody loved it. Daniel's picture cemented my prediction that he looked like a younger version of Grant Mitchell, which he most certainly did.

'Hiya Yvy.' He said happily.

'Thank God it's you, Dan. You just saved me from being recruited into a sex party tonight!'

'Am I invited?'

'You'd love that, wouldn't you?'

'Too fucking right, I would!'

'How's your morning going?'

'Dead here. Spent the morning stood outside smoking. How about you, well, besides the sex party thing.'

'Dead too. I need to sort out the lingerie Kerry brought in bin bags.'

'Bin bags?'

'Yeah, I thought it was weird too. She said they were delivered like that. Fuck knows why. It'll take me most of the day to sort all this out.'

'Yeah, glad I don't have to do that!'

The door sounded and I heard two voices near the front entrance.

'Customers. I've got to go,' I said.

'No worries. Chat later,' Daniel replied as he hung up.

I put the phone back on the charging dock and walked to the till. As I perched my elbows on the counter, I looked over at the lingerie section and saw two people walking towards me. One was a girl who looked my age, blonde hair, a curvy figure that she dressed in a thick jumper dress and leggings. She was with a guy who had the art of the mincing walk down, which I was quite impressed by given that they were walking at a slow pace yet he was still popping his hips like he was Coco Rocha at a Christian Lacroix fashion show. They came closer and my eyes began to focus on their faces. The nearer they got, the heavier the dread started to set. It was as if their approach was in slow motion as I studied their faces, making sure that what I thought was happening was actually happening. *What the fuck are they doing here?*

'Hiya,' I greeted.

'Hi,' the guy said.

As they turned the corner to peruse the toys, the girl looked over her shoulder, giving my face a double take. *Fuck, she's recognised me.* I knew exactly who she was. I knew exactly who they both were. I never thought I'd see them again, yet here they both were.

My mind went back to my college days. After leaving school without finishing my last year in 2000, I took some time out and started college the following year to complete my GCSEs. After that, I chose to study Psychology, however, as I didn't have enough credits to get on the course, I chose a different route and decided on a BTEC First Diploma in Caring. I didn't want to become a carer, but I was told that this course would give me enough credits to then study Psychology.

My first day, I walked into the classroom feeling anxious. It was my college years, and I was still presenting as Saleem, so when I walked into a classroom that was full of girls, I stuck out massively. The moment I entered, a gaze from all the girls was thrown my way, letting me know that my anxiety was just and I was going to stick out. I looked around and saw that the only available seat was next to a girl with blonde hair who appeared to not know anybody in the class, as she was being ignored by the rest of the cliques who looked like they only joined the class because their friends did. I went and sat by her and as the lesson went on, we were asked to buddy up with someone so that we could support each other throughout the course.

'Shall we buddy up?' I asked her.

'Yeah, why not. I'm Stacey.'

'I'm Sal.'

I looked over at Stacey as she picked up the giant black torpedo dildos and had a giggle, then made her way to the rampant rabbits and anal beads. I stared for a moment, remembering how close we were in college. For months, we worked together in class which then grew to going to her house every now and then. She lived in a neighbourhood in Blackburn that wasn't very welcoming of the South Asian community, unless they ran a newsagent or a takeaway. Still, I wasn't too concerned and went around to visit her every now and then.

Her house was stuffy and unkept, and her bedroom was a small box that just about fit a single bed and dresser beside her fitted wardrobe that covered the entire back wall. We sat in her room, listening to '*Missundaztood*' by Pink, an album I hadn't heard before in full so Stacey felt it was her duty as an avid Pink fan to educate me. I didn't have the heart to tell her that she was the one who was *missundaztood* when she said it was Pink's debut album, as I knew all too well that it wasn't. Still, it made for a nice afternoon sitting in her room. By that point in my life, I had already come out as gay in college, so it was no secret. Stacey and I were getting close as friends, but I still didn't know that much about her. When she told me about her circle of friends, I was intrigued to meet them.

'Have you heard of *Never Never Land*?' She asked.

'What, the club in town? Of course, I have.'

'Most of my mates go out there at the weekend. I go with them sometimes, but not lately.'

'Ah, right! I go there all the time with my mate Kayleigh. I might actually know your mates!'

'Well, we should all go out then!' Stacey was very enthusiastic at the thought of me meeting her friends.

The weekend came around and I was dressed up for a night at Never Land. It was the only nightclub I knew of in Blackburn that had a gay night and getting there without being seen was a test of stealth. I arrived at the club, dressed in combat pants and an orange t-shirt. My hair was still the same short back and sides I had done at Passerini's, which was only a couple doors down from the club.

I always got to Never's before Kayleigh, so I entered the club after signalling to the person on the other side of the door that I was a regular. He unlocked the heavy bolt and let me in, locking the door firmly once I was inside. I got a drink at the bar and planted myself at the usual corner under the balcony. Soon enough, Kayleigh arrived, then Stacey and her friends. I was surprised to find I didn't recognise a single one of them, nor did Kayleigh. Amongst them were a lesbian couple, a few single guys and two men who were very affectionate with each other, and looked like they were a couple too.

One of the guys stood out for all the wrong reasons, and at the time I assumed that was his standard behaviour. His name was Craig. I was still trying to figure out who I was, and immersing myself into gay culture was like being in a play and not knowing the script. I was constantly unsure of what to say and how to act. Watching this guy, he was flamboyant, pulling any and all attention to himself with dramatics that came across incredibly staged. Still, at least he was getting attention. All I ever did when I went to Never's was sit and try and have conversations with the people around me, which worked for a few minutes until someone louder and bigger in presence took over the conversation and it was as if I wasn't there. The only person who actually saw me was Kayleigh, my best friend.

I watched as Craig integrated with all of his friends, being provocative and flirting constantly. He never approached me or Kayleigh, which didn't bother me at all, but I couldn't help but admire how comfortable in his own skin he seemed to be.

One evening, Kayleigh and I were perched in our spot, when I excused myself to go to the toilet. Although the toilets were gendered, not many people took that as a strict rule. Only a handful of men who felt the need to stick to their own toilet used the gents exclusively. The rest of us used the ladies room instead. It was nicer in the ladies anyway.

I once made the catastrophic mistake of using the gents and it was safe to say once was enough. If men want to piss everywhere other than the damn urinal and have anonymous, unwashed cocks poke through holes in the cubicle walls, be my guest. Me, I much preferred the floral soaps and vintage mirrors in the ladies that had plenty of loo roll, good lighting and bitchy secrets. If you ever wanted to know the dirt on what went on in *Never Never Land*, all you had to do was lock yourself in a cubicle and listen to the gossip from the people congregating around the sinks.

I entered the ladies room and saw Craig. He was distraught and surrounded by his friends, including Stacey. I had barely spoken to Craig since I initially met him, so it was a bit weird for me to try and inject myself into a situation I had no knowledge of to see if he was okay. Stacey saw me enter and flashed me a smile as she came over.

'Is he okay?' I asked her discreetly.

'Yeah, yeah, he's fine. He's just a bit—'

'Oh my God, Stace!' Craig shrieked. 'I need you!'

Stacey turned to me apologetically and I got the message that they needed some privacy. I pushed through the door and Vengaboys was blaring as the music filled the air. I watched as skinny guys in mesh vests danced stiffly whilst lip-syncing '*We like to party. We like, we like to party*' with glee. I made my way over to Kayleigh to tell her what I saw in the ladies room.

'What the fuck is he crying about now?' Kayleigh asked.

'I have no fucking idea. I didn't want to ask!'

'Don't blame you.'

We saw them both come out the toilets, Craig wiping his eyes. He made his way to the bar and some of his friends crowded around him as he bought himself a blue WKD. I took a swig of my own WKD as Stacey came over to me and Kayleigh.

'Can I talk to you for a second, Sal?'

'Uhh, yeah. Sure, you can.' I gave Kayleigh a look she fully understood. *Here we go, let's find out what the fuck's going on.* Stacey pulled me across the dance floor, through the dancing twinks and to the other side of the room. She stood close to me and leaned in.

'Craig really wants to speak with you,' she said in my ear. I was confused. That was last thing I thought he wanted, I mean, why would he want to speak to me, given the lack of interaction we've had?

'Me? Why?'

'He really needs to talk to you. Can you meet him upstairs?'

'Urrm, okay.'

I made my way to the balcony and sat at an empty table. Before long, Craig approached from the other stairs on the far side. He looked panicked, something

I hadn't seen from him before. Usually, he was confident and unbothered, but now he looked like a dry leaf on the verge of crumbling.

'Hiya,' he said seriously.

'You okay? What's all this about?' I wanted to cut to the chase.

'Can I talk to ya?'

'About what?' It was hard to hear over the base of the music pounding in my ears.

'I want to ask you something.'

'What?'

'Will you go with me?'

'Go where?'

'No, I mean will *you* go with *me*.'

I didn't understand what he was trying to ask. *Where the fuck does he want me to go?* He looked at me strange and then rephrased his question.

'Do you want to go out with me?'

I was stunned. *Did he just ask me out?* I had no idea where this was coming from. At first, I thought it was practical joke. Of all the shirtless, buff guys he slathered over every time we came to Never's, why would he want to ask me out?

'Well?' He asked with a slight worry in his eyes.

'Okay, sure.'

Craig's face lit up as he leaned in and gave me a kiss. He was sloppy and uncoordinated with his lip movements, like he was trying to eat a bowl of jelly without using a spoon. Once he planted a kiss on me, he turned and scurried back downstairs, leaving me standing alone by the balcony rail. I made my way back downstairs, one heavy foot after the other, and went back to join Kayleigh.

'So, what was that all about?' She asked.

'I think I'm Craig's boyfriend now.'

***

I leant on the counter in the sex shop, watching Stacey and Craig walk around, laughing and joking with one another. It was surreal, seeing them after all this time, and neither one of them had changed. My relationship with Craig was short-lived, mostly because I barely saw him and when I did, he was in a constant state of exaggerated emotion which wore incredibly thin. For the most part, he was jealous of my friendship with Stacey. He absolutely loathed the fact that she knew more about me than he did.

I attempted on many occasions to point out that if he actually spent some time with me, he would know more about me too. But that just pushed him even further into a jealous, adolescent hissy fit. It got to a point where I didn't want to be around such an infant and the relationship died on its arse. I never had sex with him or even fooled around. I could only imagine just how terrible he was, given that his kisses felt like I was snogging flubber.

'Excuse me!' Stacey said as she directed her gaze my way. I snapped back into reality and saw that she was waiting for a response.

'Hiya.'

'Do you sell cock rings?' She asked.

'Yes, far back in the corner.'

'Thanks.'

They both turned away and carried on with looking around. Then it dawned on me. Stacey didn't recognise me. Could it be that she doesn't even know who I am? *No, it can't be.* I may have grown my hair but my face still looked the same. She couldn't have forgotten me, given how much time we spent together in college. They both walked over, cock rings in hand and dumped them on the counter. I smiled and scanned them into the till to ring them up. Stacey stared at me for a moment and then turned to Craig.

'Doesn't she look like that person?' She said indiscreetly. I felt my cheeks warm with embarrassment.

'Who?'

'That guy, you know, I can't remember his name.'

I hated that she was misgendering me to my face like I wasn't there. I didn't know what to say.

'You went out with him for a bit,' she continued. Craig looked unbothered as he scanned me.

'I don't know.'

'Did you go to Blackburn College?' Stacey asked me.

'No, I didn't. You probably know my twin brother. He went to Blackburn College.'

'Oh right.'

'Can we go now?' Craig asked rudely. 'I'm bored of this.'

They left abruptly, leaving me stood at the counter. The door chimed and they exited the shop. I had a thought about what had just transpired. *Have I changed that much? Or was I not worth remembering?* The fact that Craig didn't recognise me was no surprise. He was so up his own arse that I was convinced he was searching for fucking Narnia. He barely paid attention to the people around him unless it involved him in some way. Stacey on the other hand was someone I had spent so much time with. We were in college classes, spent time at her house, went to Never's and still she couldn't remember me. *Do you care?*

In some ways, it hurt to stand in front of someone I knew so well and have them completely dismiss me. I felt my emotions brewing up, hearing them talk about me like I wasn't there. Then I realised that they weren't talking about me, they were talking about Sal. The last thing I wanted was to be associated with Sal. He was something I had buried. I remembered how much Sal wanted to be loved and understood for who he was, even when he was struggling to do that himself. I remembered the isolation from the world, the loneliness. When Craig asked Sal out, it was as if he was finally going to have some form of relationship, not just a one-night stand. Sal was full of love, but had nobody to share it with. Craig was unworthy of such love, therefore got fuck all.

I smiled. I knew that them not recognising me meant I had evolved so much that I was barely recognisable. Both of them were exactly the same, nothing had changed. I imagined Craig being the same self-absorbed person and Stacey still having to take care of him every time he had another one of his mood swings. I had moved past that part of my life and into a new one that it was as though we were in different worlds. I thought about what lay ahead for me and it made me excited. The love I had inside was still there, only now I was starting to use some of that love on myself. I was confronted with my past, and I saw just how much I had evolved from it.

Let your past stay there, Yvy. Your future is already here.

Chapter Seven

Sunday Man came to the shop at the usual time. He was an early bird who liked to arrive just as we opened, often waiting in his car in the gravel carpark behind the shop for me or Kerry to unlock the shutters and open the door. Sunday Man's ritual was always the same. He wore his beige duster and hat, greeting us upon arrival and asked if we had any new trans titles. Kerry always said that if we ever got any new trans titles in, we should keep one under the counter for when he visited.

Every Sunday when his wife was at church, he would visit us and buy a new movie. He always wanted it in a sleeveless box, paid cash and did not want a receipt. Each time he came back, he returned the title he purchased the week before and exchanged it for a new one. That's why we always gave him a discount on movies, given that we were making money on films he returned that were then re-sold. We never threw away the sleeves we took out of the boxes.

I arrived at work just before 10:00 am and started bringing up the shutter at the back entrance. As the clunky sound of the metal shutter rattled its way up, a voice boomed from across the car park.

'Morning Yvy!' Sunday Man said.

'Morning! How are you this morning?' I asked.

'I'm very well, thank you.'

I made my way into the shop and Sunday Man waited patiently outside. He was always respectful and gave me the time to turn the alarm off and switch the lights on before asking if he could come in. The alarm was switched off and I motioned for Sunday Man to enter. It was a cold morning and I could tell that he was feeling the chill through his duster, positioning the collar up higher to block out the breeze. We made our way upstairs and the shop had already been tidied by Kerry the previous day. *One less job for me.*

Walking into the office, I popped the kettle on and watched Sunday Man walk steadily to the transgender porn section. I never quite understood why he felt the need to peruse the trans porn, given that he never bought anything from the shelves and always expected us to have a new title waiting for him under the counter to buy. Thankfully, he never asked us about the title, he just took our word that it was the type of adult entertainment he enjoyed.

I always found it strange that customers actually asked me about a movie as if they wanted a recommendation. I avoided doing that as much as I could, but Kerry often insisted that I at least watched a few titles in the shop to familiarise myself with the style of them in case someone was asking for a particular kind of film. On the plus side, at least I knew which movie to recommend if someone ever asked me if we have anything Lara Croft like with plenty of guns and tuckus lingus.

I pressed play on the CD player and made my way out of the office and onto the shop floor. Sunday Man was still hanging around the DVDs, scanning them intently. I listened as the slight delay of the CD player left the shop silent for a few seconds until Justin's voice started flowing from the speakers. *Future…Sex…Love…Sounds.* The album started playing with those four words and I watched as Sunday Man jumped a little. He made his way over to me with a smile.

'Oh, that made me leap out me skin, love.'

'Aww sorry, it happens to everyone who hears it.' *It didn't.*

'Just having a look at the old ones I've seen.'

'Oh yeah? You thinking of getting another one of those again?'

'Oh no, love. Once I've seen it, I feel terrible watching it again.'

'Yeah? Why's that?'

'Oh, it takes the joy out of it.'

I wasn't quite sure what he meant. I paused, not quite knowing what to say.

'It might sound a bit foolish…' he continued '…but I like to watch a film the one time. It's like I'm experiencing it the same way the girls do.'

I paused for a moment, taking in what he said. I suppose it kind of made sense that he would only want to watch a movie once. Plenty of people came in to buy movies that featured a certain person or involved a certain fetish, and a few prefer to move on to the next movie once they'd seen it rather than re-watch. We had a policy for customers to return a movie they bought in exchange for another DVD at a discounted price, and I always thought they did that because they didn't want to be caught with a porn stash. It never occurred to me that maybe some of them felt the same way Sunday Man did. Here stood this old man, clearly attracted to trans women, but afraid to act on it. Maybe he genuinely does see these movies as a way of experiencing something he never could act on in real life.

'That's an interesting way of putting it,' I replied.

'Love, I've been around a long time, been married 52 years, but life doesn't turn out the way you want to.'

'I guess so.'

'I knew a girl a long time ago, before I were married. Absolute beauty, as beautiful as you, my love, and I was totally smitten with her.'

I leant on the counter, listening intently He wanted to tell me a story and I was happy to listen.

'She was a lady, through and through. No doubt about it. But she had a body she said wasn't hers. Wasn't her fault how she came into this world. I met her and when she told me, I didn't believe her. I never came across anyone like her.'

'So, she told you she was transgender?' I asked.

'She didn't need to though. She was selling to make money, if you catch me drift. Couldn't have been a nicer lady but her family wanted nothing to do with her.'

'So, what happened?'

'I fell in love with this lady, but we couldn't be together. Biggest regret I've ever had.' His voice began to crack as he attempted to hold a tear from falling. 'I was brought up differently to you, my love. A man's job was to raise a family and provide.'

'Not much different than how it is now, to be honest.'

'I love my wife dearly, do anything for her, but you can't stop what the heart feels. I wish I could love the way I did all those years ago, but it's too late for me.'

He took out the DVD from inside his duster and placed it on the table. I knew that this was his way of wanting to complete his usual Sunday transaction. As I took the movie he returned, I reached under the counter for the new DVD and placed it on the table, sliding it towards him.

'Too late for what?'

'There's not many things in life I regret, my love. But letting that girl go was one of them. It may look silly, me coming in 'ere for something to watch, but people are quick to judge. Nothing wrong with admiring a special kind of woman.'

A special kind of woman.

I couldn't help but take his words as a compliment. Sunday Man had no idea I was trans, yet he felt comfortable to tell me something so personal. I understood what he meant about society's judgement. I've seen so many customers come into the shop with a cloud of shame, thinking that being interested in sex is something disgusting. Of course, I encountered a few that took it that step too far, but for the most part I never felt the need to judge.

I suppose the only issue I had with people like Sunday Man was whether they thought of us as special kind of women behind closed doors but then didn't speak up if they saw an injustice against a trans woman. I thought about all the times I had faced horrendous people, attacking me for who I was, and whether he would've said something or came to my aid if he could. Does he really care, or is he feeding me a story to cover up the real reason why he buys his DVDs while his wife is at church and wants me to understand? *Do you care, Yvy?* I guess I didn't in the grand scheme of things. To me, Sunday Man is just another customer. I heard many stories in this place, and he was a nice enough man who treated me with respect. Maybe that's all that mattered.

'Well, my love. Lovely to see you again.'

'You too. See you next weekend.'

He left with a smile on his face and his movie tucked in his duster. The sound of the door filled the room as he exited through the rear, as the track on Justin's album came to an end. The string intro to 'What Goes Around' started playing and a smile formed on my face. *Love this song.* I opened the DVD Sunday Man had returned and found his £15 for the exchanged movie inside. He insisted he put the money in the DVD and we trusted that he would always pay. Kerry and I knew that he'd return to the shop for another movie, so we had no reason not to trust that he would pay for his films.

***

I waited for John to message me. I didn't want to message him again. I had already got back in touch with him so I didn't want to come across as too eager. I didn't know why I wanted to hear from him, but all I could think about was John. The last time I saw him was the day before I was admitted to Charing Cross for my gender surgery. I loved the fact that he had no idea that I was trans and treated me in a way that I wanted to be treated. Like a woman.

We only had the one date, but it was an amazing one. I could tell he was trying to impress me with his wealth when we dined in the restaurant at the Kensington Hilton. I knew that the night was a fantasy that couldn't go any further. Even though he didn't know that I was about to have gender surgery, I didn't see the point of bringing it up with a man I had just met when I knew that the evening wasn't going to go any further.

I expected to never see him again, but after returning to Blackburn after my surgery to recover, I had a lot of time to think about him. His smile, the way he dressed, the way he smelled. Everything about him was intoxicating. He had a presence that took over an entire room. It didn't bother me that he was in his forties, he was an incredibly handsome man that I met by chance on a train to London.

Sunday Man left the shop, leaving me alone with Justin and a nagging feeling that maybe I shouldn't have messaged John. I didn't know if I was ready to see him, I didn't know if I was ready to see anyone, but the evening we spent together played over and over in my head. The way he treated me with such admiration was magical. A huge part of me yearned to have an experience with someone that was uninhibited. For so long I wanted to be with someone and completely let go, giving in to the impulses screaming inside that wanted to be fulfilled.

After what happened that night at the sex club with Jason, I learnt that I wasn't ready, and that I needed to be very careful about who I chose to open up to. The last thing I wanted was to be taken advantage of. John was different though. I already knew him, and unlike Jason and Craig, he was older and much more distinguished. He never made me feel as though he didn't know what he was doing. He was in charge, but not intimidating. He was rugged, yet I felt his softer side. He was a perfect blend of masculinity that never felt forced, as if he was trying to prove something. He made me feel safe, and fuck me he was so gorgeous.

Craig was a fucking whiny little shit stain that I couldn't stand. Always trying to prove that he's the gayest, the most fabulous, the best dick-sucker. All that told me was that he was incredibly insecure. When I met Jason, he seemed sincere too, but I soon discovered that to not be the case when he preyed on a vulnerable moment. He took advantage of a weakened state I was in for his sexual pleasure. He made one huge mistake thinking I was some weak bitch. Maybe John could be the refreshing, welcomed presence I needed in my life right now. All of a sudden, my phone vibrated next to the Karma Sutra playing cards.

J: Hello! It's wonderful to hear from you

My muscles jumped when I saw it was from John. I didn't hesitate and replied to him.

Y: You too! How have you been?
J: Very well thanks. Just come back from another trip to Monaco. How are you?
Y: Good thanx. I was hoping maybe I could see you again?

John didn't message back as quickly as I'd hoped. *Shit!* Maybe I was being too forward. *Fuck's sake!* It would've sounded better if I said *we should meet up* rather than *I want to see you.* Saying I wanted to see him may sound desperate. *You've definitely messed things up.* I looked down at my phone. Still no message. *That's it, he thinks you're a needy mess who's going to ruin his life.* I felt dizzy, then realised I was holding my breath for no reason.

I exhaled, and willed my phone to buzz. Still no message. Then again, there could be any number of reasons why he hasn't responded straight away. Maybe he's on the phone, or making a cup of tea, or maybe he's on the toilet. Yes, that's it, he's doing a number two and it's taking a little longer than expected. He has too much respect for me to text back on the toilet. *Phew, of course!* I smiled at my surprising ability of judging a situation so accurately and started sorting the nurse lingerie that Kerry asked me to iron and put on the sale rails. I looked over at my phone with a quick side eye. No message. *Just put your phone in your pocket.* It felt like an hour had passed since he messaged, then I felt my phone vibrate and looking at the time, it had only been five minutes.

J: I'd love to see you again. Shall I come to you?

I waited by King George's Hall for John. He was so insistent to come and see me in Blackburn rather than me meeting him. It worked out fine considering I wasn't about to take a train all the way to London, but a part of me was still apprehensive for him to come and meet me here. I was never comfortable going out in Blackburn, especially during the day.

When I started my transition, I struggled so much with not being seen. Funny, given that I spent so much of my life wanting to become invisible. This was different because when I had such a clear vision of myself, it broke my spirit every time I was seen as something other than who I really was. The hardest struggle I had to face during that time was having to push through the pain of trying to conceal who I was and still being seen as a joke.

Once I moved to Manchester, it was easier to step outside my door. Although I still had certain obstacles to overcome, at least there was a significantly less chance of bumping into somebody I knew. In Manchester, nobody knew me other than the people I initially worked with at the bank. Every other week, I spent a weekend in Blackburn and Feroza usually came to pick me up. Although I wanted to hold onto everything I had built in Manchester, I knew what I was going back to. I knew that the moment I returned to Blackburn, it would feel like taking one giant step back. I stripped away Yvy as much as I could and journeyed back to a place that I felt no connection to.

If it wasn't for my family, I would never return to Blackburn. The real shame was that I never hated Blackburn, I hated the memories that came with being there and the people that were insistent on making me relive old wounds. I couldn't walk through the town centre without people I didn't even know looking at me in that intrusive way. It was simpler to just try and butch it up every time I returned, or better yet, avoid going out. *But what about when I'm at home?*

My family knew that I was transitioning, but I couldn't draw attention to myself in my old neighbourhood. Just getting out of the car drew attention to the nosey bastards that lived on the same street as us, as they always wanted to know what was going on. Better to stay indoors and avoid the world.

So why did I return after I had my gender surgery? Why didn't I continue living in Manchester, you say? Well, it's simple. I was tired of letting the shadow of Blackburn consume me. I was a strong woman. I wasn't going to be ruled by a town I had every right to be in. I was born in Blackburn, so why should I be pushed out? If I want to return, I bloody well will do. Every day I went to work, I didn't hide away. I was a completely new person and I was tired of repressing who I was.

Maybe that was why Craig didn't recognise me when he came in. Have I changed so much that I was barely recognisable? Or was Sal so determined to be nobody that he was barely worth remembering? Either way, that part of me was no more, and now I wanted to move forward. One thing's for sure, John saw me. The moment we met; he couldn't help but see the woman I had worked so hard at becoming. Blackburn may still have been casting a shadow over me, but it no longer threatened to consume me. Those feelings of uncertainty still rise inside me every time I walk out the front door, but it soon fades away when I remember that I truly couldn't give a fuck what anybody thinks of me.

It was a chilly evening waiting for John. Sitting on the bench outside the Hall, I watched as couples and groups of people gathered to go inside. *Must be a show on.* Other groups were trotting along to some of the clubs. The bar where I used to work with Kayleigh was just across the street, the music pumping into the air. I pulled up the front of my duffle coat to try and keep warm when I felt my phone vibrate.

J: Just arrived. Are you at KGH?
Y: Just sitting outside.

I saw John approach and my heart fluttered as I felt a pull in my stomach, the way one does when driving over a hill and descending into the dip. He advanced further, not noticing me staring at him. Everything was in slow motion as I examined him with my eyes. His hair lifted gently as he took big strides. He was wearing a black coat that covered most of him, but I could tell he wasn't wearing a suit this time. He was much more casual, yet still so sophisticated.

I smiled as I watched him look around to make sure he had the right place. He looked anxious; I could tell he wanted to find me. He pulled out his phone and dialled. Suddenly, my phone started to ring.

'Hiya,' I said gently.

'Hi, I'm here, I think. Are you nearby?'

'Look in front of you.'

His gaze pointed my way and saw me on the bench. I gave him a subtle wave and he smiled. My body warmed at the sight of this wonderful man smiling at me. I stood up and was about to make my way over to him when he approached at speed. I didn't get a chance to walk towards him because before I knew it, he was standing in front of me.

'So good to see you again, beautiful.'

He ran his hands down my arms and kissed me. In an instant, I was pulled into his embrace and his lips warmed against mine. I couldn't believe I was kissing him in the middle of Blackburn. Any reservations I had about this town; any shadows that remained were melted away. All I could feel was John. He didn't let me go, letting our kiss last. When he released, he watched as I slowly opened my eyes and I saw just how happy he was to see me. He smiled and gave me a quick kiss on the nose and took my hand.

'It's so good to see you again, Yvy.'

'You already said that!' I said jokingly.

'And if you were me, you'd repeat it, trust me.'

Okay, that was a good one. He deserves another kiss for that.

I took his hand and we walked into town. The street lights lit up the concrete and we watched as people passed us by, not caring that we were walking hand in hand. Nobody was looking at me strangely like I was usually accustomed to. It was as if I was just another woman, just another person living her life in a way that didn't require the leering stare of onlookers. *I could get used to this.* We passed by Nigel's Hair Salon and then went on past the library.

John was taking in his surroundings, having not ever been to Blackburn. His eyes were lit up at the sight of me by his side. We continued walking, towards the Town Hall and then turned left to the Apollo cinema. I knew where to take him for dinner and wanted it to be a surprise. We eventually reached our destination, a small restaurant just across from The Grapes, a pub I frequented during my college years. I hadn't been to this restaurant before, but I had always seen it every time I went down Richmond Terrace and figured it was a classy place.

We walked in and took a seat at a table. John looked over at me and smiled, laying his hand on mine before I could remove it from the white linen table cloth.

'This is a nice place,' he said.

'Yeah, I haven't been here before but I thought it would be nice for us.'

'They sell meat and potato pies here?' His mouth did a little half smile.

'Sorry?' I was confused why he was asking about meat and potato pies in an Italian restaurant.

'You don't remember, do you? You said you'd be happy with a meat and potato pie if I ever took you out to eat!'

It all came back to me. I remembered sitting with him in that fancy restaurant in London, eating incredibly pretentious food and telling him I would have been just as happy if he had taken me to a chippy for a meat and potato pie with chips. I burst out laughing at the thought. Why didn't I think to just take him to a chippy? *It's not too late!*

Just as I gained a bit of composure, the waitress came over with the menus. We studied them, thinking about what we wanted to order. Although it all sounded delicious, this just wasn't me. Why was I trying to impress him with a classy restaurant that I've never been to before? I should be myself, that's what he likes about me.

'Looks good, what do you fancy?' John asked, his eyes scanning his menu.

'Meat and potato pie, chips, peas and gravy,' I replied. John looked up from his menu, flashing that adorable smile again.

'I don't think they have that on the menu.'

'I know,' I said, grabbing my coat. 'Come on, let's go.'

It didn't take long to find a chippy and we stuffed our faces with food served in a polystyrene tray wrapped in thin, white paper. Once we were done, I decided to surprise him with something I knew he'd like.

'So where exactly are you taking me?'

'You'll see.'

He looked around as we walked along Preston New Road. I could tell he noticed that we were walking further away from town and the absence of any shops or restaurants was obvious. We were just across from the Blackburn School of Music and heading towards the gravel carpark when I saw John's face looking flummoxed.

'Okay, now I'm getting worried. Where are you taking me?'

'Over there.' I pointed at the steel shutters to the sex shop. He saw the sign above the shutter and suddenly caught on to where we were.

I knew that taking him to the sex shop was not allowed. The shop had been closed for a few hours and I had no business going in so late in the evening. Still, I knew first-hand that the security cameras hadn't worked in months, and once I opened the door I knew exactly where to go to turn the alarms off before they sounded. This was going to be easy and I wasn't going to get caught. Besides, it was going to be fun. I turned the key for the shutters and the clanking sound as they pulled up automatically blasted through the night air. It almost seemed louder at night, possibly because I knew that what I was doing was wrong and the slightest of noises put me on edge. Once I was in the shop, I swiftly disengaged the security alarm and locked the back door once John was inside.

'Jesus fucking Christ!' He exclaimed. I turned from locking the door to see him staring at the bondage furniture that was housed behind metal dungeon bars. He looked to his right and saw the huge bondage bed, covered in PVC sheets and leather cuffs hanging on the side.

'What's that?' He asked, pointing at the cuffs at the bottom of the bed attached to a leather-covered pole.

'That's a leg separator, John. Shall we go upstairs?'

With each step, he studied the posters on the wall of all the adult DVDs we'd recently got in. He couldn't believe that I brought him here. I wondered whether he thought I was bluffing when I told him I worked in a sex shop, which may have explained his reaction. I wanted to impress him, I guess. He was such a successful person and I was only starting out, yet I had to appear as though that wasn't the case.

The last thing I wanted was for John to think that I was inexperienced in life and had no direction. I wanted to be perceived as a woman who knew what she wanted and went for it. *But that's exactly what you are, Yyy. Stop trying so hard.* John saw the shop floor and was completely enthralled by everything he saw; it was as if he'd never been in a sex shop before. Or maybe he had and it just wasn't as good as this.

'So, this is where the magic happens then?'

'I wouldn't exactly call it magic,' I replied. 'But it's definitely an interesting job.'

'Do you enjoy it?'

'Yeah, actually. I get to run the shop and I like how open it is. I get people telling me that I shouldn't work here, but I just call them out by telling them I get paid to be here, unlike them.'

'I bet that shakes them up.'

'It does, actually.'

He stood near the wall across from the DVDs, lined from top to bottom with sex toys and I watched as he examined some of them, picking a few boxes up and then hanging them back on the wall. I looked behind me and lifted myself onto the counter, perching on the edge. When I looked up, John was gazing at me.

'You're beautiful, you know that?'

'Thank you.'

'No, I mean really beautiful.'

I was slightly uncomfortable for some reason. I didn't know how to respond to his remark, instead I just smiled.

'You're not just an attractive woman, you're a beautiful person. I've been in relationships with women who I've cared for, but I've never been excited by them. Not like when I first met you.'

'Really?' I said softly. He walked towards me and stopped when he reached my legs hanging off the counter. He rested his hands on my knees, sending a shiver up my spine.

'All this is definitely interesting, and I love how frank you are when it comes to sex. But I can tell there's so much more to you that I want to get to know.'

'I wouldn't know where to start. What if you hear something you don't like?'

'I could say the same thing about me. We've all done things we might regret, but that's what makes us human.'

'I'm not talking about regrets. There's not a lot about my past that I regret. It still doesn't mean sharing it will help.'

John grabbed my hands and I pulled him closer to me, wrapping my legs around him. I could tell he was pleased with how I was making all the moves.

'If you don't regret anything, and it's made you to be this wonderful, how can that be bad?'

I could feel the words about to come out of my mouth. I wanted to tell him the truth about me. I wanted him to know that I was trans and that I was happy with who I was. I wanted so badly to see his face light up and for him to tell me that he didn't care and still wanted me. His arms wrapped around my back and his lips gently touched mine. With every pause between kisses, he whispered to me, 'I can't stop thinking about you.'

His kisses deepened and I started to lean back as his weight pressed onto me. He felt so good on me, his scent filling me the same way it did in London. Our bodies were locked perfectly, every move synced in unison. I didn't want him to stop, I wanted him to take me. *Are you ready though, Yvy?* I was unsure whether I could actually have sex with him. I was still healing, and after what happened with Jason, I was still reluctant to give myself to anybody until I was truly connected with myself. We kissed harder, barely catching a breath, when I decided to stop. Who was I kidding? I knew I wasn't ready to have sex yet. How could I be? I was still dilating three times a day, still discharging and having to wear a sanitary towel every day. I was in no position to have sex. John felt my reluctance and released his arms from around me.

'You alright?' He asked.

'I am, but I'm not ready. I'm sorry. I can't really explain it but there's a lot that I just need to—'

'It's okay,' John interrupted. 'You don't have to apologise. I don't want to rush you at all.'

'Really?'

'Yes. Look…' He paused for a moment, looking down at his shoes for a few seconds. He looked slightly anxious, like he was worried that what he was about to say might offend me. 'Can I ask you something? I don't mean this to be rude, I want to be completely respectful.'

'Of course.'

'Have you always been a woman?'

Fort Belvedere, Florence, Italy, 2018

Brighton, 2019

Little Sal, Blackburn

Canal Street, Manchester, 2011

Yvy and Chelsie, Manchester, 2019

Manchester, Pride 2019

Yvy and Ellis, Coyotes Manchester, 2014

Yvy and Zohra, Christmas 2016

Chapter Eight

I laid in bed, not wanting to get up to dilate. It was part of my daily routine to dilate once before work, again when I finished work and lastly before I went to bed. I could probably go down to just doing it twice a day now, but the morning routine was the most important. If I missed dilating in the morning, a dull pain in my lower abdomen built up and lasted for hours. I hated that feeling.

Dilating wasn't the only thing on my mind. I couldn't stop thinking about John. The way he asked me whether I was trans completely threw me. I had no idea he knew, or could tell that I was. I didn't know what to say to him in that moment, I mean, what if he was asking because he wanted the validation to kick the shit out me? For the first time, I didn't feel safe around him. I didn't know if the switch in his head was going to go off and unleash someone dangerous. Something came over me in that moment, a defence mechanism that told me to protect myself and lie to him. Up until now, I didn't feel that I was lying to him per-se.

The first time we met was a chance encounter, I had no need or obligation to tell him when I knew the night wasn't going any further. Now that I had my surgery, I didn't feel the need to say anything because I wasn't hiding anything from him. This is my body. *Mine.* Still, somehow, he could tell that I was trans. Am I that obvious? Am I always going to be seen as trans? My head started spinning with questions I didn't want to hear. All I knew for sure was that I was in no position to see John.

I arrived at work to find Kerry already there which I was surprised at. Usually, it was either Kerry or myself working the shop, seldom both of us unless something big needed to be done that required us both there. She hadn't mentioned that she was going to be opening up, and when she saw me, she had a slight look of stress that concerned me a little.

'Morning Yvy,' Kerry said. 'You alright?'

'I'm alright. What are you doing in today?'

'Oh, I needed to catch up on a few things and I wanted to talk to you about something.'

This was intriguing. I couldn't for the life of me guess what she wanted to talk to me about. Kerry went on to talk about her sister, who also happened to be the Area Manager for our shop.

'Gemma's opening up her own lingerie shop in Darwen with the stock she bought from that warehouse the other week. She needs help setting things up so I'm going to be helping her out with that.'

'Okay cool. That's fine.'

'So, are you able to do a full week shift from now on to cover here?'

'Of course!' I was ecstatic at the thought of doing full-time hours. I was only contracted to work weekends and Wednesday evenings, so any extra hours were a great help with my saving up some moving money. I was determined to move back to Manchester but was struggling to save enough to cover bills and get a deposit together.

'I could do with the overtime!'

'Well, that's what I wanted to make you aware of. You'll get paid overtime so make sure you fill out your timesheet as extra hours, but if anyone calls, don't let on that I'm not here.'

The phone rang and Kerry picked it up, as I sorted out more of the lingerie she had asked me to iron and hang up. She barely spoke a word before she put the phone down.

'Who was that?'

'Don't know, they put the phone down,' Kerry said. 'Keep an eye on that in case we have ourselves another weird one.'

It had been a while since we heard from the weird guy who called the shop and hung up every time we answered. That slowly developed, the more confident he became. He then started calling to ask if we had a product in store, then proceeded to tell us what he wanted to do. For example:

'Hello, Yvy speaking.'

'Hello…urrrm, I'm looking for a dildo.'

Exhales soul out gently.

'Okay. What type are you looking for? We have a wide range.'

'Urrrm, well, I need a big one. What do you recommend?'

Inhales soul back in.

'It's really up to you want you want. It's not for me to recommend what would be best suited.'

'Well, urrm, what do you like to play with?'

Sharp breath in and ready to shut this shit down.

'That's not something I wish to discuss.'

'Oh. Well, you sound sexy so if you want to try a toy and tell me what it's like, I might buy it.'

Click.

It got to the point where he requested I use a toy on myself and then let him purchase it after use, unwashed. After Kerry spoke to him, he stopped calling. I had a feeling he may have started up again and slammed the phone down when he heard Kerry's voice.

'Okay Yvy, I'm off to Darwen. If you need anything, I have my phone on me so just give me a bell.'

As Kerry left, I sat on the step that led to the office and felt the sunshine through the window. It was another clear day and the warmth of the sun was hitting my face. I closed my eyes and let my thoughts drift away, but they all went to John. I pictured myself with him again that night we met. I saw him take me home to his flat, just as I did when I dreamt about him in Charing Cross Hospital. I stood in his living room, looking out of the window when he came over and took me to his bedroom. I saw us making love on his huge bed and could feel myself getting excited sitting on the step.

It was too soon to tell, but I often wondered whether Missy was ever going to feel sensation. Sure, my body felt sensation before my surgery, but I was so disconnected from it that I hadn't orgasmed in so long. I remembered dreaming about John and feeling myself climax when I felt him deep inside me. I didn't know if it was legit or not, but I woke up in the hospital bed and somehow through the pain of just having surgery I could feel a pleasurable sensation between my legs. Something awakened inside me.

Even as the nurse took out the yards of gauze, I still felt pleasure. This excited me. My body had gone through the trauma of surgery, and dilating further extended the trauma by having to put Missy through an experience that was far from pleasurable. Believe me, using dilators was not remotely erotic. In fact, it was a three-hour drive and an overnight flight away from anything remotely resembling an orgasm. I worried that I wouldn't feel that pleasure tingle between my legs ever again.

I leaned against the porn and let my mind go back to my fantasy of John and felt him take me. The same eroticism stirred inside, warming my veins. *I want to see him again.* Suddenly, the phone rang. I jolted and felt reality rushing back. My eyes stung from the daylight streaming through the window, having had them closed for so long. I searched for the phone and answered.

'Good morning, Yvy speaking…hello?' There was no answer. It dawned on me that it might be the weird guy again.

'Hello?' Still no answer. I was about to put the phone down when I heard a voice.

'Hey Yvy, it's me.'

'Daniel?'

'Yeah, course.'

'Oh, thank God for that!'

'Happy to hear from me then, gorgeous?'

'No, I mean yes, I am. You didn't answer when I picked up. I thought you were that weird dildo wanker guy.'

'Has he been on again?'

'Possibly. Someone rang earlier. They put the phone down on Kerry.'

'Sounds like him. Don't blame him though. I'd put the phone down on Kerry and speak to you any day.'

Eye roll.

'So, how's your morning going?' I asked, changing the subject.

'Not bad, been quiet so far. How about you?'

'Same, Kerry just left.' *Shit!* Maybe I shouldn't have told Daniel that she left the shop after she just told me not to say that.

'So, I have you all to myself. Even better! I was thinking, I've been looking for flats around Oldham Mumps and I thought that—'

'Wait,' I interrupted. 'Oldham Mumps? Did you just make that up?'

'You've never heard of Oldham Mumps?'

'No, I haven't! That's a real place, is it?'

'Yeah, that's the nearest tram stop to 'ere.'

'Fair enough!' I exclaimed. 'Sorry, what were you saying?'

'I've been looking at flats and found a really nice one I want to move to.'

'That's good! Gets you out of your mum's house.'

'Yeah, but it's a bit pricey. I was thinking, what if we moved in together?'

I eye rolled again, taking in what he just said. I knew for a fact that this wasn't just some innocent suggestion to become roommates.

'Dan, you realise we've never even met. I don't think moving in with each other would work.'

'Why not? I mean, we practically know each other. We talk every day. I think it would work.'

BEEP, BEEP. The front door sounded which was a welcomed relief.

'I have to go, Dan; I've got a customer.'

'Promise me you'll think about it. You'd be helping me out and at least you can move away too like you want to.'

'Okay, okay, I'll think about it.' I stood behind the counter and looked ahead at the customer walking towards me.

'Really? You really promise? Yvy?'

My nerves were on edge as I watched the elderly gentleman walking past the PVC nurse outfits, looking down.

'Yvy, you still there?' Daniel said. I realised that I was frozen on the spot with the cordless phone to my ear. I forgot to respond to Daniel.

'I'll speak to you later.' I said in a faint voice and hung up.

***

Mum made keema and roti for dinner. The aroma of the fresh chapati dough cooking slowly on the tawa was heavenly. Fareed was out with his mates and I could hear Feroza moving around in her room which was directly above the kitchen. I liked to keep Mum company as she cooked. I stood by the corner of the worktop as she added a little extra flour to the surface, ready to roll some more chapatis to cook. Mum placed them on the tawa, slowly watching them rise. Mum was authentic in the way she cooked, using her tea towel to move and press down the roti, then flipping it over with her bare hands to cook the other side. The end result was a chapati that was light and fluffy with a traditional familiarity. The keema was already made and on a low heat to evaporate the water a bit more.

My stomach was rumbling, I couldn't wait to eat. When I was living in Manchester, it gave me a sense of independence, but it also gave me a bigger appreciation of my mum. Not only as a mother, but as Zohra, her own person. She was an amazing woman that did so much for us, and I didn't want to come off as ungrateful. Being back home in Blackburn, I liked to stand in the kitchen or be around when she cooked. I didn't like to show up when the food was ready and disappear when I was done eating. She deserved more respect than that. I was still reeling from my day at work, but I wasn't quite sure if I could speak to Mum about it. In fact, I didn't want to speak about it at all.

Mr Peters, or James as he always asked me to call him, started coming to the shop and he appeared to be just another customer that I was used to seeing. He'd come in to buy a movie or two, then leave. I didn't have much in the way of conversation with him, mostly because he would come in on days when Kerry worked so I seldom interacted with him.

He was elderly, my guess would be mid-to-late seventies, and wore a thick wine coloured coat and black gloves. He always had on a charcoal trilby hat made of tweed that had a wine-coloured trim matching his coat. He looked distinguished, and was well spoken. As time progressed, we began speaking. Often, we spoke on many subjects, and every time he was respectful and cordial. Then it all changed.

A couple of weeks ago, Mr Peters came in when I was working the Wednesday shift. I usually worked the evening from 5 o'clock until we closed at eight, but Kerry had asked me to also work the day shift which made it a particularly long day. The door sounded and I saw Mr Peters come in. I greeted him and went back to tallying up the days sales as he perused the DVDs as usual. His thing was lesbian porn, made by low-budget filmmakers. He had a routine of looking at other DVD titles, then going back to the lesbian section, then repeating the cycle until he finally picked something. He finally decided on buying a copy of *Sex in the City* and brought it to the counter. I searched under the counter for the disc which was stored in a large DVD suitcase.

'How are you doing this evening, my love?' He asked.

'I'm fine thanks. How have you been?'

'Oh, not too bad, my love. Better for seeing you.'

'Awww that's sweet.' I never took his compliments to heart and assumed he was just being polite. 'It's been a long day today. Been working the day shift too.'

'Ooh that's a long day. You got any plans for tonight?'

'Lots of sleep!' I said laughingly.

'Ever take any of these movies home?'

'No, I see enough of this stuff at work. Don't need it at home too.'

'Aye, I see your point, my love.'

I smiled as I ran the sale through the till. An air of uncomfortable silence fell on the moment. I wasn't sure what to say so I remained quiet. It was Mr Peters that broke the silence.

'Do you like porn or is it just for us old timers?'

'Awww no, that's not true. We get all sorts of people coming in to buy some.'

'I find it fascinating that a young girl as pretty as you would like a bit of porn.'

I always felt uncomfortable when anybody referred to me as a young girl. It didn't happen much until I started working in the sex shop. It made me feel like the person saying it saw me as this youngster that they wanted sexually. Being called a young girl made me feel like they didn't want to acknowledge that I was a grown woman in her twenties. They wanted the fantasy of young flesh.

'I don't mind porn, but once you've seen one, you've pretty much seen them all.'

'Fair enough, my love.' He wasn't sure how to respond, which I was hoping would be his reaction. Something about him changed when he spoke to me. He no longer came across respectful or cordial. He had an intrusive tone that was dirty and unwelcome.

'Well, it was lovely to see you, my love. You have a good rest tonight.'

The shop was closing in ten minutes when he left, but I decided to lock the doors the moment I heard the chime as Mr Peters exited. I was in no mood to see anyone else and I didn't want to risk a last-minute customer. I was done and closed up.

I tried to sleep. My body was exhausted, but I just couldn't drift off. I had to work another day shift the next day and I knew that if I didn't get some shut eye, I was going to be a zombie in the morning. I opened the drawer next to my bed and pulled out my iPod nano. Searching through the artists, I stopped when I got to Alanis Morrisette, playing her acoustic version of *Jagged Little Pill*. Her voice soon filled my head and drowned out the thoughts and feelings that were plaguing me.

Thoughts of John and what could have been. Thoughts of creeps at work that wanted nothing but to fulfil some selfish sexual need. Thoughts of whether my mind and body would experience a pleasure that came with feeling love. All these things I couldn't process. I couldn't stop them from infecting me, making me question whether love was something I would get the chance to experience.

What if the very fact that I was trans was forever going to hinder me from experiencing love? What if every time I find someone I wanted to get close to, they were going to find out I was trans and leave? What if I stay in Blackburn and the only interactions I have are with the filthy customers at work that I had no interest in? What if I remain unrecognisable, even to the people I once had relationships with? I didn't have the answers to any of these questions. I opted to block them out and let Alanis take over my thoughts and help me drift to sleep.

The next day at work, I was emotionally drained. I picked up my mobile, desperate to message John. I wanted him to make me feel the way he always does. Being around him was like magic and I hated that things had become awkward between us. I should've just said I was trans and seen how he reacted. It wasn't like he was angry or standoffish right before he asked me. We were passionately kissing. *God, I miss kissing him.*

Before he asked me, I didn't feel like I was lying to him because the subject had never come up. It was something I had debated with myself for so long, the question of whether to tell someone I was interested in about me. I made the decision to not tell anybody after I had my surgery because I felt there was nothing to tell. My past was exactly that, mine. It had been over a week since I heard from John and I was growing ever more certain that I wasn't going to hear from him again. I messed up my chances.

The door sounded and Mr Peters walked in. I immediately let out a sigh of frustration as he was the last person I needed to see right now. He approached the counter with a smile on his face and I just knew he wasn't here to buy anything.

'Hello, my love.'

'Morning Mr Peters.'

'Please, call me James.'

'Fine.' It came out blunter than expected, but I was in no mood to chat.

'Did you get some sleep last night?' He enquired.

'I did, thanks. Feel much better today.'

'And you look it too, my love.'

Ugh, wish he would stop calling me 'my love'.

'I was busy last night too,' he confessed.

'Good.' I knew he wanted me to ask him what he did, but decided not to.

'I made something for you.' He pulled out a small camera and messed around on it for a moment. 'You said you'd seen them all.'

I was confused at first, trying to recall what we spoke about last night. My mind wasn't paying much attention to this old man so it took a moment for me to register what it was Mr Peters was referencing. He handed me the camera and a video was playing. I looked at what seemed to be a living room, with a dining table, a bay window and dated furnishings of a man stuck in the 1970s.

'What is this?' I asked, not looking up at him.

'Just keep watching.'

I did as was told and watched as Mr Peters appeared in the reflection of a wooden framed mirror. He was holding the camera up, trying to catch his smile in the lens. The camera turned down to show his hard penis. My hands froze and I couldn't move my head. I was shocked at what I was seeing. He zoomed in, showcasing his wrinkled, unpleasant-looking cock that resembled that piece of dried foreskin hanging off a branch in Summerisle. I was disgusted. The moment I saw his hand wrap around it, I knew where this was going and handed the camera back to Mr Peters.

'Why would you show me that?' I asked way too politely.

'You liked it, didn't you, my love?' His voice deepened to a slightly sadistic tone. I felt his words creep under my skin.

'That's not nice to show someone.'

Why the fuck are you being polite, Yvy?

'Oh, come on, my love, do you know how hard you made me? That was for you!'

I had enough. I put my hand on the camera and pushed it towards him.

'Here, take it.'

Before I could pull my hand away, Mr Peters put his wrinkled hand on mine with pressure. I knew that he didn't want to let go.

'This one's for you too.'

He grabbed his crotch with his other hand and began stroking himself through his pants. He stared at me, sucking his tongue in his mouth in rapid succession, creating a grotesque squelching sound, as if he was trying to catch the attention of a dog. I pulled away from him and he saw the anger in my eyes.

'You need to leave. Right now.'

He stood back and I could see that he was hard. Before he could speak, I raised my voice to stop him.

'RIGHT NOW.'

I sat in the living room with Mum, eating her delicious keema and fresh roti. The keema was always lovely and spicy, the really hot kind that I had grown accustomed to over years of eating homemade curries. I loved eating it with a slice of banana to cool my mouth with every bite. It was Mum that got me into eating keema with banana, which at first sounded horrendous; however, it turned out to be absolutely amazing. The television was blaring as Fareed had come in and switched on *Top Gear*, which he insisted on watching on a high volume. I zoned out as I ate, thinking about seeing Mr Peters again today.

I hung up on Daniel and watched as Mr Peters approached, only this time he didn't have the usual spring in his step, his shoulders hunched and his hat covering his eyes. My mind went back to him exposing himself to me and it made me sick. Unlike last time, I wasn't frozen on the spot. This time, I was going to give him a piece of my mind if he even attempted to do what he did again. He reached the counter and greeted me under his breath.

'Hello.' He dropped the 'my love' this time.

'What do you want?'

'I-I wanted to apologise.'

'Fine.'

'I shouldn't have done—'

'I don't want to hear it,' I said, 'you've apologised so there's nothing left to say.'

'I understand.' He reached into his pocket and took out a forest green, velvet box. 'I want you to have this.'

'No thank you,' I replied.

'Please, I feel terrible. I don't know what got into me. I don't usually act that way.'

I looked at him sternly. I wasn't about to entertain his bullshit and rejected his attempt at a polite gesture. I wish I had reacted this way the last time he was here. I should've called him a disgusting prick and thrown his arse out.

'I don't want it, Mr Peters.'

'Please call me Jame—'

'I don't want to call you James. I don't want anything from you. Now if that's all you came in for then I suggest you leave. I'm not going to make you feel better just because you feel shit. How do you think you made me feel?'

'I know, I feel terrible about it.'

'Then carry on feeling terrible.'

I folded my arms and walked off into the office. I knew he was still stood at the counter, but I refused to come out. I waited, sitting on the office chair and putting the kettle on so he could hear I was busying myself like he wasn't there. After a few minutes, I heard the door chime and I emerged from the office to see that he had gone. The kettle boiled and I poured myself a cup of tea, taking it out to the shop floor.

Placing the mug on the counter, I saw the green box sitting by the novelty gifts. *He didn't take it with him.* I resisted at first, but I decided to open it and found a watch. It was old and used, probably something that meant a great deal to Mr Peters. Looking at the condition of it, it looked as though he must've taken special care of this watch over the years by keeping it in the box. Maybe it was a family heirloom or it was gifted to him by someone special. I picked it up and in one swift move, I threw that piece of shit in the bin.

Chapter Nine

I stood in the bathroom, staring at my jawline in the mirror. I spent so much money on laser hair removal that my facial hair had all but ceased to grow. The use of make-up was unnecessary which was fantastic, but I couldn't help but notice the stubborn areas around my chin that just refused to stop growing. I still had to shave those areas to keep it as smooth and faint as possible, which I loathed.

The thought of putting a razor to my face to shave was such a masculine act which made my old self feel vehemently present. Getting laser hair removal was £70 a pop and although my Indian heritage had blessed me with lovely, thick hair, it was also seen as a curse when it came to facial hair. I needed so many treatments to achieve the desired result of smooth skin.

Still, after months of shelving out cash to have the treatment, I still had the stubborn patches that simply wouldn't succumb to the intense heat searing through my skin to burn the root and send it to a fiery grave. With that said, I was one sexy bitch and there was no denying that.

Kerry was once again at work when I arrived which was becoming a common theme for the past week and a half. I knew she was still working at her sister's shop in Darwen, and I was still covering for her any time someone from Head Office called. I was tired of working there. At first it was exciting and I enjoyed my job, but a part of me knew I wasn't supposed to be there anymore. The reason I returned to Blackburn after living in Manchester was to be at home while I recuperated from my gender surgery.

Of course, I needed to work and pay bills which was why I took the job at the sex shop, but I knew that it was temporary, and eventually I would move away again. Manchester wasn't the goal per-se. I had lived there already which gave it a familiar, comforting pull, but it wasn't my only choice. Moving to a new city didn't scare me and I wanted to keep my options open. Leeds was tempting, or possibly Nottingham. Definitely not Oldham Mumps.

Having the opportunity to be around Mum every day was wonderful. I missed her so much when I was in Manchester, but I felt stagnant in Blackburn. A part of me will always remain there, but that part of me also belonged in Blackburn and not with me. I left that person behind and I was needed elsewhere. I needed to start my life again somewhere different. I wasn't anxious about moving away again, not like I was the first time. I knew now that I was more than capable of taking care of myself.

When I moved away the first time, I was riddled with thoughts of whether or not I could support myself, but I proved that I could do it, and moving back to Blackburn was no reflection of my capabilities to live independently. Money was still a huge issue for me. I was working extra hours at the sex shop, but it wasn't anywhere near enough money to cover my bills, pay for more laser hair removal, cover the costs for trips to Charing Cross whenever I was asked to go for a follow-up consultation and also try and save a big enough deposit for a flat somewhere else. But I had no choice but to keep working. At the end of the day, I didn't have much choice given the circumstance.

Kerry was hunched over the counter, filling out her timesheet for the week, when I arrived at work. She seemed pleased to see me, with an eager look on her face.

'Yvy! You alright?'

'Hiya! What are you doing in so early?'

'Just sorting my timesheet out, have you done yours for the week?'

'Yeah,' I answered. 'It's in the folder.'

'Good, I'll fax it over to Head Office before I leave.'

I squeezed past her and headed to the office to drop my bag and put the kettle on. I didn't have to ask Kerry if she wanted a brew, as the moment I clicked the kettle on, she immediately indicated that she'd like one. She nodded at me to drop a tea bag in her cup next to the sugar.

'How's it going in Darwen, Kerry?' I asked.

'Okay, just a lot of work. It's driving me fucking insane though.'

'Why, what's going on?'

'We need the shelf units putting up and the whole thing is a disaster to sort out. We can't keep storing all the stock downstairs, but we've got nowhere else to put it.'

I knew what she meant. We had bags and bags of lingerie that Kerry's sister purchased from a warehouse stored in the dungeon downstairs next to the metal bed. They'd been there for weeks, carefully hidden behind some boxes but still taking up at lot of room.

'Oh, before I forget, have we sold any of the sale rack stuff at all?'

'No, not yet,' I replied.

'Right, good. I need you to do something for me.' She lifted a small, red security box from under the till. 'If you sell any of the sale stuff, if they buy it cash, put the money in the box and don't run it through the till.'

'What do you mean?'

'That stuff belongs to Gemma, so if anyone buys it in cash and gives you the exact change, put it in the tin.'

'What if they want a receipt though?' I enquired.

'Write them a paper one and say the till's broken. It's fine, Yvy, most won't ask for receipts for sale stuff.'

I wasn't sure how I felt about what she'd been asking me to do lately. First, she's asking me to lie about how many hours she actually works here in order to go set up her sister's shop and still get paid. Now, she wants me peddle her sister's skanky sale items and not run it through the till. I was starting to feel as though both Kerry and Gemma were using me to cover their arses and do their dirty work. What was I getting out of it? Sure, I was working more hours, but I didn't feel like I conveyed to Kerry that I was not okay with what she was asking me to do. Kerry took a few sips of her brew and dashed off to Darwen, leaving me in the shop.

I sipped my brew and thumbed through the latest Leg Avenue catalogue, writing down all the lingerie and stockings I wanted to order with my 50% staff discount when the door chimed. I glanced up and saw a gentleman walking towards me. He seemed familiar, but not enough to hold my interest as I gave him a greeting smile and went back to my catalogue.

'Hello again!' He said rather loudly.

'Hiya, you alright?'

'Yes, thanks. Thanks for your help the last time I was here.'

I paused for a moment, studying his face. Then it dawned on me that this was the man who bought the Tera Patrick Sex Doll.

'Oh yes, I remember you,' I said. I didn't want to acknowledge the thanks, not because I didn't want to, but because I had no idea what I did to help him.

'Jenny has really settled in so well at home. We get on well good.'

'Jenny?' I asked and then immediately regretted it.

'Yeah, you know her, from here.'

'Yes of course. I'm glad you two are getting on.'

'She's lovely. She really is.' His smile was radiant. I could tell the doll made him genuinely happy.

He walked towards the DVDs and went down the aisles looking for the titles that weren't as hardcore. After choosing three, he brought them to the counter and I looked for the discs to put in the cases.

'Have you ever been in love?' He asked me.

'I haven't, no,' I said as I turned momentarily whilst looking for his discs.

'I feel like I am.'

'With Jenny?'

'Yeah, she's perfect.'

'In what way?' *Why the hell did you just ask that question?*

'She just is. She listens to me, takes care of me. Other girls laugh at me. I-I don't mean, I mean. I'm just, well, it's hard for me to—'

'I get it.' I could tell he was spinning a little. I didn't want to distress him. 'So, you get along with her, do you?'

'I do!' His face lit up once more. 'I tell her things, and she listens. I'm not stupid. I know she's just a doll, but does that really matter? She makes me happy so what's the big deal?'

I didn't know how to answer that. Many people came through the doors of this shop, and most of them were quick to judge me for simply working here when most of the time they were the ones cheating on their partners or hiding a side of themselves or being absolutely disgusting towards me. Here this guy stood and the only thing he had done was fall in love with a doll that gave him what he needed when he needed it the most.

'I'm sure I'll meet a nice girl like you who doesn't judge me. But when that time comes… I don't know. I'm not going to lock myself away though. I've got lots of love to give, and I can share it however I want.'

I couldn't help but smile. His words floated through the air and whistled in my ears. *I've got lots of love to give, and I can share it however I want.* I never thought of love that way. I always felt that love was something you worked for, that you had to seek out and then hold on to. I never felt love for myself. My entire life was plagued with confusion that I barely had room for love. The love for my family was different, that was something I was instantly brought into the moment I took my first breath in this world. But for those seeking a different kind of love, I expected it to be something you find in someone and fall in love with.

It never occurred to me that one could already possess that love before sharing it with anybody else. I suppose it made a lot of sense. Loving myself was such a foreign concept that it never dawned on me that I should work on loving me before someone else does.

'I'm sure you will,' I responded.

'I mean, if it makes me happy and I'm not bothering anyone, what's the harm?'

I shrugged and smiled at him reassuringly.

'Anyway, sorry, I'm talking your ear off!' he said, changing the subject.

'It's alright, I don't mind.' I put his movies in a bag and placed it on the counter. 'That's forty quid for those three, hun.'

'Thanks, I don't need a receipt.' He handed me two twenties and smiled as he exited the shop. I stood holding his money, about to process the sale in the till. The door chimed and he left the shop when a thought ran through my brain. *Pocket the money, Yvy, no-one will find out.*

***

Nearly three weeks had passed since I heard from John. It was pretty clear that he didn't want anything more to do with me and I didn't want to message him first. I messaged him first the last time and doing so again might come off desperate. I missed speaking to him though, but I was pissed that he just stopped messaging me because I said I wasn't trans. Was it that he was only interested in me because he thought I was or am I thinking too deeply and he might have a genuine reason why he hasn't got in touch? He might be in the hospital, or dealing with a family emergency. I needed to stop stressing about it. The phone rang and before I answered, I knew it was going to be Daniel.

'Morning, Yvy speaking.'

'Hey, it's me!'

'You alright, Daniel!'

'Better now. Have you thought more about us moving in?'

'Yeah,' there was no way I could word this without being totally honest, 'I don't think it's a good idea. I don't want to share a place with anyone.'

'Oh,' he said disappointedly, 'okay then.'

'We're still okay though, right?'

'Yeah, of course!'

Usually, Daniel kept me on the phone for at least thirty minutes, but not this time. He kept it short and sweet and we were done after ten minutes. I knew his feelings were hurt by my rejection to his offer, but there's no way I was going to move in with him. I wanted my own place, my own life. Saving up was getting a bit easier. Over the past week, I had made enough money from unregistered sales that I could afford another IPL treatment on my face and still save a bit towards a deposit.

I didn't feel guilty about what I was doing. I was still putting money in the tin whenever I sold Gemma's lingerie and covering Kerry's shift while she got paid anyway. The easiest way for me to pocket cash was to sell the discount DVDs and the sex toys in the sale bins. They were all items that the shop wanted to get rid of and wouldn't be ordering again, so I didn't have to include them on the inventory. If they went missing, nobody noticed. I figured they wouldn't miss the money.

My desire to leave Blackburn was growing immensely. All I could think of was getting my own place again and building my life up to something that resembled one that Yvy could comfortably live in. One that didn't involve bumping into people I knew or having to avoid social settings to avoid the 'that's her' looks I couldn't stand. I was growing tired of trying to prove that I belonged in Blackburn and really didn't want to stay in a place I had so obviously grown out of. I heard my phone vibrate on the sales counter and flipped it open.

J: Hello

I stared at my phone and my nerves tingled sharply, sending a shiver up my spine.

Y: Hi

I didn't want to seem too eager. After all, I hadn't heard from him in weeks. Then again, I hadn't messaged him either so we were both on even playing fields.

J: How are you? Sorry I haven't been in touch. Missed you
Y: I've been okay. Thought I wudnt hear from u
J: Sorry. Been away in Monaco. Bit crazy at the moment

Of course! That's why he hadn't gotten in touch with me for so long, he was probably busy with his public relations job. My phone vibrated again with another message.

J: I really want to see you.

I agreed to see him again. It was a no-brainer, as I missed him terribly. The last time we saw each other was incredible and we didn't part on bad terms. We decided to meet on a Wednesday, after I finished a late shift and we could go somewhere in town. I sat opposite King George's Hall, waiting for him to arrive. He knew the area well from the last time he was here, so it took no time for him to find me. He approached and gave me a kiss on the cheek, a gesture that chilled me to the bone. *He doesn't want to kiss you on the lips.* I wasn't sure if that was a bad sign, but things were already off to an awkward start. His gesture to kiss me prompted me to attempt a kiss on the lips, but resulted in an uncomfortable series of movements when we didn't connect.

'How are you?' He asked.

'Confused if I'm honest.' I couldn't hold back my frustrations. 'It's been a while since I've heard from you.'

'I know, I'm sorry. I just felt so bad for what I said to you. I didn't think you wanted to hear from me.'

I paused to look at his face and saw sincerity.

'Oh, well, you don't have to feel bad. I mean, I wanted to talk to you about that.'

I sat back down on the bench and John followed shortly after. He shuffled closer to me in an effort to stay warm as the sun settled and a chill breeze set in.

'I didn't want to apologise over the phone,' he said 'I wanted to tell you that I felt awful for springing that on you.'

'Listen.' I responded, I was tired and wanted to be honest with him. 'About that, I was thrown by it, don't get me wrong, but not for the reasons you probably think.'

I felt ready to tell him. I wasn't ready when he blurted the question out to me because I wasn't in control. I wasn't about to reveal something I didn't want to. This was my journey and nobody will have access to it without my say-so.

'I am transgender.'

I waited for his reaction, but only saw a motionless face. He remained content, taking in every word I just said. 'You put me on the spot and I didn't like it. The only thing I could do to shut it down was lie. I'm not sorry I did it, but I feel comfortable telling you now.'

'I'm glad you did,' he said. 'I don't have a problem with you being transgender. I could've worded it better than blurting it out. I had an idea you might be.'

John saw the frustration on my face when saying that to me.

'No, I didn't mean you look like one. I think you're very beautiful.'

My frustration grew even more. *Did he just imply that trans people are ugly and I'm beautiful because I don't look trans?* He began fidgeting in his skin and I could tell he knew he was digging himself a hole.

'I didn't want to make a big deal, I just wanted to tell you. But if things are going to start getting weird between us—'

'No, no, they certainly won't. You're one of the most amazing people I've ever met. I think you're fantastic. All I could talk about was you in Monaco. I wanted everyone to know you.'

'That's sweet.'

'In fact, that's something I wanted to talk to you about. I've landed a PR contract with a major firm there and they need a twelve-month commitment from me. It's big money, really big money.'

'That's great.' I could see where this was going. I was about to get the *I like you but this ends here* speech.

'Would you want to join me?'

It took a moment to take in what he just said. I went from staring at nothing to focusing on John's certain face.

'Join you?'

'Yeah.'

'You want me to come with you to Monaco?'

'Yes.'

'For a year?'

'That's right!'

'As what exactly?'

He was stumped for words. John didn't know how to answer that. We had never discussed what we were to each other when it came to our relationship.

'As my woman.'

'*Your* woman?' A term I wasn't comfortable with.

'Yes, I want you on my arm there. We'd have such an amazing time. Imagine seeing all the beauty there and you'd have no worries at all. I'd take care of everything. All you have to do is be there. Be there with me.'

I couldn't deny that it was a tempting offer. Living in Monaco with a handsome man and no cares in the world. Not having to worry about anything. But then on the other hand, what would I be giving up? Yes, I'd be with a man who knew I was trans and I wouldn't need to keep it a secret, but was that all I was to him? Every time I met someone who found out I was trans, it either ended badly or they saw me as a sexual fetish of sorts.

I didn't want that to happen with me and John. We hadn't slept together, but would I inevitably become his fetish? Would he still see me as Yvy or will he only see the label? I'm sure Monaco was a wonderful place, but being there under his care meant I would be completely dependent on him. He was a lovely man, but to move to a different country and not have control over my own money, my own job, my own life scared me.

He had already bragged about me to his friends and colleagues which made me feel like he was setting the groundwork for my arrival before I had even agreed to go. There was so much going around in my head and none of it was pleasing. This was too big a step. I was on the road to recovery from the biggest step I had ever made, I wasn't willing to give up my own journey to make another person's journey better.

It was a week since I had seen him on the bench, huddled up in the cold as he proposed an adventure I wouldn't regret. I sat in my bedroom with my sketch pad and watercolours, letting my hand guide the brush in waves of green. I wasn't sure what I was painting, which was always good. I preferred to let my imagination take over and watch the art unfold. My hand twitched, causing a sharp, more deepened shade of green sink into the paper. Just then, my phone vibrated and I already knew who it was. My body knew who it was. The deep green looking back at me signalled who it was.

J: Hello beautiful. Have you thought about Monaco?
Y: Hi. Yeah, I have
J: Will you join me?

I stared at the phone, pondering his question. It was a question I had pondered for days and no matter what angle I came at it, no matter how I tried to rationalise it, I still ended up in the same place. I picked up the phone and replied.

Y: You should go without me. I'm sorry

I waited for a response, but one never came.

I Owe to My Mother

Chapter Ten
Christmas, 1987

Zohra walked through Blackburn town centre towards the department store, knowing full well that she couldn't afford a single thing she actually wanted to buy. The shops were decorated with Christmas cheer. Lights were twinkling and tinsel covered the entrance amid shoppers wearing festive winter attire. She watched as children grew excited, walking hand in hand with their parents in the hope that maybe they would succumb to their tireless pleading and buy the very thing that made their hearts swell. It was Christmas. A parent's job at Christmas was to put the biggest smile on their children's faces, the biggest smile of the year no doubt. Zohra knew this. She knew that for Feroza, Fareed and her three-year-old baby, Saleem, they too deserved to have the biggest smiles on their faces for Christmas.

She approached the entrance of the department store and picked up a metal basket. The lights were bright, flooding the entire store in a glow that left no place to hide. She glared at the pick and mix section, showcasing an array of sweets wrapped in shimmering foil that twinkled in the eyes of every child that tried to pull their parents towards the colourful confections. She walked past and started towards the household items.

Zohra felt a sense of dread wash over her. She knew what her intentions were when she walked into the store, but it was one thing to think it and another to actually go through with it. Zohra was a good person, through and through, and she knew this. In fact, it was the one thing in her life that she was certain of without any doubt. For years, she was subjected to the world taking pieces of her and giving nothing in return. Nobody saw her, not even her own siblings. Growing up in Tanzania, Zohra was the youngest sibling and under the tightest restraint. She never got the chance to do the things her brothers and sisters got to do. She had dreams. She had thoughts and visions of what her future would be,

123

but a dream needed a chance to flourish, something that was never afforded to her. She did the only thing she could do and took moments in her life that she found to be hers and held on to them.

Zohra loved school, and was the brightest in her class. She learned to speak English so well that even her teacher was unsure where she learnt it. She marched in parades in front of the President of Tanzania and felt more alive than ever. Her opportunities to live her life were limited, but whenever she had a chance to shine, she was blinding.

The store was busy with families as Zohra navigated down the aisles, one heavy foot in front of the other. Her gaze on the items sitting on the shelves was dense, barely registering what she was looking at. Her focus was not on the items, but on the people around her. She studied the faces of the people passing by, noting their expressions, their emotions, their eyes when they locked with hers for a split second. She turned a corner and almost bumped into a lady pushing a pram. Zohra was startled as the woman came around the corner and almost crashed into her. Her bones jumped beneath her skin and her heart skipped a beat.

'Oh, I'm so sorry,' said Zohra.

'No worries, love,' the woman replied as she manoeuvred the pram around her.

Zohra took a moment to gather herself. She knew she was overreacting, but with good reason. *I am a good person.* Zohra always did for others, never putting herself first her entire life. It's hard to know any better when that's all she did. Moving to the UK as a teen meant a new life, the possibility of things getting better and her emancipation imminent. Instead, the restraint haunted her like a ghost. All she ever wanted to do was live her life, but things were different now. She had her children. Her love for them was just as blinding as the light she had for herself. She would do anything for her children, even if their father wouldn't.

Zohra reached her intended destination as she stood staring at an array of children's toys. She scanned the shelves and saw everything that would make a young child burst with happiness. Remote control cars, Jem and the Holograms dolls, Thomas the Tank Engine toys, plush teddy bears. She picked up a toy car set and studied it carefully. She imagined Fareed ripping off the Christmas wrapping and finding the box beneath it. He'd love it.

Just take it, Zohra.

She knew she couldn't afford to buy a single toy in the store. How could she? Her husband had cleared the bank account once again and left her with nothing. *I have nothing.* The thought of her children not having anything for Christmas made her feel sick. She couldn't do that to them. Zohra had to withstand the hits life threw at her over the years, but the three precious lives she had a responsibility for shouldn't have to feel those same hits. They deserved to enjoy being children, just like every other child. They deserved to have the biggest smiles on their faces on Christmas Day. Why should her children miss out just because their father couldn't care less whether they had any joy at Christmas?

Just take it.

Zohra inhaled and held her breath, contemplating what her heart was telling her to do. It was screaming inside her chest. She exhaled sharply when a voice sounded to her right.

'Excuse me?' A gentleman said, grabbing her attention. 'Am I alright to squeeze past?'

Zohra glanced and saw that there were a few people now perusing the toy section.

'Sorry,' she said softly as she moved to let him pass. She placed the toy cars back on the shelf and walked away.

What are you doing, Zohra?

I can't do this.

Why not? Do you want your children to go without this year?

No, but I—

So just do it. Take something for them and leave. It's that easy.

I can't! I just can't.

And what's the alternative? Do you really want to see the three of them so upset?

Of course I bloody don't. What do you take me for?

I take you for a woman who does what she needs to for her kids. Is it your fault that bastard at home has left you with no money again? Do you think this will be the last time, huh?

She knew what her heart was telling her was right. This wasn't the first time he'd done this and it certainly wasn't going to be the last. He may have fathered her children but he wasn't stepping up in the way that she wanted him to, nor did she expect he ever would. It was all up to her. *It always is.* She returned to the toy section and saw that the crowd of people picking gifts for their young ones had left, leaving an empty aisle. The toys she knew her children would love still remained. Toy cars for Fareed, a teddy bear for Sal, a doll for Feroza. If she were to put them in her bag and walk out, would it really matter?

Of course, it would.

Her head suddenly overcame her heart and refused to be blocked out. Her hands began to twitch and her skin prickled underneath her heavy coat.

You do this and you'll get caught.

No, I won't. It's just a few toys, it's nothing big.

To you it might not be, but what do you think will happen if they catch you?

I don't want to think about that?

I understand why you want to do this. I know. You can't hide it from me. I felt how upset you were that day you took them to town during Summer.

Zohra's cheeks flushed. Her nerves were on fire, making her skin burn. She knew exactly what she was recalling. It was a sweltering day in Summer when she and her children were at home. Sal was playing with Feroza, who was feeling the warm air that was building in the house as she played games with her siblings. Zohra wanted to do something nice for them. It wasn't fair to keep them cooped up in the house on such a wonderful day. They deserved a treat.

'Feroza, Fareed, come on!' She said as she picked up Sal from the sofa 'We're going out!'

Feroza didn't need to ask where they were all going, she knew it would be a treat and she thought right. Zohra knew that they would love a nice walk into town for some cold drinks and ice cream. She dressed her children in Summer clothes and got everyone together. The walk from Hancock Street to town usually took about 20 minutes, but having a baby in a pram and a child on each side to take care of meant that it took Zohra a little longer today. The roads were busy along the way, which was usual for Bank Top. It was always a busy road which required Zohra to take special care of her treasures as they made their way on foot.

Thankfully, neither Feroza or Fareed complained about walking into town, and Sal simply enjoyed the ride in the pram. Zohra couldn't take the car, their father had taken it to work, but she didn't want that to stop her enjoying the day with her children. She knew the smiles on their faces when they got their hands on a deliciously cool ice cream would be enough for her.

Fareed held her hand tightly and Feroza walked beside the pram. Being that she was eight years old and the eldest of the three, she didn't feel that she needed to hold her mum's hand. She preferred to help her mum by making sure her littlest sibling was safe in the pram and walked beside the turning wheels. Zohra didn't mind, given that none of her children ever left her sight and were always obedient. They knew to listen to their mum and not wander off.

They eventually made it into town, walking through the centre where it was even busier than Bank Top. Zohra needed to take some money out of the cash machine before heading somewhere for ice cream. She could already see plenty of families enjoying the sun, sitting outside with their children enjoying an ice-cold dessert. *They're going to love this treat!* She made her way to the cash machine with the children and waited in the queue. It wasn't too long, but the sun beating down on her felt unbearable as she waited her turn to use the machine. She looked down and saw that Fareed's brow was damp with sweat and Feroza was swaying from side to side to make her Summer dress dance. *Come on, hurry up.*

She knew her baby was safe in the pram and well protected from the sun's rays. Finally, her turn came and she wheeled the pram to the cash machine with her children. She could tell Fareed and Feroza were getting a little bit tired from being out in the warmth and needed to cool down. As she inserted the bank card and punched in her PIN number, her heart sank once she pressed the button to check the bank balance in the joint account. She couldn't believe what she saw, taking in the seconds that slowed down as she stared at the balance of the account.

He took it all.

Zohra felt her emotions taking over, the memory of that moment eating away at her. She couldn't help but think about her children and how it felt to let them down. *All I wanted was to make them happy.* It took a lot to make her cry, but Zohra felt her body reacting at the memory of that Summer day. Looking down at her children, the pressure behind her eyes built as tears formed in an attempt to fall down her cheeks. *Don't do it, Zohra. Don't you cry.*

She held them back as hard as she could, letting out an exhausted gasp into the air and away from her children. She had no other choice but to take her children home. Feroza was confused as to why her mother had taken them all into town, only to go back home. Zohra had no money and no choice. With not a penny to her name, she couldn't even buy a drink for her children. All she could do was hold back her sadness and take them back home.

It was those emotions that were brewing up again. The thought of her children having the same confusion as they did on that Summer day was too much for her to bare. She didn't want to feel the same sadness that she felt. But at what cost?

You know it's the right thing to do. Just take the toys and walk out the door.

Zohra paused, contemplating what her heart was telling her. She knew it was wrong, but not providing for her children because of their father putting her in this situation couldn't be an excuse. But then again, why was it always her responsibility? Why was it that she had to do everything?

Because you're their mother, that's why. It became your responsibility the moment you brought them into this world.

It was true. She was responsible for her children. It's only a few toys, it's not like she was robbing a bank or something.

Exactly. You're making a big deal out of nothing. Imagine their faces when they open their presents!

Zohra didn't struggle to see their faces beaming from ear to ear. She smiled discreetly as she continued to stand in front of the toys. She pictured Fareed and Feroza ripping their presents open and gasping at their new treats to play with. She saw her eldest helping to open Sal's present as he stared curiously at what lay beneath the snowflake-covered wrapping. Feroza opening the present and making the teddy bear dance before Sal's eyes, his face lit up with excitement. *That's it. It's decided. I'm doing it.*

She picked up the toys, glancing around constantly as she put them in her carrier bags. She moved discreetly and swiftly. She didn't want to procrastinate, just get the toys in the bags and move. The toys were secured in the bags when she started around the corner and back to the homeware section. The intention was to head straight for the exit and get the hell out, but something was stopping her. Instead, she walked slowly around the lighting section, pretending to be interested in various lampshades and different sized bulbs. Her pace slowed, almost to the point of standing still, as she clenched the handles of her carrier bags every time someone passed her. What if they walk past and see the toys in there?

Okay, you're thinking too much about this. You know what you're doing is wrong.

But I've done it now.

You haven't left the store yet. You don't have to go through with it. Save yourself the trouble and put them back. The children are small, they won't care if you haven't got them any presents.

I'll care.

What you think doesn't matter. What matters right now is that you're going to get caught. There's no way you're going to walk out of here.

Yes, I will. No-one noticed me taking them. How will they notice me walking out with them?

Because they just will. You know what will happen. They'll search your bag. Call the Police. Brand you a thief. Do you want that?

Zohra moved away from the lighting area to the open space between the aisles and stood frozen on the spot. The blaring department store music ceased and the shoppers were all stood still, like statues. The store was silent, not even a child's cry or wheezing cough could be heard. Every customer was frozen in place, stuck in position like living mannequins. Some were pushing prams, others paying for goods, children mid-motion as they ran towards the pick and mix.

Zohra didn't understand what was happening. She stood for a moment, listening to the silence that rushed through her head like an empty echo. As she looked over her shoulder, she saw a door at the far side of the department store. It was painted white with a fire exit sign on it. She wondered whether that was the room the Store Manager took people in who were caught stealing.

But you're not stealing, you're providing for your family. Any mother would do the same.

She turned to face forward again. Her heart shuddered in her chest as she noticed that everyone was now staring at her. Their eyes were empty, like glass marbles left outside in the cold that turned to frosted orbs. Zohra felt the pressure building behind her own eyes once more. *Don't cry.* She couldn't stand the people looking at her, judging her, tearing her apart. All she wanted was to be a good mother. She took a step forward and her shoes clicked, the sound bouncing off the walls.

As she moved through the customers, each one remained frozen in place, just their eyes following her. Zohra tried her best not to look at them. *If you don't look at them, they can't see you.* She felt their presence, even though she refused to look up. Each body was like a jagged rock she was forced to manoeuvre around in a raging river that wanted nothing but to see her destroyed. She proceeded with caution, painfully aware of every movement and sound she made. She thought she had her technique down until she made an attempt at increasing her pace. The empty shopping basket she picked up upon her entry bumped into another woman's basket. Suddenly, the music in the store played and the sound of the hustle and bustle of the store rushed into her head like a full-on assault.

'I'm so sorry! Didn't mean to bump you like that!' the lady said.

Zohra was stunned and gave her a smile and continued walking. The exit was right in front of her. She stood for a moment, readjusting her shoulder bag and taking in her surroundings for the last time. She saw that there was no security staff by the exit, they were busy walking through the aisles.

You can do it, Zohra. Just walk out the store and don't look back.

Chapter Eleven
Christmas, 2009

It was a freezing Winter in Morecambe. The streets were buried beneath a thick blanket of snow, coating every tree branch. It was the coldest Winter I ever experienced. Never had I seen such silence as the snow fell. Not a sound from a neighbour or people in the streets. Everyone knew better and stayed home where it was warm. Although the snow was beautiful, beneath it lay thick layers of ice that made every step a treacherous one.

The house Benjamin and I lived in was situated at the bottom of a hill, which meant any decision to leave the house to go to the shops or to see his friends was one we didn't take lightly. My disciplinary hearing at work was delayed once again, which meant I was still out of work and stuck at home with Benjamin.

Living in Morecambe for the past few months was really getting to me, to the point where I barely left the house other than for work, and now I no longer even did that since the grievance was put in against me and I was sent home on full pay. It sounded sort of good at first. Yes, accusations were made against me by staff, well, one particularly manipulative bitch, but I couldn't help but appreciate the fact that I didn't need to work over Christmas.

Being with Benjamin was growing increasingly frustrating. I moved to Morecambe for him, and for a chance to live a life where being transgender was a non-issue, especially since he had no idea of my past. At first, I felt a responsibility to be upfront and honest with him, but in the end, I decided not to take that step to tell him. I didn't want to risk him looking at me and just seeing me as a trans woman. Then again, I could be wrong. He might turn around and accept me completely, but a part of me thought he would secretly think differently and nothing he could do or say would make that feeling go away.

You never know what a person really thinks about you and it can eat away until it consumes you. Better to keep it to myself. After meeting him at the sex shop and him living in Manchester at the time, we quickly went from being casual to a relationship and then to living together when circumstances forced him to moved back to his home town. I didn't want to be so far away from him. I knew it was a rash decision to move to Morecambe when I didn't know a single soul except for Ben, but that was a risk I was willing to take. The opportunity to start again in a brand-new place with a clean slate was too good to pass up. I had no idea if living together was going to work, but then again how would I ever know unless I just jumped in and did it?

I hated working in a supermarket. It was something I never saw myself doing, but I had no choice. There was fuck all when it came to jobs where we were. My only options were either working in a supermarket or in a residential home, and since I had no actual qualifications to enable me to work in a residential home, I had to go with a supermarket.

When I moved to Morecambe, I used all the remaining money I scammed from the sex shop to get me there. Ben had no job and no money, so I had to depend on myself to make things happen. When I finally moved, the first priority was to find a job. We managed to snag ourselves a nice two-bedroom house to rent at a reasonable price, but I didn't have enough money to sustain us for long, so I was out in full force and applying for every job I could find. After countless trips to different stores in the area, I finally got two job interview offers. One was for a small supermarket, the other for a new chippy that was opening down the road. I was in no position to throw away a potential job offer, so I went to my first interview at the chippy.

The morning of the interview, I dressed in a smart outfit comprised of a blazer and pencil skirt, with a white blouse and court shoes. I looked like I was applying to be Maggie Gyllenhaal's replacement in *Secretary*. I made my way to the interview, confident that I had nothing to worry about. *Why wouldn't I get the job?* I arrived at the chippy, which hadn't actually opened yet. I looked in and saw some lights on in the back as I pressed my hands against the glass and peered through the circle I formed like a telescope. Movement in the corner of the room caught my eye and I saw that a worker had noticed me too, motioning me to come in. I wasn't sure how to open the door, as it appeared to be one of those fancy automatic doors you see in a hotel. The man realised that I couldn't open the door and pushed a release button that made the glass slide open.

'Sorry love, I thought it was already open!'

'No worries.'

An uncomfortable second passed before the man spoke to me again, 'What can I do for ya?'

'I'm here for the interview.'

He stood staring at me, looking me up and down in a quick motion. It appeared as though he wasn't going to speak again so I cut through the silence.

'The job interview. I'm Yvy.'

'You're 'ere for the chippy job?'

'Yes, I am.'

'To work in *this* chippy?'

'I hope so, it pretty much looks like a chippy in here!'

'No, I just mean, well, I didn't think someone like you would apply to work 'ere.'

Instantly I thought this was going down a route I really hoped it wasn't. I already noticed when moving here that I barely saw any people who weren't white.

'I mean,' the man continued, 'you look very posh!'

I let out an internal exhale, thankful that this wasn't turning into a racial discussion.

'Well, it doesn't matter what the job is, I always think it's best to dress properly.'

I walked behind the counter and followed him to the staff area in the back, where I was greeted by another gentleman.

'Hiya, thanks for coming in for a chat.'

'Not a problem,' I replied as I took a seat.

The two men seemed very upbeat, wearing smiles on their faces throughout the entire interview. The man I met first then spoke.

'I'm Gary and this is Luke. We're looking forward to starting this place up and want to find someone who can do the counter stuff.'

'Great!'

'Can I ask,' said Luke, 'why are you applying for this job?'

I knew they were confused by my presence. To be fair, even I was confused as to why I was there. Working in a chippy for rubbish pay was the last thing I wanted to do, but I couldn't turn down a potential job, any job for that matter.

'If I'm honest, I need the money.'

'Fair enough! Just didn't expect someone like you wanting to work 'ere!' Luke said surprisingly.

'Work's work, I guess!'

'So,' Gary interjected, 'we've had a look at your CV and I have to be honest, I think working in a place like this just wouldn't suit you.'

'Why?'

'I'll be honest, it's a pretty basic job and the stuff you've done for work you can easily get a job somewhere that can pay you better.'

I knew he was right, but I had been looking for work for weeks and gotten nowhere. At this point even a shit paying job is better than nothing, but I could tell that Gary and Luke had made their minds up that I wasn't going to get the job. I didn't want to beg for it, so I took their words on the nose and politely walked away from the interview, knowing that I didn't get it.

I arrived home to find Benjamin sat on the reclining sofa, his laptop balancing on the arm of the chair. The familiar tone of *Dog the Bounty Hunter* boomed from the television. A tone I had come to loathe after being subjected to hours of Ben's favourite television show.

'How did it go?' Ben asked, turning his head to me but still looking at Mr Dog.

'I didn't get it.'

'What?' His eyes focused on me. 'They already told you that?'

'It was pretty obvious from what they said. Doesn't matter. I'll figure something out.'

'Well, the supermarket job called and asked if you could give them a ring.'

We planned on having a quiet Christmas this year. I was in no mood to spend it with Benjamin's friends or family, and I didn't want my family to come here. I wasn't ashamed of being here, it was more that I was ashamed of what I had become by being here. I went from an energetic force of nature to a frumpy girlfriend who did nothing but work and take care of a boyfriend who had no job and relied on me to keep everything afloat, which I was barely doing.

I was sick of my job too. I had my interview for the Sunday job at the supermarket and I somehow impressed them so much that they ended up offering me the role as a Team Leader. They felt that bringing in new blood would breathe new life into the store and I was more than happy to accept the job. I thought I was applying for a job stacking shelves one day a week and instead they offered me a full-time job and bigger salary.

Initially, the job was going well. I got to know the staff pretty well and they seemed to be accepting of me, something I was anxious about given that I was an outsider, and I knew for a fact that at least one of the staff had their eye on the job I snatched. In the store there were two other Team Leaders, Dhalia and Viv. A couple of young girls in their early twenties, Natalie and Alice. Two women in their thirties, Denise and Steph, and a university student working part-time called Colin. Two elderly employees who had retired and only worked the tills a few days a week, Stuart and June, were the only staff I didn't get much chance to speak to, except on my first day when the Store Manager, Paula, introduced me to them.

For the most part they all seemed okay with me, asking me plenty of questions about my past. At first, I grew a little paranoid when I was being asked so much. *Do they know about me?* However, I soon discovered that I was branded 'the sex girl' after Viv and Paula told everyone that I had worked in a sex shop. It wasn't exactly the reputation I wanted before I even had a chance to introduce myself, but it beat being seen as the he/she in Blackburn whenever I bumped into someone I knew.

The first few weeks involved getting to know the job and how things ran in the store. The hours felt long, given that I was either starting work at 5:00 am until mid-afternoon, or starting work at 2:00 pm when the morning staff were done and working until past 11:00 pm when the store closed and all the nightly duties were completed, ready for the morning shift to pick up the next day. As time passed, I had to adjust to being a Team Leader. I never had a job where I was directly responsible for other members of staff, let alone ones that were already established and didn't know a thing about me.

I could tell that the younger girls, Natalie and Alice, weren't particularly fond of me, Natalie most of all. I noticed how stand-offish she was around me, only livening up when other people were around. Viv was her aunt, so I knew to be careful what I said around either one of them. Of everyone I worked with, I had the least trouble with June and Colin.

June was a lovely lady with short red hair that enjoyed working a three-day week on the tills. Just like Stuart, she did no other job but the tills. This really pissed off the younger staff, mostly when we had delivery orders and we needed help with bringing the crates in. Natalie and Alice constantly complained that June should be getting her arse outside to help, but I always defended June. She was too old to be pushing heavy crates of goods around, and I wasn't about to take her off the tills just because Natalie couldn't be bothered and wanted an easy shift serving customers instead of doing what I asked her to do.

She hated taking orders from me. If Viv told her to do something, she'd listen to her aunty and do as she was told. I was finding it difficult to step into the authoritarian role. It wasn't in my nature to give orders to people; I just didn't find it comfortable. Nonetheless, it was my job and I had to get used to it. The best I could do was not come across as a dick and always be polite and nice, a trait Natalie needed to adopt.

It wasn't long before I started noticing things going wrong. It was small things at first, but they had a huge impact on me. One shift, I came into work and went to the office. I greeted Paula and put my keys on the side counter of the office while I did the handover with Dhalia.

'Yvy,' she said pointedly, 'you need to make sure the front facing is done properly on every shelf.'

Front facing was making sure every product was facing forward and taking up the full space of the shelves every night, ready for the morning shift. This was usually done by a member of the night staff, but I always helped out to get it done faster.

'I always do, Dhalia.'

'Well, the dairy section was a mess this morning, so you don't always do.'

There was no point arguing. I knew that I had asked Alice to do the dairy section the night before and she clearly didn't fucking do it.

'Fine. I'll make sure it all gets done.'

My day shift continued and I was busy in the back, rotating stock and counting the seconds until lunch.

'So, I hear you've done porn?' Colin stated as he helped me.

'No, I haven't. I've worked in a sex shop. Big difference.'

'Aww that's a shame! Was gonna ask if you could get me in!'

'Seriously?' I asked.

'Yeah, I'd be well good at it!' He said proudly. Just then, Natalie, Steph and Denise walked in.

'Well,' I said, continuing to talk with Colin, 'it's not difficult if you ever wanted to put yourself forward for something like that.'

'Put yourself forward for what?' Steph asked.

'To do porn!' Colin replied excitedly.

The group started laughing hysterically, cheering Colin on to go for it. Colin asked a few more questions that I was happy to answer and then we all went back to work. He started unloading boxes of hair conditioners when one fell off the top of the crate and burst on the floor, covering my pants in the creamy white conditioner that exploded from the broken plastic bottle.

'Oh shit, I'm so sorry, Yvy!' Colin said.

'It's okay, I'll clean it up.' I grabbed a towel and tried my best to wipe it away. Natalie tried to hide her laughter as she walked out of the back room. After cleaning the conditioner off my pants, I returned to the staff office to retrieve my keys to unlock the back gate and store the empty cages when I saw that they were missing. For hours I searched the store, even returning home to see if they were there at the instruction of the Store Manager, even though I explained that I had most definitely brought them with me to work. I was in deep water, given that losing the keys meant having to change the locks to the store as a security measure. The keys never showed up and I was given a warning.

Over the next few months, I kept my head down and did what I needed to do during my shift, nothing more. I wasn't there to make friends and had no desire to socialise. I was civil to the ones I didn't like, and friendly to the ones who gave me no hassle. I usually worked the evening shift, as it gave me more reason to not spend much time at home. I was growing tired of living in a house that never felt like home. Every moment I caught myself with nothing to do, my first thought was of Mum. I couldn't help but feel cold without her.

Living with Benjamin meant having to hide so much from him. I hadn't told him I was trans, so that meant having to hide things from him that I had to face on a daily basis. Dilating was almost impossible. I never had a good enough reason to tell him why I needed time in the bedroom without him interrupting. Instead, I had to dilate in the shower, holding my dilator inside me by clenching my thighs around it to keep it in place. Having to wear sanitary towels every day was also becoming an issue. The healing process was slow and arduous and using sanitary towels was necessary, but not always explainable.

I often thought of being at home and seeing Mum in the kitchen making us something delicious to eat. I thought about how much I loved spending time with her, even when we did simple things like sitting in the living room with a hot cup of tea, or when she came into my bedroom to hang out because she loved how cosy I made the downstairs front room. Being in Morecambe, I felt so far away from anything warm and inviting. Instead I was left feeling the chill of loneliness. I didn't feel remotely connected to Benjamin; he was just a person I had to take care of. I loved him, but I wasn't in love with him. *So why don't you just leave?*

I arrived at work one day for my evening shift when Steph came running over to me, looking flustered.

'Yvy! Come here, I need to show you something!'

'Show me what?' I asked.

'Shh, shh, come here.' She grabbed my hand and pulled me past the freezer section and into the back staff room.

'What? What is it?' I looked out the round window and could see Viv and Dhalia at the tills trying to see why Steph had just dragged me into the back.

'Look at this!' Steph said, shoving her phone in my face. I looked down and saw that it was a Facebook post. I took the phone from her to read the comments that she was trying to show me. I was shocked to see that the comment was from Natalie, asking Alice if she knew if 'Fudge Bar' was working tonight. I knew that she was referring to me. In that moment, a light came on in my head. It dawned on me that I had spent so much energy into not wanting people to know that I was trans, that it never occurred to me that I could be faced with something like this. To be reduced to a racist slur all because she didn't like me for getting the job. What was worse was that it was all over Facebook and both Natalie and Alice still felt confident to write it. I felt my insides twist with rage.

'Can you do me a favour, Steph? Screenshot that and send it to me.'

That evening, I sat at home and wrote out a letter of grievance against Natalie and put in all the incidents that had occurred that I believed she was behind, including my keys going missing. Ben helped me put it together, as he could see I was distraught and had had enough. I handed in the letter to Paula the next day.

'Thanks, Yvy. Listen, why don't you take the rest of the day off?'

'Who's going to cover my shift?' I asked, surprised that she was going to let me go home.

'I'm here today so I can cover for you.'

'Thanks!'

I walked out and made my way home, feeling optimistic that my voice was going to be heard. I wasn't going to stand for this. There was a lot of cattiness at work that I was willing to put up with, mostly because it was someone else's drama and I had no interest in getting to know the people there. But this was something else. I wasn't going to sit back and be referred to as a *fudge bar* and not call this bitch out. I included a printed copy of the screenshot with my letter to show I wasn't trying to stir up shit. *She'll see, Yvy, just watch.*

I sat at home on Christmas Day, my hair wet from just having a shower, dressed in my white nightie that Mum had given me. *I want to give her a call.* I hadn't spoken to her in weeks, and with good reason. I missed her so much, but I couldn't bring myself to pick up the phone and speak to her. The first thing she was going to ask me was if I was doing alright. If I heard her say those words, I knew I was going to break down. I was trying to hold everything together, but I felt the cracks in my armour getting bigger. I wanted so badly to give up and go home. *Why don't you, Yvy?*

I stared down at the huge lever arch file that contained all the interviews conducted with the staff. I pictured them all, Colin, Steph, Viv, the lot of them, sitting in that small office answering question after question about me. I read every word each member of staff had said and I couldn't believe what they came out with. Literally a day after I put in my grievance against Natalie, I found out that she put in one against me, accusing me of sexual harassment. It sickened me to read the lies she came out with.

Saying that I tried to feel her breasts when she was working the tills one evening. That I brought in sex toys that were still in their original packaging to see if they would scan on the till. That I was handing out porn applications to staff. I just couldn't believe it, she made over twenty allegations of sexual harassment and sexual assault without a shred of evidence. Paula told me that my grievance did not take precedence over Natalie and was automatically rejected, despite that the fact that I had tangible evidence.

The day I was asked to come in to discuss what was happening, I had no clue who they had spoken to or what was going on. I only knew that Natalie put in a grievance against me. I had the option to bring someone with me to the meeting, however I was told it could not be someone from a union or a relative or spouse. In other words, they didn't want anyone coming in with me. I didn't want to give them the satisfaction of being by myself, so I asked the only person who I was friends with at work, June.

We sat in the office at a neighbouring store down the street and waited for whoever it was that was going to be interviewing me.

'How you feeling, love?' June asked.

'I don't know, June. I'm just shocked this is even happening.'

A staff member came in and introduced themselves and the person taking the minutes of our interview. As the interviewer proceeded, she ran through the twenty-four allegations against me, asking me to comment against each one. As she worked her way through the list, I felt myself getting furious. *I can't believe this is happening.*

'I'm sorry,' I said interrupting the interviewer 'but how is it that I'm being interrogated when you've got no evidence of what she's saying?'

'That's not what we're here to discuss. We're here to discuss the allegations made by Natalie.'

'What do you mean? You're just going to believe her then?'

'These are serious allegations.'

'I'm aware of that. But have you not checked CCTV? I mean, if I allegedly felt her up at the tills, there would be footage of this. Have you actually checked CCTV?'

'No,' she replied.

'Don't you think you should?'

'Let's get back to the allegations.'

I exhaled sharply and turned to June, who looked equally as perplexed by the interviewer casually dismissing me.

'Natalie has said that there was an incident where a conditioner bottle spilt on you and you said, let me read here, you said 'look Natalie, Colin has come all over me'. Can you tell me about that?'

'Are you kidding me with this?'

'This is a serious matter, Yvy. Please answer the question.'

I was a lit fuse. I had already spent nearly ninety minutes answering questions, but I knew this bitch had no interest in what I actually had to say.

'That didn't happen. Yes, conditioner did spill on me but I *never* said that to her. Ask Colin, he was there!'

'We did and he says he doesn't recall you saying this. But why would Natalie lie?'

'You'd have to ask her that! But what she's saying isn't true.'

'Put yourself in her shoes, Yvy. She was very shaken up by this and there are staff members that back her allegations.'

'No, I'm not going to put myself in her shoes. That implies I believe all this rubbish she's saying.'

'Well, Vivienne and Alice have gone on the record to say that—'

'Wait, these are the staff that back her up? Her aunt and her best friend?'

'We've taken that into account and we don't see that as an issue.'

I was done. I knew where they were going with this. They made up their minds. They wanted me out.

'If we can carry on, Natalie says you brought sex toys to work to scan through the till.'

'What? That's ridiculous! What possible reason would I have to do that? And why haven't you checked CCTV?'

'Alice says she also saw you do this.'

'Again, why don't you check CCTV?' My eyes started to tear up. I couldn't hold in my emotions any longer. June could see I was getting upset and gave my hand a squeeze.

'I'm sorry,' June said, 'I know I'm not supposed to talk, but I have to say this. I work the tills and I've never seen Yvy act in any way other than professional.'

I turned to June and gave her a weak smile, knowing that her kind words weren't heard by this woman sitting in front of us.

'I'll be honest, Yvy,' the interviewer said cutting through the silence, 'these allegations made me feel very ill. I saw Natalie and she was shaking as she went through these and I felt for her.'

'And what does that say about you? Are you just going to believe her and not me then?'

'That's just my opinion.'

After a couple of interviews, I was told to stay home on full pay and wait to see whether the matter would be resolved or if it was going to be escalated to a formal hearing.

December soon arrived and the snow started to fall. Although I had so much on my mind, it was a welcome break to not have to step into that place with the same people every day. I was getting paid, but we were struggling so badly that we just about covered bills and rent. We didn't have much to spend on food, let alone on myself. What was driving me crazy the most was staying home.

Spending so much time with Benjamin made it even more clear that being here with him wasn't for me. Dilating had become increasingly painful, and whenever Ben and I had sex, I just couldn't manage it. It wasn't often that we did have sex, but it wasn't for my lack of trying. Whenever I was in the mood, I'd kiss him and tell him I loved him, but the most I got out of him was a kiss on the cheek or a not-so-subtle invitation to suck him off. *What do you expect, Yvy? He can't even fuck you properly.*

I tried my best to please him, but I couldn't ignore the fact that he gave me nothing in return. I never felt truly loved, but something about him was pulling me in. I didn't know how to shake it. I knew I had to do something about us not having sex, so I decided to make an appointment at Charing Cross to see my surgeon. I figured I could get checked out and get Missy stretched so she wouldn't be so tight. *That'll work, Yvy.* After I returned from London, nothing changed. He was still distant, watching porn rather than touching me. I never felt so undesired in my life. Here I was, trying to take care of him, pay the bills, fight false allegations and what was I getting in return? But something inside always tried to rationalise the situation so it made sense.

Of course, things were hard, but at least you're living your own life. *Isn't that what you wanted?* As for Ben, I was convinced he was a good man under all the issues we had, he had to be. Otherwise, why would I stay? There had to be a reason, and just because I couldn't figure out what that reason was, I shouldn't give up on us.

I picked up the phone to call Mum to wish her a Merry Christmas. I figured if she didn't hear from me today, she would find that strange and call me anyway. The phone rang and she eventually answered.

'Hello, my Preity Zinta!' she said with glee.

'Hello! Merry Christmas, my beautiful mother!'

'Merry Christmas to you too. How are you doing?'

'I'm fine,' I lied, 'we're planning on having a lovely quiet day today.'

'Awww, that's good. How are things with work? Did you hear back from them yet?'

'Yeah, I got a letter delivered from the Store Manager last week. They're passing it to the Area Manager to make the decision. I don't know what they will say.'

'Did you give them all the evidence you found in that folder? Did you bring up the CCTV thing?'

'Yeah Mum. I put it all together in a case file and sent it to them. I made it clear that they have no basis to accuse me of all this without any evidence. I doubt they'll fucking listen though.'

'Well, they fucking have to, the bastards. They can't get away with this.'

'Yeah, you're right, but I'm going to push it out my head for today.'

'You're right, forget about it for today! Anything else going on with you.'

I paused and thought about what to say. I looked down at the folded piece of paper that sat on top of the lever arch folder and picked it up. *Don't tell her, Yvy. She'll flip out if you tell her.*

'Nope. Everything's okay here. Ben's cooking dinner and I'm just relaxing.'

'Aahh good!' She said with relief. 'Did you get any nice presents?'

My heart sank in my chest when she asked me that. I glanced over at the wrapped Christmas presents under the tree, knowing that each one was completely empty. We couldn't afford to buy anything, so Ben and I decided to wrap old shoe boxes in wrapping paper and put them under the tree so it appeared that we did have presents if anybody ever came around to visit.

'I haven't opened them yet. We'll do it after dinner. I'm going to go help Ben in the kitchen but I thought I'd give you a quick call. Love you.'

'You too, bye.' Mum hung up the phone.

I unfolded the piece of paper that was on top of the folder and read the words plastered all over it.

YOU BETTER GET THE FUCK OUT.
PAKI BITCH!

Benjamin walked in from the kitchen and saw me holding the letter that was shoved through our letterbox on Christmas Eve. He looked concerned when he saw me.

'Did you tell your mum about that?'

'No,' I said, not looking up from it. 'There's no point worrying her.'

After dinner, the rest of the day was spent watching reruns on UK Gold and trying my best to close off from the world. It didn't work though. I felt like I couldn't breathe in the house. I looked out the window and saw the night sky set and the snow falling, thick and untouched. I convinced Ben to go for a walk to clear my head. I heard the snow crunch with every step, which felt marvellous, but I knew that I didn't belong here.

Morecambe had turned on me in such a harsh way that I knew I didn't deserve. We walked through the streets, listening to the blissful silence as the icy chill of the air ran across my face. I felt free. I didn't feel like all the things I had been labelled as over the years. *Khusra. Tranny. Paki.* None of that could touch me. In that moment, as I looked up to let the snow hit my face, I felt like Yvy. Just then, Ben grabbed my hand and I rushed back to reality.

'Come on, let's go home. It's fucking freezing out here.'

We got back to the house and I had a shower before sitting back in the living room, my head occupied once again with an intrusive reality. My phone buzzed and I saw it was Mum texting me.

M: Have you opened your presents yet?

I knew I had to do something to hide the fact that this day was an absolute sham. I couldn't bear to tell her the truth. I didn't want her to know I was drowning. I asked Ben to take pictures of me opening the empty presents under the tree.

'Why do you want me to do that?'

'Just as a laugh!' I said, masking the real reason.

After he took the pictures, I sent them to Mum and waited for a response. Within seconds, she responded.

M: Awww, looks like you've been spoilt! Merry Christmas!

Chapter Twelve

Our journeys to London were a treat, which was strange considering we never visited for an actual holiday. Mum was insistent on accompanying me to my hospital appointments, which she didn't need to be, as I never wanted to go without her when I had an appointment at Charing Cross Hospital. She had been with me throughout my whole transition, except for when I went for my gender surgery. It was the one and only time she didn't come with me and that was more than enough for me.

When I made the decision for her to not come with me to London for my surgery, my only thought was that it would be a complete waste of money for her to stay in a hotel while I was in hospital, only for her to see me during visiting hours and then leave. I didn't like the thought of her sat around by herself with nothing to do until the time came for her to come and visit me, of which she wouldn't be able to do anything to ease my pain from the surgery. It made sense that she stayed home and let me go by myself and come pick me up with Feroza once I was ready to come home. For a while that made sense, until the time came when I was being rolled into surgery.

It was then that it hit me like a lightning bolt striking me through the chest. *Mum was right.* She didn't give a fuck about sitting around by herself or having to spend money on a hotel. She knew that I needed someone there with me. I never felt such a void before when I looked around as I was taken to theatre, seeing nobody there to hold my hand, to tell me they loved me. I never wanted to feel so alone again.

Benjamin had no idea about the real reason for my visit to London. With the news that that tangerine-tinted bitch had put a grievance in against me, Ben and I had been getting on quite well for once. I knew it was all on the surface though. Beneath the smiles and pleasant exchanges, I knew that Ben and I had some serious problems. I knew he was surfing the web for porn constantly, and I was growing suspicious of what else he could've been doing. Sex between us was almost non-existent. We hadn't been physical in weeks, if you didn't count me wanking him off whenever he requested it and getting nothing in return.

I was tired of feeling so undesired. I knew that the major issue was caused by me. It was my fault. I was still healing from a surgery I couldn't tell him about and it was beyond painful every time he entered me. My muscles tensed and I felt the sting of every raw nerve as he pushed himself deeper inside. Even he could feel how tight I was, to the point where it was too much for him too. *It's your fault, Yvy.* I didn't want it to carry on like this.

Sooner or later, he was going to get sick of trying and find someone else, and then where will that leave me? I didn't want to go back to Blackburn, but the alternative was falling apart. I felt the strain of our relationship, and being with a man who never shared his feelings with me other than being dismissive and hurtful was breaking me down. I had to do something about it, I wanted to feel comfortable having sex. I wanted to enjoy my body, not battle with myself every time I tried to be intimate. I mean, how much more do I have to fucking endure? Am I doomed to have these problems forever? The only thing I could think of that made me feel more in control was to speak to my consultant and ask if he could help me. Apparently, there was a procedure that could help loosen me up, and since I was due another follow-up appointment, he said this procedure could be done as an inpatient and I only had to stay one night.

'Did he explain what he'll do for the procedure?' Mum asked as she sat across from me on the train.

'I didn't ask. As long as it works, I really don't care what he does.'

'Well, at least you'll feel better and won't feel so sick.'

I lied to my mum. I told her that the tightness was making me feel ill constantly. I just couldn't bring myself to tell her that the real reason why I wanted this procedure was so I could please Ben. I knew it sounded pathetic. Sex was so important to me, and struggling like this was messing me up. My body was the one thing in my entire life that I both celebrated and loathed. The love/hate relationship with my body consumed my every thought for so many years that it was the only real relationship in my life. I knew my body's every curve, every secret, every insecurity.

The moments of pleasure my body experienced were few and far between, and it became a hunger I couldn't satisfy. It made so much sense to me why I felt so comfortable working in a sex shop, or why I became obsessed with watching erotic thrillers instead of straight up porn. Watching the way other people's bodies reacted and moved during sex became an art form. The way a back can arch, the way the hairs on the back of your neck respond to touch, the heavy breathing as the anticipation of heightened pleasure builds. I longed for all those things to happen to me, to my body.

Ever since having my surgery, I slowly saw the lights go out and my body grow dark, like a lonely house that nobody occupied. I felt a cold chill inside that I so desperately wanted to warm. Being with Ben had become something I feared, not because he scared me, but because I was scared of what he was beginning to figure out about me. Whenever he was on top of me, struggling to get inside, I saw his face and the look of disappointment that he tried to hide. I knew he loved me and that his disappointment wasn't in me per-se, but with each time we attempted to make love. I hated that he inadvertently experienced something about me that I never wanted anyone to know.

Mum and I arrived at the vegan hotel in Hammersmith which was only a few minutes away from the hospital. After having had enough of staying at the crazy cat bed and breakfast we usually stayed at, we switched and found a much more pleasant place to stay. I wasn't quite sure what exactly a vegan hotel was, until we arrived and saw that there was a vegan restaurant attached to it and all the toiletries in the hotel room were vegan. We walked in and saw two single beds, covered with beautiful white cotton sheets. The dressing table had an array of chocolate treats and a selection of teas. On the walls hung faded paintings of religious figures that were hauntingly beautiful.

'Bloody hell!' Mum said, dropping her bag on the bed 'This place is nice!'

'And look, we have a kettle! We can make our own teas!'

'And I won't get shouted at by that fucking bitch!'

We chuckled at the memory of Mum asking the lady at the cat place for a cup of tea and being told sharply to go outside to get it, even when Mum offered to pay for a cuppa.

'What time do we need to be at the hospital?' Mum asked.

'Another three hours.'

'Oh good! Let's go gallivanting!'

***

I took a shower the moment I got back from the disciplinary hearing. I knew that Ben heard me walk through the door, but I couldn't bring myself to tell him

I had just been fired. Even with all the evidence I gave them that completely discredited that lying bitch, they still decided to get rid of me. I wasn't going to take it lying down and I planned from the second they escorted me out of the store that I was going to take the whole fucking lot of them to court. But in this moment, I couldn't comprehend what had just happened. I hated that those bitches won. They managed to take me down in a way that made me feel violated.

I knew the moment I moved to Morecambe that I didn't belong here. Now I was being told that very thing to my fucking face. *Get the fuck out, paki bitch.* I had enough. I heard a faint greeting from Ben as I walked up the stairs and told him I wanted to take a shower as I closed the bathroom door behind me.

The water heated up, spraying from the shower head as I took off my clothes. I pulled down my underwear and as usual, the sanitary towel fell and I quickly picked it up and bundled it in some tissue to throw away. I went to grab my dilators that I hid in the sink cabinet and stepped in the shower. The water was so hot, just the way I liked it. Feeling it beat down on my skin felt hard yet comforting.

As I picked up the first dilator, I stared at it through the waterfall running across my face and couldn't bring myself to put it inside me. After my trip to London a few weeks ago, I thought things would feel a little better. When I was there the consultant made some minor corrective surgery around Missy's hood and stretched me inside in the hopes that my muscles wouldn't be as strong. The stitches around the hood had dissolved, leaving a sensitive area that looked neater and less unfinished than when I initially had my gender surgery. Stretching me did nothing, or at least it felt that way. I felt a constant tension in my body and willing Missy to relax was an exercise in futility. How could I relax when I'm having to hide the very thing from Benjamin that requires understanding and patience for me to do? I couldn't tell him I was trans.

Every time I mildly brought the subject up, he'd say or comment in a way that made it clear that telling him could possibly end badly. I wasn't willing to take that risk, not because I was afraid of him, but because I was afraid of what it could result in. The last thing I wanted to do was go back to Blackburn. I didn't want that to happen. The only thing that I missed from Blackburn was Mum. I missed that feeling of not worrying about how to act around her. When I was with Zohra, I felt like myself. Nothing about her made me insecure or doubtful about the choices I made in life, never a moment went by when I didn't feel her strength.

I knew being in Morecambe was wrong for me, but I couldn't bring myself to tell Mum how I was feeling. I didn't want to acknowledge the bullshit that was happening to me. I was embarrassed by it.

So, what to do? I towelled off and wrapped my hair in a wet bun, making my way downstairs. I saw Ben sitting in his usual seat watching a blaring television when he turned and saw me enter the living room.

'You alright? What happened?'

'They fired me.'

'What!' He said surprisingly, which pissed me off.

'It was obvious this was going to happen,' I said, shutting down his surprise.

'Yeah, but you fucking showed them all the stuff we put together to prove them wrong though.'

'They didn't give a shit about what I had to say. They wanted to get rid of me and they did it. End of.'

'So, what now?'

'I guess I'll have to find another job around here, won't I?'

'What does that mean?' He responded, acknowledging my sarcastic tone.

'How are we supposed to live here if I don't have a fucking job? You haven't fucking worked since I moved here, have you?'

'You know I've tried finding work, there's nothing here.'

'Well, you're not trying hard enough! I'm sick of taking care of everything myself. Why am I having to fix everything?'

Ben became increasingly agitated with me, and frankly I didn't give a shit. I was sick of this house and I was sick of him. When we first met, he was so different. I suppose it was the veneer that gave off the false version of himself that enticed me with his charm. Once that veneer peeled away, all I saw was an insecure person who took it out on me in his own irritatingly passive-aggressive way. I tried to ignore it for as long as possible, but I was reaching my limit.

Then again, who was I to him? Was I any better? I mean, wasn't I putting up a constant veneer to hide the real person I was determined to keep from him? I was so confused, I didn't have the strength to care anymore, but I just couldn't find the will to let him go. Something tied me to him that held on like a clamp with no release. It didn't make any sense, but he was the only thing in my life that didn't see me as a trans woman. That was enough for me to stay.

New Year's had been and gone, the snow was still thick on the ground but ceased to fall from the sky. I loved experiencing the icy cold as the sun shone brightly against the snow. It felt fresh, like new beginnings after heavy clouds that loomed for so long. Something inside me felt a sense of renewal. A sense of purpose. I knew I had to pick myself up and carry on, no matter how defeated I was feeling. So much of last year went wrong, and I didn't want to carry it into 2010.

I started looking for work and found a vacancy at a mini supermarket similar to where I worked before and decided to give it a go. It was a long shot, given that I was fired from a store that was more or less next door, and everyone knew everyone's business in this shit hole, but I put that aside and gave in an application. It wasn't long before I was offered a job interview. I dressed smartly and was greeted by a woman who took me to the staff room.

'Thanks for coming in, Edie.'

'Thanks, it's Yvy.'

'Oh, I'm so sorry—'

'That's fine.'

'So, the position is to work full-time over the entire opening hours and will include weekends, but from looking at your CV I can see you're pretty used to working supermarket shifts.'

'Yes,' I replied, 'I worked both the early and late shifts at my last job.'

'You were a Team Leader there?'

'Yes, I was responsible for the running of the store and the usual team leader duties. Cashing up, managing staff jobs, getting the weekly orders put out.'

'Sounds like you know your stuff then!' she said pleasingly.

'Yeah, I got to know how to run the store really quickly.'

'So, what was your reason for leaving?'

I knew this question was coming. I didn't want to lie about it, so I decided to be honest. *Just tell her, Yvy.*

'I was dismissed.'

'On what grounds?'

'Allegations were made against me by a member of staff that weren't true. I was let go anyway.'

'I see. May I ask what they were?'

I told her the truth without going into detail. It was tough to sit there and hear the words come out of my mouth that despite everything I tried to do to disprove the claims, I still wasn't strong enough to beat them. Still, I wasn't going to let it drag me down. It would've come out if I got the job if one of those cunts found out I was working here. It's better all-round if I laid it out on the table now. If it means I don't get the job, so be it. After I finished telling her what had happened, she paused for what felt like a minute.

'That sounds like a terrible ordeal to have to go through,' she said.

'It was, still feeling it a bit if I'm honest.'

'This girl who said these things about you, what's her name?'

'Natalie; she's—'

'I'm aware of who she is,' she said, her face turning. 'I know her aunt who works there. I'm not at all surprised she would say something like that.'

I was puzzled by what she said and wondered if Natalie had tried to pull this stunt before. I watched as the woman's demeanour became more relaxed, like I had stumbled across a common ground that made her see me differently. After a few more questions about my work experience, she ended the interview.

'Well, thanks for coming in, it was lovely meeting you,' she said kindly.

'Thanks for seeing me. I look forward to hearing from you.'

I left my interview feeling optimistic. For the first time in a long while, I felt my sense of purpose coming back. I hadn't felt so energised in such a while that it put a spring in my step. As I crossed the street to make my way home, I glanced over at my old work and saw the girls helping the delivery men take the order crates in the store. I felt so far away from all of them and it felt great. I no longer had to fake pleasantries or listen to their bullshit. I wasn't going to be scared off by them, even when threatened. I knew I wasn't wanted here, but they could all fuck off. I couldn't think of a single thing now that could make me move and let them win.

I was almost home when my phone started buzzing in my pocket. I pulled it out and saw that it was Ben.

B: You done at your interview?
Y: Yeah. On my way home.
B: Could you pick up my prescription from the chem, plz?
Y: Yeah, will do.

I totally forgot that he had already asked me to pick it up. I made my way back around the corner and to the pharmacy which wasn't too far. I entered and asked for Ben's prescription and stood by the toiletries, waiting for the chemist to shout his name. As I stood waiting, I noticed a gentleman behind the counter looking at me. He kept glancing at me sporadically as he busied himself with sorting prescriptions. He was a tall, South Asian man with a slim build. He looked a little familiar, but I couldn't quite place him.

He continued with his work, occasionally peering over the partition that held an array of pills and medical products. I felt uneasy. I was beginning to feel as though he recognised me from somewhere. As he approached and gave me my boyfriend's prescription, a sudden rush hit me in the face. *I know him.* I know this man from my past. My heart sank. I couldn't believe he was here. *Why the fuck is he here?* Of all places for me to find someone from my past. Everything I felt good about began to crash down around me. I couldn't stay here any longer. I couldn't risk anyone finding out about me. *Not here.* I had no other choice. *I have to leave Morecambe.*

Chapter Thirteen
Christmas, 2016

The food from the kitchen smelt delicious. Jack was great at cooking a wonderful Christmas dinner, and this year was no exception. He was preparing a beef joint with all the trimmings, except for the vegetables which he avoided like the plague. Jack and I had been together for five years, and in all that time he's tried to enjoy eating vegetables, but it never took. I usually just prepared one of those steamed vegetable bags in the microwave whenever we had a roast dinner. I walked into the kitchen and saw my husband checking on the roast in the oven. I reached behind him and put my arms around his waist, resting my head between his shoulder blades.

'You alright?' He asked with a smile.

'Yeah, just wanted to see if I can help with anything.'

'Everything's cooking nicely so it should be done in about 10 minutes.'

'Cool. I'll sort out the stuffing and set the table.'

I started setting the table when Mum walked into the kitchen. I was so happy that she decided to spend Christmas with us. I loved living in Manchester with Jack, but one thing I didn't like was that I barely got the chance to see Mum. She was still living in Blackburn with Fareed and Feroza, and I seldom got the opportunity to go down and see her, especially recently. Mum had visited quite often this year, which pleased me as it gave us more time to connect.

'Ooooh, it smells lovely in here!' Mum said excitedly.

'It's almost ready so go and relax and we'll let you know when it's time to eat!' I said.

The table looked exquisite, in a humble sort of way. Jack and I weren't one to fancy it up with tacky Christmas ornaments that got in the way of reaching for the gravy. Jack prepared the plates with the beef, some roasties and honey-glazed parsnips. I topped up the wine glasses with some Vimto and set them on the table. Got to be a bit classy at Crimbo! I called Mum in and we sat down around the table, ready to eat.

'This all looks amazing, Jack,' Mum said as she took her seat.

'I'm bloody starving!' I replied.

'Well, Merry Christmas, and it's so great to have you here with us,' Jack said, as he raised his bottled beer to toast.

Our glasses clinked and we pulled our Christmas crackers before tucking into the wonderful dinner.

Outside the living room window stood a tall tree in the communal courtyard. Our flat was on the first floor and the living room overlooked the part of the gardens that were more secluded and less used by the rest of the residents living in our building. It was like having our own private garden to look upon. The tree outside our window was wrapped in a coil of blue fairy lights that lit up beautifully, their twinkling reflections touching the living room walls.

Our Christmas tree stood at the opposite side of the room from the window, nestled in the corner by the sofas and in front of the DVD collection that took up the entire back wall. It stood covered in shimmering ornaments, all unique for a very special reason. For years, I had my own tradition of choosing a Christmas tree ornament to hang on the branches that symbolised that year. The year I started dating Jack, I bought myself a gingerbread cookie ornament. In 2012, Jack and I bought a toy soldier, and the following years we found every Christmas ornament on holiday, as I had an impressive ability to sniff out a Christmas shop wherever we went.

A glass sweet in Bruges, a bell in Prague and a very special Disney wedding ornament that I found in Sleeping Beauty's castle when we visited Disneyland on the last day of our honeymoon in Paris back in 2015. This year was different though. Although we did holiday in Amsterdam in June, I didn't find a nice enough Christmas ornament, and we didn't get much chance to look anywhere else. This year had been rough for me, in fact, it was one of the most difficult years I experienced in a long while. Still, I was safe at home with Mum and Jack and that was more precious to me than anything else after the year I had.

Mum knew how important it was for me to keep up my tradition of getting a Christmas ornament, and chose to contribute and buy us an ornament from the Manchester Christmas Markets. We decided on a ceramic ornament of two reindeers that had our names on it. A sentiment I could tell meant a lot to my mum and I was very happy to hang it on the tree.

Jack was in the kitchen, sorting out the pots, while Mum and I were in the living room. I grabbed the box of strawberry mint candy canes from the book shelves and began opening it up.

'I saved these for you! Hang them on the tree!' I said, handing Zohra some wrapped candy canes. As she placed them on the tree, I couldn't help but notice how serene she looked.

'I don't get to do any of this at home!' She said.

'See, it's nice here!'

'So, you do like your present, don't you?' She asked.

'Of course, I do!' I picked up the gorgeous faux fur animal print coat she got me. 'I absolutely love it!'

'It'll keep you nice and warm.'

'Oh, I've got a better idea than that! Wait here!'

'Where are you going?'

'Just wait here! I've got an idea!'

I quickly disappeared into the bedroom and got changed. When I returned, Mum's face dropped as I entered the living room, dressed in a red and black corset with thigh high boots and Fendi shades.

'Bloody hell!' Mum exclaimed. 'You look so good!'

'Grab my phone! Let's do a video!'

I shut the living room door and started playing Lil' Kim's *Crush On You* through the computer. Mum couldn't hold in her laughter watching me manoeuvre around the living room in six-inch heels. I loved the fact that she didn't even question why I owned clothes like this, which just shows how cool she was with her daughter's raunchy ways. The music started and Mum pressed record on my phone. The moment I knew she was recording, I channelled Lil' Kim, a woman I admired for so long.

The music flowed through me with every hard beat. Once Cease was done with his verse, I knew Kim's verse was coming up. I walked forward, moving my hips seductively and popping the collar of my faux fur. As soon as Kim started rapping, I looked straight into the camera and gave my mum a performance.

Ayo shorty, won't you go get a bag of the lethal
I'll be undressed in the bra all see through
Why you count your jewels thinkin' I'ma cheat you?

The only one thing I wanna do is freak you

Mum watched through the camera, bouncing away to the song like she was Regina George's Mum. I swear I was waiting for her to do the *Jingle Bell Rock* movements, bouncing her behind out from the side.

Keep your stone sets, I got my own baguettes
And I'll be doin' things that you won't regret
Lil' Kim, the Queen Bee, so you best take heed
Shall I proceed? Yes indeed!

I was getting into the performance, grinding my hips and flipping my long hair. Mum was living for it and couldn't contain her laughter as she signalled me to keep going.

I'ma throw shade if I can't get paid
Blow you up to your girl like the Army grenade
You can slide on my ice like the Escapade
And itchy-gitchy-yaya with the marmalade

I knew the verse was coming to an end so I gave it a little more attitude, opening my coat up a bit more so my corset was exposed and my breasts peaked up from the top. *Fuck it.* You've shown Mum this much, might as well make it a fucking show!

Who me? Not, you, oh yes, who's he?
I even dig yo' man's style, but I love yo' profile
Whisper in your ear and get you all shook up
But don't blush, just keep this on the hush!

As Biggie sang the chorus, I kept on dancing, turning my lips down and moving like a snake for the camera. I couldn't keep a straight face any longer and burst into laughter with Mum. My heels were killing me and I collapsed onto the sofa arm, taking off the Fendi glasses I found on sale in TK Maxx a few years ago.

'That was so bloody bastard good!'

'I need to get out of these heels! I'm bloody knackered after that!'

I changed into my comfy pyjamas and got cosy on the sofa with Mum. Jack popped his head around the door and offered to make us a couple of brews and soon enough, Mum and I had a hot cuppa in our hands.

'I can't believe how much has happened this year,' I said.

'You've gone through a lot, but look where you are now! I just think about you only a few months ago having to stay at home with all those tubes coming out of you, and now you're dancing around!'

'I know. It's crazy. I never saw it coming and I honestly didn't know if I could make it through.'

'I knew. But I know you, you're too strong to give up.'

***

Jack and I were so looking forward to our honeymoon in Paris. The day finally came to catch our flight and I couldn't have been more excited. The first few days were incredible, visiting places like Sacré-Cœur and Café des 2 Moulin, to the Louvre and the Arc de Triomphe. It was as if we walked into a romantic painting that became more beautiful with each day. But as the holiday progressed, something started to change. I was beginning to feel tired and dizzy, which were symptoms I suffered with for some time.

I knew this feeling well, and most of the time it meant I had low blood sugar. However, at times it got quite scary as this feeling often resulted in collapsing from exhaustion. I tried to fob it off as nothing to worry about. I always tried to calm myself down any time I felt this way. I felt like my mind made it worse by going straight to the worst-case scenario which made me panic and before I knew it, I was blacking out and crashing to the ground.

Jack and I were spending a romantic evening, taking a boat ride and then to dinner. We decided to dress extravagantly, which meant Jack threw on a suit and I took nearly two hours carefully accessorising and making sure I looked perfect. I decided on an elegant silk dress that Mum gave me to wear, pairing it with gold bangles and a jewelled necklace Feroza gave me. We boarded the boat and sailed along the river, floating past Notre Dame Cathedral and the Eiffel Tower, my husband's arms wrapped around me. I felt so loved.

Once the boat ride was done and we headed to a restaurant for dinner, my head began to feel dense. It was a hot day, so I figured it was due to being out in the sweltering heat for so long on the boat. We were shown to our seats in the restaurant and the dense feeling soon escalated to dizziness. All I could think of was the time I collapsed in the shower at Charing Cross after my blood pressure dropped so dramatically that my legs gave out.

I awoke on the floor, looking sexy in a soaking wet towel with the nurses frantic that they'd found me lying naked and unconscious. I knew I was being silly, focusing on how I thought I looked hot when I came to on the hospital floor and caught a glimpse of myself in the mirror, but it took my focus away from the reality that I felt like I was about to go again. However, this time I wasn't in a hospital where someone could help me quickly. I suddenly felt scared.

'You okay, Yvy?' Jack asked, noticing I wasn't looking too good.

'I feel rubbish. I'm getting dizzy.'

'Do you want to leave? We can go back to the hotel.'

'I don't want to get up. Can we eat first? Maybe that'll help.'

I managed to eat, which did make me feel better, but instead of our intended plan of a night on the town, Jack insisted we called it a night and he took me back to the hotel to rest.

A few months passed and I experienced more episodes similar to the one in Paris, so I got myself checked out by my GP. I wasn't surprised at what was happening to me to begin with, as I experienced episodes like this before, but not as frequently as they were happening now. I had a blood test and was told that I'd hear back if anything was wrong. It was the beginning of September and I just started a new job for a surveyor. I couldn't for the life of me figure out how I even got the job. I had no background in that kind of work, but it paid well and I figured it was better than no job. The role was tough to understand, sitting in the training room with my head spinning. I felt my skin warm uncomfortably as I attempted to soak in the information being thrown at me by the trainer. *Calm down, Yvy.* I knew what was happening, but I didn't want to focus on it, I didn't want to lose control. I managed to get through the day and made my way home, safe and sound with Jack.

'How are you feeling?'

Before I could answer him, my phone started to ring. I picked up and within a few seconds, Jack noticed my demeanour change. He saw the concern, the uncertainty, the fear. I put the phone down and stared at nothing.

'What's wrong?'

'That was the GP. They said my kidney function has dropped to 12.'

'What does that mean?'

'It's not good,' I said, still not able to stop myself from staring at nothing. 'I have to go to hospital.'

'When?'

'Right now.'

***

I sat opposite Mum, thinking back over the last year and a half since returning from my honeymoon in Paris. My head filled with the memory of having to rush to the hospital after my GP told me I had to go immediately. Being told that my right kidney was completely destroyed and that my left kidney had almost become permanently damaged. I thought about being in Salford Royal, having a nephrostomy tube fitted in to my left kidney and spending the entirety of my time as an inpatient hoping that my kidney function improved so that I could have surgery. For the most part, I had absolutely no idea why this was happening to me. How the fuck could I not know that my kidneys were being severely damaged? Why was this happening to me? I had so many questions but nobody gave me answers.

'I'm so tired of things being so fucking difficult all the time,' I said softly as I watched Mum take a sip of her tea.

'Listen, what were you doing last Christmas?' She asked.

'What do you mean?'

'What were you like when I came down last Christmas? You still had your tubes and your catheter, having to sleep in the living room, couldn't go out or do anything. You faced all that, plus not having a job, and you still pushed through.'

'I'm pissed off though. When the consultant told me that the damage was caused by tissue scarring from a previous surgery, I couldn't believe it.'

'I know, but you can't let that get you down. You don't regret having your gender surgery, do you?'

'Not at all. I just hate the thought that all this time I didn't know that something may have happened during my surgery and now look at me. If they did fuck up with something, why didn't they just tell me? I would've—'

'I know, but listen, all you can do is face today. That's it! That's all you have. Stop getting down on yourself over things you can't change.'

I could feel the tears building up and I forced them back, the lump in my throat getting harder to swallow.

'I've seen how hard this year has been for you,' Mum continued. 'You thought it would get better but it got worse after your surgery.'

My thoughts were a million miles away from the beauty of my Paris honeymoon. Instead, all I could think of was the Spring of this year when I finally got my surgery date after waiting eight long months from when I was rushed to hospital last September. The surgery involved reducing the ureter by cutting through my bladder, a procedure that was incredibly invasive and scared me to no end. I knew that in order to heal, they would need to put a stent inside me so that the ureter could mend after they removed the damaged part.

What I didn't expect post-surgery was the consultant deciding to leave the stent in and discharge me. By this point, they already took out my nephrostomy tube that I had in for months and was helping with passing water through a catheter, but now I had to go back to normal. What ended up happening was the stent started folding on itself, causing the ureter to block and my left kidney to flood.

To say the pain was excruciating would be an understatement. I was in extreme agony, screaming my lungs out in pain in the emergency room. Jack felt helpless as he watched me suffer on the hospital bed. In the end they had to put another nephrostomy tube inside me while the consultant tried to repair the damage the stent had made. By mid-May I was beginning to feel more like myself, but my life had completely changed. I struggled so much over the years, and I honestly thought I would get a break.

'Do you know what's stupid, Mum? I remember the night before I had my surgery in Charing Cross, I sat on the bed and prayed.'

Mum was surprised. She knew I wasn't religious in the slightest, so hearing that I would do something like that threw her.

'I didn't pray, really, I just talked. Nobody was in the room, and I didn't even know who I was talking to, I just needed to get the words out. I said that I didn't care what goes wrong in my life, all I wanted was for this surgery to go well and let me feel whole. Whatever happened after that, I didn't care. Just let me be me and I'll face whatever life throws at me.'

'I know how hard it is. I've been through so much but I'm still standing. Do you know why? Because we have no choice but to keep going. When all of you were little, I struggled so much, but life doesn't slow down to wait for you to catch up.'

'I know. I'm just tired of the reminder.'

'What reminder?' Mum stood up and went by the radiator, carefully warming her hands as she placed them behind her.

'There isn't a day that goes by that I'm not reminded that I'm trans. It's getting to a point where I'm sick of it.'

'What do you mean?'

'Look at you. You stood over there. I'm a woman and I know I am, and so are you. But the day will never come where I can stand next to you as a woman. I can get as close as I can to you, but I'll never be there, next to you. Every day I'm reminded of that. All I want is to be treated as a woman, but all I get is reminders that I'm trans. That's even why I left Morecambe. I saw someone from high school working at the pharmacy near my house and I almost died when he saw me. And then when all this shit happened it felt like yet another reminder. "Look! Yvy! You're sick because of the gender surgery you had!" I'm just so tired of it, Mum.'

'You are a woman. Who cares about where you stand and all that? You just stand for who you are. You worked so hard to get here. Don't throw away this time. It's this time you fought so hard to get.'

'I'm so glad you're here.' I snuggled with her as she returned to the sofa, her hands warm from the radiator.

'Do you remember when I was at primary school and every Christmas, my class would have those Christmas dinners?'

'The ones where you lot had to bring the food?'

'Yeah, and I always took the chocolate Yule log!'

''Course I do! You always hounded me to make sure I got you a good Yule log to take to school.'

'That's because the team I was on always won the dinner prize because of that!' I said laughingly.

'I remember! You'd always have a big smile on your face when you came home.'

'It was one of the rare times I was actually happy in school. I can't remember ever celebrating Christmas back then. We didn't do much for Christmas when I was little, did we?'

'I always tried,' she said, her tone turning sombre. 'I'd see the three of you get all excited for Christmas. I always tried to…' Mum paused, glancing at the twinkling tree outside the living room window.

'What's wrong?' I asked.

'Nothing, I, you know what? I haven't told anybody this before.'

'What?'

'You three were only little. Your dad never cared about getting you three anything nice and he was a bastard when it came to money. I'd check the account and there'd be nothing in it on his payday. I was sick of seeing you three go without things.'

She stopped talking for a second, then proceeded with what she was saying.

'I knew that you three deserved something for Christmas, but I had no money, I had nothing to give you. I didn't want you to see other kids getting presents, especially Fareed and Feroza 'cause they were older. You were still a baby, but I still wanted all three of you to have something.'

I sat listening, wondering where she was going with this story.

'I went to town, thinking I had no choice and went to some shop to steal some presents for you.'

'Really?'

'I was so bloody scared, but I couldn't bear the thought of you three not having something to open at Christmas. I went in and put some toys in my bag for you lot.'

'And what happened? Did you actually take them?'

'I couldn't go through with it. I was right there, about to walk out, but I knew it was wrong. I felt so bad afterwards, like I let my children down.'

I stared at Zohra for a moment, examining her features. Her delicate nose and warm eyes. Her beautiful Indian gold jewellery. Her brown skin that was always soft to the touch. I smiled, thinking about how much love I had for this woman.

'How come you've never told me this before?'

'I never thought I'd tell anyone. You know what our lot are like. All gossipers. I didn't want to be seen as a bloody thief.'

'Mum, do you have any idea how strong you are?'

'What do you mean?'

'Any good mother would do the same for their children. You loved us that much that you risked so much just so we had a present to open on Christmas Day. Of all things you could be called, a thief is not fucking one of them.'

'I know, but you know what people are like—'

'Listen,' I said. 'Do you remember when I was younger and every time it was your birthday or Mother's Day, I always bought you tons of presents?'

'Of course, I do! I couldn't believe you got me so much every year!'

'I did that because it was my way of telling you that I'm so proud of you. It was my way of showing you how much you do for me. I was struggling so much back then but I couldn't talk to anyone. Even though you had no idea what was wrong, you never stopped loving me.'

I grabbed her hands and cradled them in mine.

'Do you remember that plaque I got you when I was about thirteen? It had a little wind-up music box on the back. Do you remember that?'

'Ooooh yeah I do! What did it say on the front of it? I can't remember.'

'It said *Everything I am or hope to be, I owe to my mother*. And it's true. I owe everything to you. All my strength, my resilience, it came from you. Don't ever feel bad about anything you've done for us. I wouldn't be the woman I am without you.'

I gave Zohra a tender hug, feeling her soft cheek against mine and planting a kiss on her face.

'Can I make you two another brew?'

Jack popped his head around the door and we broke our embrace to find him looking at us, slightly concerned that he just walked in at an inopportune moment.

'Yes please!' I said and watched as he slipped back into the kitchen.

I turned to Mum and gave her a comforting smile.

'I'm so proud of you, Yvy,' she said. 'I'm so proud that you're mine.'

This is Our Space

Chapter Fourteen
Manchester, 2019

This was the first time in a long while that I ventured out to the Village for a night out. I was feeling a bit nervous about going out on the town by myself. Usually I'd be out with friends, but this time I couldn't find anybody to go out with. What is it about turning thirty that flips a switch that makes your regular party self suddenly crave a hot cuppa and a good movie rather than partying all night? To be fair, I was exactly the same. I would've much rather stayed home and done nothing, but that was steadily becoming the problem. I needed to shake things up.

Summer had passed and September was soon here, and I was feeling very magenta, a phrase Blanche Devereaux once explained as that feeling when you have all sorts of emotions tumbling around but you can't quite put your finger on what you're actually feeling.

I sat in my bedroom applying my make-up and listening to Brandy, wondering why I was so hellbent on going out tonight. *It's just a drag show!* But I already promised a drag queen who was performing that I would be there. Her name was Vanta Black. The first and only time I saw her perform was a few weeks ago when I went to the Black Pride Vogue Ball at Gorilla. I knew some of the performers at the show and figured it would be a fun experience.

When I arrived, the room was filled with queer people of colour, performers dressed immaculately and a hungry audience waiting to experience a spectacle. As the show began, performers came onto the stage, voguing, posing, lip-syncing, the lot. It was incredible to see such amazing talent, the likes of which I seldom saw around the Village. I felt connected in some way to these queer people of colour. As the drag artists came on, they performed their hearts out to a crowd that couldn't stop cheering. I positioned myself at the corner of the stage so I wouldn't miss a thing.

Vanta was introduced and I applauded as she strutted onto the stage, with her dangerous curves and slick, black boots that screamed sex. As she started the intro to her performance, I waited to see what number she was about to do. Suddenly, the room began to shake to the booming bass of the hip-hop beat and I lost it! As Vanta performed, I thrust my hand up and punched the air, cheering her on with uncontrollable enthusiasm. The evening was spent recording the performances of the artists I knew. I figured with how things are these days with Insta celebs and fanatics only caring about who was on Drag Race rather than actually going out and supporting local artists, I wanted to capture some of their performances to share and show some love for what they do.

By the time Vanta took to the stage, I had already spent so much of the show recording and figured I should take some time to just enjoy it without being glued to my phone. The moment Vanta stepped out, I knew I was in for a treat, and when the beat dropped it was as if I was transported back to 2012 when my good friend Ellis and I practically lived in the Village every weekend. As the show came to a close, I was totally buzzed. Feelings previously absent were surging through me, awakening a dormant passion I once possessed. I was made for the stage, but never acted on that impulse. For so long I had been too focused on my transition and getting through everyday life that I never took the time to find an outlet to quench my creative thirst. I left feeling inspired and I couldn't wait to share the performances I had recorded.

I soon heard from Vanta on Instagram after I posted my videos, asking if I might have captured her performance too. I felt terrible that I hadn't, but I was so blown away by her that I was keen to see her perform again and offered to come to her next show to do some filming. She told me she was part of a show at Tribeca and offered me an invitation, expressing that she would love for me to be there. It was going to be a fun night out and getting the opportunity to meet some new people and also meet Vanta properly was a definite advantage.

I was already feeling pretty isolated, and in desperate need to connect with people. Don't get me wrong, I had people in my life. I had my husband, close friends who lived in the same building as us, and a small group of people I met at work that I saw as more than just colleagues. But something was still missing. It had only been a couple of months since I came back from my first trip to Brighton for Trans Pride, and I was still feeling the after-effects. The realisation of something damaging to me was that I never fully realised just how detached I was from the queer community. For the first time in a long time, I felt like Sal.

That feeling he felt when I was trapped inside him with no way out and all he wanted to was to find a place in the world.

I kissed Jack goodbye once I was ready and made my way into town. I knew that I had to go and was determined to have a good time. So what if I don't have anybody to go out with? Does that mean I have to put my life on hold? *Fuck no!* I should just go and see what happens. Who knows, maybe I'll have an amazing time! As I walked onto Canal Street, I saw the usual cliques gathering. Groups of annoying, straight white girls shrieking like hens. Twinks that had mastered the art of the side eye so sharp it could draw blood. The already steaming lads stumbling towards G-A-Y and being told by the bouncers that they weren't getting in.

Then there were people like me. I can always tell who's just like me on Canal Street. By that I mean the people who partied in the Village back in the day and now see it in a different way, quietly judging the younger generation who think they own the rights to the damn place. I avoided the cliques the best way I could and made my way through the Village and past Sackville Gardens towards Tribeca. Although Tribeca wasn't technically on Canal Street, it was still very much a part of the Village. As I walked towards Sackville Gardens, two drag queens stood amongst the many people walking through the Village.

One was wearing a long, blonde wig that housed hundreds of curls and a pink mini dress. The other had bold, orange shoulder length hair and a tight black ensemble with killer thigh high boots. The instant I saw her, I knew who it was. *Vanta.* Although I had seen her perform at the Vogue Ball, I never actually met or spoke to her in person. It was weird to see someone in real life and feel like I know them, when in fact we never actually met. I approached her and as she locked eyes with me, I could tell that she recognised me too.

'Hi! How are you?' I said excitedly. I knew very well that drag etiquette numero uno was to never get too close to a drag performer's paint, so I gave her a distant drag kiss.

'Hi, I'm sorry, is it Ivy?'

'It's ee-vee actually.'

I could tell straight away that the conversation was a bit awkward. *Maybe I'm coming on too strong!* I've always seen myself as someone who can pretty much get on with anybody, but one thing I often struggled with was meeting new people when I'm alone on a night out. The last time I felt like this was a while back when I was out with some friends in the Village and we all went to G-A-Y.

I wasn't keen on G-A-Y, mostly because it usually became overly packed with idiots who had no concept of personal space as they pushed by you with a drink, not caring if they spilt it on you. This night was no exception as I looked around at the array of plastered cliques and pilled-up girls on the dancefloor giving me the glad eye in a not so discreet way. I was out with a friend from work, Matt, his sister and her boyfriend. The night started off as expected, having a few drinks in a corner of the club that we found to go sit, instead of hovering around the crowded bar.

As the night progressed, the couple started bickering which subsequently turned into a full-blown fight. I sat uncomfortably as the madness unfolded and it ended with my friend's sister storming out of the club, followed by her boyfriend. Matt knew he couldn't leave his sister in such a state and said he was going outside to check on her and that he'd be right back. There I sat, alone and waiting for my friend to return. The club was growing more crowded and I noticed the annoyance on people's faces as they glared at the girl sitting at an area by herself that the group could be occupying. *Fuck off!*

Minutes rolled by like hours as I waited for Matt, with nothing but my phone to keep me company. After waiting for thirty minutes, I was getting worried and decided to go outside to make sure everything was okay. I stepped outside and was hit with a barrage of people, but Matt was nowhere to be found. I looked down at my phone when I felt it vibrate.

M: Sorry Yves. Had to leave. It's a big mess. Real sorry.

That fucking cunt! Did he actually leave me in the club without even fucking telling me to my face? I was so fucking pissed off that I was basically ditched by my friend and was standing in the Village with nowhere to go. *Fuck it, Yvy, just go home.* I gathered myself and figured I had no other choice but to leave, Matt pretty much decided how my evening was going to end and he'll get a fucking bitch slap from me when I fucking see that wanker again. The air was chilly and I didn't bring a coat with me, so I put my arms around my waist and made my way to the taxi rank around the corner. I started walking, feeling a little sorry for myself given how the night had turned out, when a girl crossed my path that was pretty drunk and trying her best to walk across a cobbled path in heels. Before she tumbled, I saw that she was about to kiss the pavement when I reached out and caught her.

'You alright, hun?' I asked as the girl tried to stand.

'Yeah love! Do you like chicken?' She slurred with glee.

'You okay?' I asked again. 'Can you stand up?'

'Yeah, I'm fine!' She said, her blonde hair slightly dishevelled against her pale skin.

'Good!'

'Do you like chicken burgers? I love 'em, me!' She said excitedly.

'Are you sure you're okay?'

'Yeah, let me buy you a drink!'

'Oh, no it's alright, love. I'm—'

'No please! Please let me buy you a drink. To say thank you.'

I hesitated at first, but then threw caution to the wind as this night couldn't get any worse.

'Alright then.'

She took my hand and led me to a pub where the room was even busier than G-A-Y, only the crowd was very different. By that I mean it wasn't filled with young idiots who were plastered or pilled up. Here the people were equally plastered and pilled up but much older. A few elderly gentlemen sat at the bar with a pint, their faces screaming with discontent, as if they were all wondering how the hell their favourite watering hole became a haven for middle-aged, straight white women boasting how they could turn a gay guy straight and creepy men perving on young flesh while *Bananarama* blared from the speakers.

The girl I was with took me to the bar, and before I could fall into a pit of despair, I saw that she was in fact with a large group of people, all of whom had no idea who I was. I felt so awkward meeting them, trying to find something to say other than *I've just been ditched by my friend and I saved your drunk friend from face planting in the street*. They were all pretty drunk, which I loathed.

It's so rubbish on a night out when you're completely sober with drunk friends. I found myself fumbling my words and trying to mask my insecurity with laughter. It became excruciating, but as the night progressed, it became harder to get away from them. As nice as they all were, I just wasn't in the right headspace for this and in the end, I made a lame excuse to leave and got my taxi, four hours later than I had originally intended.

My mind was spinning as I sat at the bar in Tribeca, waiting for the drag show to start. I perched myself on a stool right next to the bar and sipped on my fruit cider, scanning the whole room. I felt naked, constantly grabbing my phone to pretend to look at my social media, trying my best to not look so pathetic.

When I looked around the room, I saw a crowd of people sat in a booth close to the stage. Another group sat in the neighbouring booth and a few other people sat in a darker area to the side of the stage. I wasn't wearing my glasses so I couldn't see them very clearly.

Still, the club wasn't packed but it was early. The queens weren't on for another ninety minutes, which to me meant I had to sit alone and wait all that time. *Great!* By the time the show started, the crowds of people were getting more and more drunk, in particular the first group of people I saw sitting by the stage. I could tell they were mostly straight people celebrating something. They grew louder and louder and increasingly agitated, the kind that only comes with intoxication.

I kept reminding myself that I was a safe distance from them at the bar, so it wasn't all bad. I watched as each drag artist came on stage and performed. I stood closer so that I could record Vanta's number but decided to record all the other artists when they came out. I watched as the queen with the blonde curls, known as Kardi Blac, walked on stage and commanded the room with her Taylor Swift number. Glitter King, a spooky drag monster, performed a haunting number dressed as a gothic clown with tears of glitter, all the while handing balloons out to the audience.

Vanta came out and did a rap lip-sync that got my hips moving as I recorded the entire performance. I thought to myself that it must be hard for local drag artists to get half decent footage of their performances from start to finish. As I held my phone up to record them all, I felt at ease. I no longer felt exposed. Finally, I had a reason to be there other than to sit at the bar with nobody to talk to.

The first half of the show finished, and the host informed the club that there would be a thirty-minute intermission before the second half. I went back to the bar and sat on the stool next to two women. I flashed them a smile but all I got in return was a stern look. *Fuck you too, then!* I grabbed my fruit cider and took another sip, realising that my paper straw had been in it too long and turned to mush. I took the straw out and placed it on the bar, just as two of the boys from the noisy booth came over to order drinks. As one ordered a bunch of Jäger bombs, the other made a drunken attempt at making eye-contact with me.

I pulled out my phone and pretended I was busy, but could tell his droopy eyes were still scanning me. The two women beside me began chattering, noticing the drunken men at the bar and turning their stools away so that their backs were facing me. I felt a strong sense of vulnerability wash over me. Their drinks were ordered, made and placed on the bar. I watched from the side of my eye as one of the boys attempted to pick up all five drinks with one hand, placing their fingers on the edge of each glass and lifting them off the bar. As soon as I noticed what he was doing, I knew that he was going to spill them. He was already stumbling around and acting ridiculous, it was clear that the whole bunch of them had been drinking for hours before they even came to Tribeca.

'Thanks mate!' He shouted as he walked away.

'Excuse me,' the bartender said over my shoulder, 'you haven't paid for those.'

'Yeah, I have!'

'No, you haven't. That's fifteen quid for those drinks.'

'Fuck's sake!' he said, as if the bar staff was inconveniencing him somehow. He used his free hand to rummage in his back pocket, not noticing that the drinks he was holding in the other were slowly tipping over.

'WATCH IT!' I said abruptly. I was too late though. Two of the five drinks spilled all over me and my phone.

'Why'd you do that? That was your fault. You should pay for my drinks.'

'What?' I said.

'You fucking spilt 'em. Pay for 'em.'

I was stunned. Was this guy for real? Then I looked at him. His shirt was lopsided, his eyes bloodshot, his speech slurring. He could barely hold a sentence together. He was so drunk he probably believed that he hadn't done anything wrong.

'I'm not paying for them,' I said, looking straight at him, not realising that his posse of friends had noticed the escalating altercation.

'You what? You want me to punch that fucking thing off your head, Paki?'

I was speechless. I watched as he forcibly pointed at my jewelled Bindi and felt myself flinch away from his sticky, Jäger-soaked finger. I looked over at the two women sitting beside me at the bar. I could tell they had registered what was happening, but they did nothing. Instead, they reacted nervously and walked away from the bar.

'What's going on 'ere?' A girl said as she approached with the rest of the drunk partygoers. She was quickly informed that I spilt the drinks and that I refused to pay.

'I'm not paying for them,' I reiterated.

'Then why did you spill 'em?' She asked pointedly.

'I didn't.'

'You fucking calling him a liar?'

'Yeah, I am. He spilled them on me. I'm not paying.'

'Why not? You got no money?'

'Oh, shut up, will you.' I was growing tired of the conversation and wanted it to end. I tried to get the bar staff's attention, but his glance always missed mine.

'You got the money then?' The loud-mouthed girl stepped closer to me, her face screwed and angry. I didn't want to admit it to myself, but I was beginning to feel unsafe.

'Fuckin' joke this. Why you even 'ere, Paki?' She said, then leaned in and inhaled sharply. 'Look at her. Bet her twat fuckin' stinks of curry.'

That was it. I felt completely despondent. I was so disgusted by her vile, racist behaviour that I wanted nothing more than to smack this bitch in her fucking face. However, something unexpected happened. I did nothing.

I couldn't bring myself to stand up against them. I felt small, inadequate, pathetic. Why is it that a total stranger was able to reduce me to feel something I hated feeling more than anything? *Weak.* I stood up, grabbed my faux fur coat and made my way to the exit. I couldn't stand being there any longer. As I made my way to Piccadilly Gardens, the cold air felt like a veil touching my skin, sweetly. The Village was pretty busy, the taxis were moving along the roads, groups of partygoers stumbling up and down Canal Street.

'Oi, where you goin'?'

I turned and saw the group from Tribeca outside, shouting for my attention. *Fuck off, just leave me alone!* I was in no mood for round two of this bullshit. Just as I was ready to lift up the nearest sewer grate and jump in, a black cab with its glowing orange light turned the corner and slowly moved in my direction. Like a shot, I put my hand out and hailed it down.

As the taxi pulled away with me secured in the back seat, I watched the black night speed across the windows. Little droplets of rain ran franticly in streams and the world outside of my moving sanctuary looked fragmented through the rain. I started to feel safe again. But I couldn't shake off the feeling of vulnerability. *What the hell happened tonight? How did I let that happen to me?*

Walking into the flat, my husband's face was one of concern.

'You okay, Yvy?' He already knew what had happened as I messaged him in the taxi.

'No, I'm really not. I'm so fucking pissed off.'

I couldn't get my words out. All I could think about was getting in that taxi and feeling so defeated by those fucking idiots. Everything I wanted to say to those pricks was coming to me now, but it was too late to say it. Why does that always happen? You know, when you find yourself in situations when what you want to say doesn't come to you in the moment. Sometimes that happens out of being overwhelmed by the moment itself, and sometimes it's out of fear of what might happen if you do.

Fear.

Fear is a bullshit emotion that I can't fucking stand. Why is it that fear can have so much power? I had no idea whether the reason I didn't call those arseholes out on their racist comments was because I was overwhelmed by how unprepared I was for such a moment, or was I afraid? It's a tough pill to swallow, but I was determined to not let my mind go crazy thinking about it.

'I'll be back in a bit,' I said to Jack. 'I'm going to make a call.'

I went into the back bedroom and video-called the one person I felt I could talk to who'd understand what I was feeling. As the phone rang, I waited for Ellis to pick up. After a few seconds, his face came up on my phone.

'Waddup, dude!' I said.

'Waddup! How are you doing?'

'Dude, you won't fucking believe what happened tonight.'

Chapter Fifteen
Two Months Earlier

The train pulled out of Manchester Piccadilly and I was ready for the journey to Brighton. Deciding to go to Brighton this year was a big decision, given that I put off going down to see Ellis for a while. It wasn't that I didn't want to see him, quite the opposite. I missed his company so much ever since he made the decision to move from Manchester and I no longer had my partner in crime anymore. My reservations lay in Brighton itself.

Strange how a place I had never been to made me so anxious. The reason for this feeling was a mystery to me. I mean, Brighton seemed like a great place to visit, and even though it was pretty far to travel, I had my very good friend there which made visiting even more enticing. Yet I couldn't bring myself to do it. Manchester had been my home for a while now, and I was comfortable with the life I built, but for so long I tried to ignore a feeling that I simply couldn't shake. A thorn in my side that I couldn't get rid of.

Three years had passed since my renal surgery. Three years since I got my life back on track and was feeling somewhat stable with my health. I spent so many years focusing on myself and I wanted to give something back. After having my surgery at Salford Royal, I took the time to heal, but I couldn't stay out of a job for much longer. I had already been out of work for months and Jack and I couldn't manage all our finances on a single salary. I eventually found a job that started in June, but until then, I wanted to do something that gave me the opportunity to be a part of the queer community.

I started volunteering with the LGBT Foundation and found myself meeting new people, making new friends along the way. For the most part, I was asked to help with general tasks for their monthly events and doing their social media when Sparkle came around. I enjoyed doing it, as it gave me the chance to be in the Village, a space I was very familiar with. However, this time I was an actual part of it. The more volunteering I did, the more I realised just how much I had to offer the community. I loved helping out and meeting new people, but more than that, I loved feeling liberated, not having to hide anything. But I still felt that I needed more.

***

Ellis and I met when I was working for an insurance company in Salford back in 2011. At first, I knew him purely in passing as we were never on the same team. Ellis hadn't transitioned into the person he is today, and I was not openly trans at work even though it was nearly three years since I had my gender surgery. I walked into the break out room to meet my friend Debbie for lunch, but she was stuck on a call.

I think it's safe to say that every call centre worker's biggest hate is when you know you're going to log off the phones and some twat has the nerve, the gall and the audacity to call you a minute beforehand and cuts into your precious *doing anything else but fucking work* time. Ellis was sat alone at one of the tables in the small break area reading a book. Debbie was signalling to me from her desk that she was still on a call, so I made my way into the break area and greeted Ellis.

'Hiya! You alright?'

'Yeah, thanks,' he said, a little bit thrown by my boisterous approach as he looked up from his book.

'How's your day going?'

'Not bad, the usual.'

'Cool.'

'You up to much this weekend?' I asked.

'Not much. Might go out to the Village but haven't decided.'

I knew that Ellis' girlfriend also worked here, but I hadn't really spoken to her that much. I wasn't sure how to navigate the conversation with Ellis at this point, mostly because I wasn't exactly sure whether he was in the mood to talk or would rather read his book, wondering why the hell I was talking to him in the first place. Either way, I had my reservations about continuing the conversation. Luckily, it ceased to be an issue when Debbie walked into the break area.

'Fucking call right before lunch!' She said.

'I know, right! Rude!'

As time passed, my friendship with Ellis began to grow. It was purely in a break room capacity, but nonetheless we got chatting more. My birthday was looming, *27*, which this year was on a Monday and Debbie had planned a night out on the Friday beforehand that I was so looking forward to. Since it was turning into a birthday weekend, I decided to give the Village a go and have a night out on Saturday too.

I hadn't gone on a proper night out in the Village, well, if you don't count that night with Chris when I blacked out after way too much tequila and drugs. I wanted to experience the queer scene, an experience I really wanted to delve into as I felt that I was missing out. Jack and I had been seeing each other discreetly for nearly two months, and although I knew the Village wasn't his scene, being that he was a full-on metalhead and not remotely interested in anything that involved having to shake one's groove thing on a dancefloor, he still wanted to come out and celebrate my birthday.

A few of us decided to go out on Saturday and meet up outside Crunch for a few drinks. I made my way through the crowds as the music from the clubs played and the fairy lights coiled around the trees made the Village look magical. Walking along Canal Street, I messaged Ellis to see where everyone was.

E: We're in G-A-Y! Come meet us here!

Jack was already with me so we made our way over. Something about the atmosphere around G-A-Y always seems a bit shitty, and this night was no exception. I glanced around at the drunken groups and the frustrated people waiting in line to get in. As it came to our turn to enter, the bouncer at the door scanned us both and halted our attempt to go inside.

'Members only.' He said in a monotone voice that could rival Bebe Neuwirth.

'What do you mean?' I asked.

'Members only.'

'Yeah you already said that. What do you mean though?'

'Members only.'

'But our friends are already inside!'

The bouncer stared at me blankly. Clearly, he wasn't budging and I knew exactly what he was getting at with the whole *members only* shit. I messaged Ellis, telling him that I was outside and that they refused us entry. After a few minutes, Ellis emerged with a plastic pitcher in one hand and his girlfriend following shortly after him.

'He won't let us in!' I exclaimed.

Without saying a word to me, Ellis went up to the bouncer and explained that we were there to meet him. It pissed me off that the fuckhead was basically telling me and Jack that we weren't permitted inside because we didn't look queer enough. I mean, yes, I totally understand that clubs in the Village want to make sure that they don't let in any rowdy, drunken straight dickheads that might cause trouble, but to not let me or Jack in felt like a slap in the face. 'They're with us, so let them in!'

'No. Members only.'

'Fine, we'll go somewhere else then,' Ellis said.

'You can't leave with your drink,' the bouncer said blandly.

'I'm not leaving it here!'

Ellis walked off with us, his pitcher in hand, and we made our way to Crunch. We found a table outside, which was nice as the air was warm and welcoming. Drinks were poured and conversation flowed. A lovely evening was beginning to unfold and I was so happy to be sharing my birthday with people I cared about. I started to feel a connection to something, but I was unsure what it was. Looking around, I saw so many queer people having fun, being themselves and not giving a shit. For so long, I depended on myself and didn't get much chance to experience something like this.

I know, it sounds weird given it was just a night out and not a trip to Mecca, but it really was a shift in what I thought my life was and should be. I saw that I could be in an environment that I felt at home in. The only thing I had trouble with was owning my *transness*. I wasn't ashamed of who I was, not at all, but at the same time I never felt comfortable being open about being trans because I didn't want to put myself in danger. *Not again.*

'Who wants tequila?' I asked.

'Go on then!' Chris said, who had since joined us.

Chris went into Crunch and before long he emerged with shots of tequila and a salt shaker. Now I'm sure you're thinking that after the last time I drank tequila with Chris I would swear off it. Yes, I did black out in Baa Bar after I took a pill, did way too much cocaine in a toilet cubicle and then started downing shots. That was something I didn't want to revisit anytime soon, and I was still fighting through the urge to take drugs. This time, I was just going to have a shot of tequila, nothing else. I wasn't about to ruin my birthday celebrations and I didn't want to put myself at risk again.

'Ready?' I shouted as we all spilled some salt on the back of our hands and then took the shot. The warm poison ran down my throat and burned my stomach. Already I was feeling a little bit tipsy, and wanted to stay that way instead of getting absolutely leathered.

'Shall we move on?' Ellis asked.

'Yeah! Where shall we go?'

'We could go to Cruz,' Ellis suggested.

'Yeah, why not?'

I was happy to go with the flow. I didn't know my way around the Village and Ellis seemed to know his shit when it came to places to go.

The five of us arrived at Cruz 101 and waited to get in. A bouncer was at the door, checking people's bags, when I approached holding my brown sequin shoulder bag with metal ring hooks that I bought from a cute little boutique in Chorlton. The bouncer asked if I could open the bag, which I did willingly. I was still feeling the tequila in my system, gently warming my veins to a point where I didn't even notice the chill in the air as the temperature dropped.

'What's this?' The bouncer said. Suddenly I felt a slight chill.

'What?'

'What's this in your bag?'

'Just my stuff?'

'And what's all this white powder?'

Ellis and Jack looked over at me, a little stunned. I looked in my bag and saw that the lining was full of white trails of what looked like a powdery substance. *Shit-motherfucker-fuck-shit!* When I examined it a bit more, it suddenly dawned on me what it was.

'That's just salt.'

'What the hell are you doing with salt in your bag?' The bouncer asked.

'I took it from Crunch! See! There's a salt shaker in my bag! Seriously! It's just salt! Why would my bag be full of cocaine?'

'I didn't say anything about cocaine.'

'Yeah, but come on! That's what you meant though.'

'I said nothing like that, love. Sorry, you're not coming in here.'

'Oh, come on!' Ellis said.

'Sorry, you're not coming in.'

This was now the second club I was rejected from. You'd think it would've left a bad impression on me about the Village, but to be honest, I really didn't care. It was just nice to actually be out with people I could relate to. We eventually ended up in Vanilla, dancing to Eve's 'Tambourine' and wearing stickers with numbers on them as apparently it was Vanilla's Shag Tag night. Ellis and I soon discovered that we had a lot in common, and our friendship started to grow into something I never expected.

***

The trip to Brighton was long, but I eventually arrived at Brighton train station with my weekend bag and a nervous feeling in my stomach. The clouds were dense and a light drizzle was beginning to fall through the air. I looked around and saw crowds of people rushing off in all directions when I suddenly felt my phone vibrate.

E: Hey dude! I'll be done by 3
Y: No worries dude! I'll find somewhere and wait for you
E: Let me know where you are and I'll meet you
Y: Will do x

Being a Psychotherapeutic Counsellor, Ellis focused his attention on the needs of the queer community when it came to his clients. This was his reason for moving to Brighton in the first place, when he made the decision to study for his qualification there. I knew it was the best thing for him when he decided to go, even though it was a punch to the heart to lose the one person I had so much in common with. He was the only one out of all the people I knew when we went on nights out that I felt a bond with.

However, Ellis and I went way back which made that bond the strongest. Ellis had been living in Brighton for a few years now, and I was nervous about what it was going to be like being with him here. I wasn't familiar with anything in Brighton, except for my friend. I didn't know if I was going to fit in or if anyone was going to get my personality and humour. To sum things up, I didn't want to come across as a complete dickhead that nobody could stand.

I walked down a sloped road and into an array of narrow streets and I was fascinated by what I saw. Every street had rows of independent shops selling all sorts. Books, crystals, handmade garments. It was like I walked into a virtual reality version of Etsy. The people around me looked trendy and very much fit in with the scenery. I kept walking through the streets, turning corners and finding more shops and cafes. I wasn't sure where to wait for Ellis and stumbled across a pub that looked like a quiet place to get off my feet and settle until he was free to come meet me.

Perching myself on a big stool in front of the bar, I ordered myself a fruit cider and took in my surroundings. A group of people sat in the far corner, laughing and joking and I could tell they were regulars by how chummy they were with the bartender. Sitting alone at the bar, I felt slightly vulnerable. It's always awkward when you're waiting for someone, but in this case, I knew Ellis was going to be a while so I needed to do something to occupy my time until he came. I decided to spark up a conversation with the bartender, who was working by themselves.

'You've travelled from Manchester, have you?'

'Yeah,' I said. 'I'm here for Trans Pride and to see my friend.'

'Who's your friend?'

'He's called Ellis. I haven't seen him in ages so it's good to be here.'

'Aww yeah, Brighton's a great place.'

'So, are you from here?' I asked.

'I am, yeah. I'm a musician. I'm actually performing tomorrow for Trans Pride.'

'That's amazing!'

'Yeah, you might not recognise me tomorrow though!'

'What do you mean?'

'I'm trans non-binary. I like to perform under my female name. Sarah. When I'm at the bar, I just wear jeans and a t-shirt. When I'm on-stage tomorrow though, I'll look completely different!'

'That's great, I can't wait to see you perform!'

'It's such a great experience, Trans Pride. You'll love it.'

'I love how open everything is here. Manchester is so different. Don't get me wrong, we have the Village and it's definitely changing when it comes to queer visibility. But being here is a totally different vibe!'

'Yeah, there's definitely a big queer space here. So much is going on, especially during a Pride weekend. You'll have a lot of fun.'

I didn't realise just how long I was talking with the bartender because before I knew it, Ellis walked through the pub doors and I saw his eyes light up as he spotted me.

'Waddup dude!' He said ecstatically.

'MAMA'S HEEEERE!'

'Awww dude, it's so good to have you here! I can't believe it!'

'I know! It's so good to see you, dude.'

'So, what do you fancy doing? We're going to a queer film festival tonight to kick off the weekend, so do you want to do anything before hand?'

'You know what, dude, I'm fine with whatever we do! I'm just glad to be here!'

'Agggggh, we are going to have so much fun this weekend!'

Chapter Sixteen

Manchester was scorching hot for the 2019 Pride parade and I was thrilled to be walking the parade route with queer people of colour. I wanted to represent being a queer witch, so I went with an all-black ensemble, rocking a black skirt and camisole, and a cobweb lace bolero that tied under my bust. The one accessory I was so excited to hold was my Pride placard.

After returning from Brighton, I wanted to get more involved with the queer community, in particular queer people of colour, and I already knew of an organisation that was just that. I had known about it for some time but I never felt the urge to go to one of their gatherings that were held on a monthly basis, mostly because I assumed it was more centred around the queer black community and was unsure if they also included people like me. I also didn't want to intrude on something that was very much a necessity, which is a safe space for black queer people to celebrate and support one another. Something I in no way wanted to invalidate or take away from by being there.

When I found out that it in fact was an inclusive space for all queer people of colour, I decided to give it a try and go to a meet up. They planned a Pride banner-making evening that I thought would be the perfect place to start and hopefully get to know some new people. I arrived at the gathering in the evening one night and found that it was just a small number of people, but that didn't bother me. I walked in and saw another South Asian person, sat eating a takeaway kebab. He glanced over and saw me too and gave me the biggest smile.

In a strange way, it was as if I was looking at a familiar face, even though I had never met him before. As we sat around the crafting table, I looked at the different people preparing to create Pride banners and having a mutual happiness of coming in from the pouring rain outside. I began creating my banner and struck up a conversation with the person sat across from me. I didn't quite catch their name as everybody introduced themselves before we started, and it was a bit late to ask now without sounding like an ignorant git.

'So, what do you do?' They said, not looking up from their own banner.

'I write, I'm a writer. I have a book out and everything.'

'Ooh that's amazing!' said the woman sat next to the lad I met earlier.

'Cool. So, what's it about?'

'Me, basically. It's an autobiography.' Something about my conversation with this person felt more like an interview than an informal chat.

'Let's get inspired and create some amazing stuff for Pride, yeah?' The man who appeared to be running the group said enthusiastically. His name was Kenneth. His energy was so vibrant in a way that made the room brighter.

'I cannot wait for this!' I said. 'It's going to be so good to march with other people of colour. I was in Brighton not long ago for Trans Pride and it was so amazing to be holding up a huge photo of Marsha P Johnson and representing. I felt so powerful.'

'Mmmm.' The person to my right mumbled. I turned and looked at them, put off by their distain.

'Sorry?'

'I wouldn't bother with Brighton Trans Pride. Was it just full of white people?'

'I saw quite a few people of colour there. I was marching too.'

'Well, maybe, I wouldn't bother with it though.'

'Can I ask, if you think there's not enough representation, do you not think it's a good idea to actually march and be that representation yourself?'

'You don't get it.'

'Get what?'

'There's so many other issues with Brighton that I have.'

I was in no mood to carry on with the conversation and went back to my banner. I understood the issue of representation of queer people of colour, especially within the LGBTQ community. It's always been predominantly white in representation and people like myself are left behind with no real place that lets us have equal visibility. When it comes to my experiences, I too have had to fight to be seen.

For years I was told that being Indian and gay was wrong. Then I was told that being Indian and trans is a sin and that I shouldn't exist. After the Brexit vote, racism became the new fashion trend that hordes of white people felt comfortable wearing openly. From being told to fuck off back to where I came from as I walked hand in hand with my husband, to being physically attacked in public.

I was on my way to work one morning, waiting for the 33 bus to pull up to the bus stop. The doors swung open and I flashed my bus pass. It was a busy Monday morning and the bus was already near-full. I found an empty seat next to a middle-aged white woman, who busied herself with her phone as *The Verve* blasted through her headphones so loudly even I could hear it. The bus worked its way through traffic, slowly moving down Regent Road and towards Deansgate.

The sun was shining brightly against the windows, causing me to squint every time the rays hit my glasses. Towards the back of the bus sat a group of young lads. They were the typical type that frequent the back of buses. Noisy, annoying fucks. I put in my earphones and let Sade fill my head. The saxophone intro to *Your Love Is King* played and I felt a million miles away. My eyelids grew heavy and I was willing to drift off, when I suddenly felt a brush against my arm that made me jump.

It was that feeling you get when you miss a step walking down a flight of stairs, making your stomach collapse. I opened my eyes and saw the three boys stood in the middle of the bus, facing forward and holding onto the support rails. I looked at the stop sign behind the driver and noticed that it was illuminated. It felt odd that nobody was stood in front of the boys and they chose to stand right beside me. The first track came to an end and the sultry intro to *Hang on to Your Love* started when I noticed one of the boys was staring at me. *Fuck.* I tried to focus on the window and the sunshine instantly reminded me why that was a bad idea when the rays almost blinded me, causing a few hard blinks.

I looked forward, feeling this lad's eyes fixated on me as he chatted with his companions. The bus was waiting at the traffic lights and I stared at the McDonald's on the corner of Oxford Road as the building blocked the sun from my eyes temporarily. The red light was taking forever and I could tell that the lad was still staring at me, trying to get my attention. I made the mistake of taking my earphones out to see what he wanted.

'You alright?' I asked politely.

'Get off this fuckin' bus.'

'Excuse me?' A few people heard what he said to me but tried their best not to react.

'Are you fuckin' deaf, Paki? Get off the fuckin' bus.'

I was disgusted at what I was hearing. I tried to ignore them, which was pointless given their close proximity, almost touching me. I looked around to find anyone willing to help me. *Nothing.*

'We don't want no fuckin' dirty Pakis 'ere, do you hear me?'

'Oh, fuck off, will you?' I said. I was sick of listening to them.

'You're just a little Paki bitch!' He said. The others started laughing and one that hadn't spoken so far decided to join in.

'I wouldn't even shag that shit stain.'

I looked at the woman next to me and could see the distress in her eyes as she tried to avoid eye-contact with me. I looked back, and saw the expressions on all the other passenger's faces, telling me that they also registered what was happening, but nobody wanted to help. In that moment, something happened that I hated more than anything. Something that caused my skin to burn and my nerves to prickle until it hurt my chest. I was scared. The bus started moving and I was a few stops away from my destination, but I wanted off this bus.

Fear was setting in and I knew that even on a crowded bus, I was alone. Nobody was coming to my aid or standing up to these boys, and I knew that these were the kind that didn't give a fuck that I was a woman, or alone, or afraid. If given the opportunity, they wouldn't hesitate to do something to me. *Get off the fucking bus, Yvy.* I pushed the button to signal to the driver that I wanted the next stop, and pushed my way past them. They continued to hound me, telling me to get off the bus. The driver pulled up to the stop and came to a halt. The doors opened and I stepped off, taking a quick glance behind me. My heart jumped when I saw the boys getting off the bus too and before I could process my next move, a sudden blow to my side forced me off my feet and I came crashing down to the ground. I fell in front of the bus, just as it started to move off. Luckily, it didn't and the bus driver stopped in time.

In a flash, my mind went back to when I was a teenager walking to school. I saw the moment clear as day when that car hit me and left me on the pavement. I heard the laughter of my classmates ringing in my ear as they walked over me and left me lying in the street. As I tried to get up, I heard a man confront the arseholes that pushed me in front of the bus, but they made a quick exit and ran in different directions.

'Are you okay?' The man said as he helped me up.

'Yeah, I, I have to go.'

After somehow making it to work, it wasn't long before I was told to take the day off and to go home. I made my way home, but I couldn't bring myself to go in my flat. All I wanted was Jack. I knew he was at work so I made my way to Media City and called him.

'Hey, it's me,' I said when he answered.

'You okay?'

'No, I'm not.'

'What's wrong?'

'I'm at your work. Can you come downstairs?'

After a few minutes of sitting outside Jack's work in the sunshine, he emerged looking concerned.

'You okay, what's happened?'

I couldn't speak. The moment I saw him, I knew I was safe. I broke down and fell into his arms as the tears started to fall.

Sitting around the crafting table, I knew that every person had their own struggles. The one thing we could all relate to was the struggle of being discriminated against and attacked for the colour of our skin. I didn't like that I was being made to feel as though I made the wrong decision to be a part of the Trans Pride march in Brighton.

At the end of the day, I didn't give a fuck how many white people were at that march. What I was focused on was what it meant for me to be there. To represent me and everything that makes up Yvy. I walked in that march knowing that my trans identity, my brown skin, my Indian hair, my glittering bindi, everything that I was, was on show in a way that said: *THIS IS YVY. EAT IT!*

***

The Brighton air was light and inviting as the sun peeked through the clouds. I arrived the day before and spent the evening at a trans film festival, followed by a night at Gal Pals. The queer accelerator was in full force the moment I arrived and it wasn't letting up anytime soon. I was so overwhelmed by how openly queer the whole community was here. It was a completely different world, a world I became amazed by. The turnout for the march was huge when I arrived with Ellis at the Marlborough Pub, or The Marly as it was commonly known as.

I hadn't had the chance to visit The Marly just yet, but I knew that it was the heart of the queer community in Brighton, especially when it came to performance and giving a platform to queer artists. I stood in my acid green, snake skin dress and looked over at everyone that gathered for the march. This definitely wasn't a parade. At every turn I saw nothing but banners and signs that screamed a message.

PROTECT TRANS KIDS

TRANS, SEX WORKER
PEOPLE OF COLOUR
STARTED PRIDE

ALHAMDULLILAH FOR THE QUEERS

I stood by the edge of the road, soaking in the feeling of what it meant to be here. For the first time in a long while, I felt like I was home.

'Come on, dude!' Ellis said to me as he took my hand. 'Everyone's getting to the front of the march.'

Ellis led me through the crowd and we eventually stopped when we found the group of people we were marching with. It was clear that Ellis knew everyone, some I had already met the night before when we partied at Komedia. I was hoping they still recognised me, given that the last time they all saw me I was completely drenched from having to walk to the club in the pouring rain. It didn't let up the entire walk to Komedia and trying to keep my umbrella up was a complete mess so I gave in and went full on Missy Elliott and entertained Ellis with my rendition of *The Rain (Supa Dupa Fly)* on the way to the club. By the time we arrived at Gal Pals, my hair was stuck to my face and my purple dress clung tightly to my breasts. In short, I still looked fucking hot!

'Hi Yvy!' A few people said as they saw us approach. It had been so long since I felt like a newbie. Seeing so many welcoming queer people, it was empowering, but at the same time slightly intimidating. I wasn't quite sure why I was feeling timid, maybe it was just being somewhere new. Regardless, I was stoked to be a part of the march.

As we marched through Brighton, we chanted and screamed. The crowds around us cheered and cars sounded their horns. I held my placard of Marsha up as high as I could while Ellis wore my inclusive flag around his shoulders. The sea air was blowing gently across in waves as the sound of the water filled my head. I couldn't believe how close I was to the sea. I couldn't even recall being by the sea before, so much so that I freaked out when I actually saw the water.

'Holy shit! There's the sea! Look! Dude!'

'I know, dude!' Ellis said, laughing affectionately at my over-excitement.

I was elated. I was beginning to feel such a connection to Brighton that it almost felt like I had been here all my life. We headed towards Brunswick Gardens where the march ended and took in the rest of the festivities. Ellis and I worked our way through all the different stands and eventually moved towards the area where everyone was relaxing on the grass in front of the stage that was on the far side of the garden in front of the sea.

As Ellis caught up with people who grabbed his attention, I started towards the crowd, taking in all of their faces. Some were smiling, others looked deep in thought. And some looked angry as hell as they spoke passionately to their companions. Every walk of life from the queer community was represented here; relaxing, celebrating, socialising. I stood alone, feeling the sea breeze hitting my face harder with every step I took. Emotions started to stir inside me, something I didn't expect.

Even though I was walking alone, I didn't feel alone. Here I was in a place I had never been to, yet I felt like I knew everybody. I felt like I could sit amongst anyone in the crowd and they wouldn't think twice to strike up a conversation with me. My emotions built and I felt a lump in my throat growing when I stopped walking and stood perfectly still. *I love it here.*

'Dude!' Ellis said when he walked up from behind me. 'Do you wanna have a look at some t-shirts? I really want to get one!'

'Yeah definitely! Who were you chatting with?'

'Oh, I'm bumping into everyone I know!'

'Check you out, Mr Celebrity! Even the bartender at the pub when I first got here knew who you were!'

'What can I say, dude! Living my best life! This is why you need to move down here!'

'Can you imagine if we were both here? Brighton would be destroyed!' I said. 'They would not be able to take us!'

Ellis found himself a t-shirt and a tote bag at one of the stands and we saw that the rest of the crowd we were with had already secured a spot on the grass and signalled us to come join them. I pulled my phone out of my bag to take a picture of Ellis and I when someone came over and offered to take our picture. As Ellis held up his new find, I stood beside him, holding up my flag. The breeze blew the flag wide open and when the picture was taken, it came out perfectly.

By the end of our second night on the town and my last full day in Brighton, I was absolutely knackered. Turning thirty really switches your entire body, or mine at least, and I was craving a cuppa the same way I used to crave a swig of apple Sambuca straight from the bottle. It was a warm evening, unlike the night before, so I risked going out partying in just a t-shirt and my hair in two buns. I planned to stay in Brighton for two nights and I was saddened by how quickly it had gone.

Already I was back at Ellis's flat, knowing that the next day I would be on a train back to Manchester. It was pushing towards 01:00 am by the time we got back to the flat, and Ellis and I were wired and not remotely close to sleep. The whole day was filled with so much that I hadn't had any time to soak it all in. It was strange but this was the first time I got to actually sit down and reflect on everything I was feeling. We went upstairs into Ellis' room where I was sleeping and we decided to get comfy and light some candles. As I rested on the bed, Ellis sat in his chair by the window, opening it slightly to let the air in. My hands grasped the hot mug of tea I was holding as I folded my legs.

'How are you feeling?' Ellis asked.

'Honestly, I'm so overwhelmed, dude.'

'What do you mean?'

'It's crazy here. I can't believe how much there is here. I never realised just how alone I am in Manchester. Can I tell you something?'

'Of course, you can.'

'I went through my transition years ago. It was different back then. There wasn't any queer community in Blackburn and social media was fucking non-existent. I did it all by myself because I had no choice, which in a way I'm grateful for. I didn't look outward for how to act or think. I just got on with it and although I went through some shit, I could say to myself that at least all these experiences are mine. But being here, I can't help but think that I've totally missed out.'

'I get that.' Ellis said after taking a sip of his brew. 'Brighton has a big queer community, and although this weekend isn't an everyday example of what it's like here, it's miles more open than most places.'

191

'I've never had a queer family or a queer community around me. I mean, I didn't even have any other trans friends when I was coming up. Do you remember that night outside Vanilla when you told me about you?'

'Of course, I do, dude! I remember telling you I was trans and you told me that you had a 'cousin' or something who was trans!' He said jokingly, which made me smile.

'I know! I felt so stupid making up some cousin, but there was a reason that I did that. I said that because I knew you for a while by then and when you told me you were trans, I was so happy for you. I didn't want to take anything away from your moment. If I had told you that I was trans, I would've felt like I was taking that moment away from you. It meant a lot for you to tell me, even though we were shit-faced and I ended up with a meat package delivered to my house.'

'What!'

'Dude! Do you not remember?'

'No!'

'We were sat outside Vanilla in the carpark and after you told me, we carried on drinking. For some reason I was fucking around on Groupon and we thought it was a fucking good idea to order some meat.'

'Oh, I totally forgot about that!'

'Yeah, like a week later I had some guy come to the flat with a fuck off massive box of meat! There was absolutely loads in it!'

'How much was it?'

'It was supposed to be £200 but I got it for sixty quid!'

'Bargain, dude. Bargain!'

'To be fair though, it lasted ages!'

'We had some good times in the Village, dude. It was always us though that just took everything to another level.'

'Come on! I mean, look at who we were hanging out with! I remember coming to yours once and the moment I arrived I was like MAMA'S HEEEEERE and everyone looked at us like we were crazy!'

'Too true. It's funny because at the time I had no idea you were trans, but on some level I knew that you felt like you belonged. When we'd go to the Village, you just fit. I never questioned it.'

'It was hard, you know.' I said, my tone turning sombre. 'I was so fucked up around that time. I saw everyone dealing with all their dramas, including you, and I was just the random crazy bitch of the group that executed dance routines in the club like I was a fucking choreographer and made everyone laugh! But on the inside, I was drinking and taking so many drugs. I was in such a bad place but I didn't tell any of you.'

'But look at us now!' Ellis replied. 'After all these years, we're the last ones standing! Those days when it was just us were so good. It's built us up and now we're in such a better place.'

'Totally.'

'And I get what you're saying about community. I can't imagine what it was like for you to transition alone, but you are one strong woman. There's nothing stopping you from being a part of the community. Damnit, you *are* the community!'

'I know, I just don't know where to start. If I'm honest, I was so focused on my trans journey that I barely made room for my Indian journey. I love who I am and I love the skin I'm in, but I've been so disconnected from my culture that I have no idea how to connect.'

'Dude, you never lost that connection. It's always been a part of you, there's no way you can lose it because you wear it every day.'

Ellis was right. It made sense that I hadn't lost touch with being Indian because I see it every time I look in the mirror, or when I see my beautiful mother. It's in my blood. Yes, I was lacking in the friend department when it came to trans people of colour, but looking over at Ellis, I couldn't help but notice just how amazing he looked. His short black buzzcut, his broad shoulders and his mustard yellow striped shirt, his beautiful brown skin. I saw an amazing human being that I had been friends with for almost a decade. We had our ups and downs, but something kept us connected. Something always pulled us together, even when we didn't speak for long periods. Every time we connected; it was as if we had seen each other every day. He was like a brother to me.

'I know what you should do, dude. I know what will make everything so much better,' he said.

'What's that?'

'Move here!'

'Can you imagine me moving down here, seriously?'

'Yeah, I can! You need to be here! This is where you can really shake things up! When your book comes out you've got so many opportunities to make things happen. Plus, it would be so good to have you here, dude!'

'I can't deny that it's fucking tempting, dude. I love it here.'

'All jokes aside though, dude, if you need or just want to see what's out there community wise, have a look at what's going on in Manchester.'

'You're right. I mean, I meet people all the time at the Foundation when I volunteer so I don't know why I'm feeling a certain way about going somewhere new to meet people.'

'Exactly. Don't forget that you're Yvy!'

My last day in Brighton arrived and I was on the train waiting for my long journey to Manchester to begin. My time here was well spent and I left Brighton with a new sense of direction. Spending time with Ellis was fantastic. For so long I had put off coming to Brighton to see him, and now that I had done it, I couldn't have asked for a better experience. To me, it was an awakening of something inside me that had been dormant for so long.

I knew who I was and was proud of that, but there was a piece of the puzzle that was missing. I knew who Yvy was. I devoted years and so much energy into understanding her and building her up. What was missing was the connection to my Indian heritage. When I was young, my connection was strong because I never felt that I needed to prove that I could be both queer and Indian.

However, the older I got, the more I was told that I couldn't be both. I knew that my journey to transition was undeniable, but did that mean I had to leave being Indian behind? Did that mean I could no longer connect with something that was very much a part of me? I knew things needed to change.

As the train pulled out from London Euston, my journey to Manchester had begun. Being in Brighton filled my heart with so much joy. I honestly wasn't sure if I was going to enjoy myself, as I thought my presence wasn't needed, but my time in Brighton surpassed everything I ever could have imagined.

Now it was time to go back home and do my part to represent who I am in my community.

Nyssa and Pirlo

The BollyWitch, 2021

The BollyWitch, Lock 91, Manchester, 2019

Misty Fye and Glitter King, Lock 91, Manchester, 2019

Christmas, Morecambe, 2009

Jack and Yvy, Florence, Italy, 2018

Sweet Constancy, Pisa, Italy, 2018

Jack, Florence, Italy, 2018

Chapter Seventeen
Manchester, 2019

The crowds around the Roman Gardens just off Liverpool Road were growing bigger as the heat continued to beat down on us. It hadn't been long since I arrived and found the group I was going to be walking the parade with, when I started to feel the strain of the intense warmth. Wearing all black might not have been the best idea, but I looked good so I didn't care. The group I was meeting had already set up at their assigned area at the back of the gardens.

As I made my way towards them, I noticed the group from my place of work had also gathered in their spot not too far from where I was supposed to be. Lucky for them they were given a spot in the shade, whereas my group were sweating it out under the blazing sunshine. I manoeuvred my way through the vast amount of Pride organisers, photographers and people sitting on the grass until I reached my group. Everyone was pumped up and ready to go, holding up their banners and quenching their thirst with bottles of water.

Standing under direct sunlight was becoming unbearable. I figured the best thing I should do was take a walk to clear my head and maybe find a little shade.

'Yvy!' A voice boomed from behind me. As I turned, I saw that it was Kenneth. He was so nice when I met him at the banner making evening and I really got on with him. When we first met, I learned that he was responsible for a lot of the costumes that were worn during the Black Pride Vogue Ball, so I knew he had some serious fashion skills.

'Hey Ken!'

'How are you doing, Yvy?' He said as he gave me a hug.

'I'm good thanks, just sweating in this heat!'

'I know, right! Listen, I've brought some stuff for people to wear and I keep hearing your name when it comes to a skirt that I've brought along.'

'Yeah?'

'I hear you'd be perfect to wear it! Wanna try it on?'

'Umm, yeah sure! Will it go over the skirt I've got on?'

'Oh yeah that'll be fine.'

Kenneth rummaged through the bags that were laying on the grass and lifted up the skirt. I was completely blown away by what I was looking at. The skirt was long, all the way to the floor and flared out towards the bottom like a vintage petticoat. Black squares were sewn on in rows, and each square had a raised fist that was designed differently. I studied each fist and could see so many designs, from trans and non-binary pride, to black pride, queer representation and individual pride flags.

'Did you make this?' I asked, completely astonished.

'I put everything together but the group all chipped in to make the squares.'

'This is incredible! I can't believe you all made this!'

'Do you want to wear it?' Kenneth asked with a smile.

'Of course, I do! I'd be happy to wear it!'

'Fantastic!'

I stepped into the skirt and lifted it up to my waist. *Perfect fit!* As Kenneth worked on tying a Pride flag around my waist to secure it, I noticed how everyone around was looking at it in amazement. I couldn't wait to wear this during the parade. Luckily, my skirt underneath made Kenneth's creation flare out even more.

'There! Got it!' He said as he fastened the final pin on the flag. I watched as he smiled with every twirl I did, making the skirt come alive.

I took a walk around the garden to clear my head. One thing I was fully aware of was my tendency to feel dizzy whenever I was under the sun for too long. Walking around the crowded groups, I saw that a lot of different organisations were here, ready to march in the parade. I needed to find some shade and the only place I could see was the area where my work colleagues were congregating.

I didn't want to go over there. It wasn't that I didn't want to see some of my colleagues, it was more because I was still angry about something that happened at work a few days earlier. Actually, that was putting it mildly, I was fucking pissed the fuck off by what happened. My head was spinning, but not from the heat. What happened was still on my mind and part of me was angry because of how I handled it. *Don't do that to yourself, Yvy.*

When one of my colleagues noticed me, I had no choice but to go over. As I made my way through the crowds and towards the shade, my enthusiasm for the day slowly started to decline. Luckily, the shade from the trees cleared my mind and helped me calm down.

***

Jack sat comfortably on his side of the sofa, another episode of *NYPD Blue* blaring from the television. I unzipped my art folder to look for my pencils and placed the white sheets of paper I took from work on the table.

'What is it you're doing again?' Jack asked.

'They asked me to help decorate the office for Pride. Figured I'd make some banners instead of what usually happens. I'm a bit sick of just seeing rainbows and unicorns!'

'You got any ideas on what you want to do?'

'Yeah. I'm going to make protest banners. Kind of like ones you'd see in a proper march. It'll give everyone something to think about.'

'That's a really good idea.'

As soon as I put pencil to paper, the ideas for different messages flowed out and before I knew it I had already drawn over ten different protest messages. I made some finishing touches and put them safely away to take to work in the morning.

Nyssa was fast asleep next to my pillow just before 06:00 am. The sky was already bright and the bedroom lit up. I turned onto my side and saw that my cat was stirring, wondering why I was moving around. Once I settled, so did Nyssa as she rested her delicate chin on my arm and fell asleep again. I gave her a little tousle between her soft ears as she drifted off to sleep. Clutching my pillow, my head sank deeper into the comfy groove and I felt my mind drifting off. It only felt like a few seconds before something woke me.

At first it was just a light feeling across my face, but soon it became a persistent touch that was soft yet demanding. I opened my eyes and saw Pirlo, his black fur and marble eyes staring at me. The moment my eyes opened, Pirlo instantly knew he had my attention and began to purr. His happiness rumbled loudly as he pressed his wet nose against my ear in an excited effort to get me out of bed. I knew exactly what he wanted. Stepping over his sister, Pirlo stood on my chest, his weight pressing against my boobs and reminding me that I went to bed with my bra on as the underwire dug in. Another nose dive from Pirlo prompted me to break out of my sleepy haze.

My phone alarm was about to sound, which was pointless given that Pirlo had become my new alarm. He never let me forget that 06:00 am meant it was time to get up and feed him and Nyssa. His sister never did the work though. Nyssa was clever and let her brother wake up Mum while she relaxed in a tight little bundle next to my pillow, only getting up when she saw me out of bed and heading to the kitchen, this morning was no exception. I fed Nyssa and Pirlo and started to get ready for work. My outfit was already hanging on the wardrobe when I walked into the back bedroom that I turned into my witchy room.

The office had a whole Pride-themed day planned and wanted everyone to dress in Pride colours. I didn't want to wear a rainbow outfit because, well, you know, too obvious! Instead, I opted to go a little bit more Sasha Velour and used block colours to represent the rainbow. I decided on a red dress with frilled sleeves, purple tights, green shoes and pink socks. I finished it off with an orange flower pinned to my hair bun and a rainbow feather boa for added effect just in case I wanted to serve a little bit of camp throughout the day.

Jack, being the rocker that he is, was way too metal to dress in rainbow colours. Instead, he settled with wearing a t-shirt that he wore when I threw my last Pride party at the flat. He put on his black t-shirt that showcased a big picture of the gayest, most fabulous queer icon of contemporary cinema. An icon that was instantly recognised by the queer community…*The Babadook.*

I wanted today to have a message. I felt like I had a real opportunity to bring some queer history to work and hopefully enlighten my colleagues on what it took to even have a Pride celebration.

Arriving at work, I saw that they had put up the Pride flags I brought in the other day. In between the pods of people sitting in front of computer screens, I saw my trans flag, my rainbow flag and my inclusive flag that I took to Brighton. It made me smile to see them hanging proudly amongst my colleagues, however I knew that what I had in store was going to take the Pride decorations to a whole new level.

'Yvy!' I heard as a young woman with flowing hair came bouncing towards me.

'Hey Katie! I've brought you some goodies!'

'Ooh, did you make some posters?'

'Yep.' I pulled out the posters to stick on the cabinet doors at the end of each pod. Katie's eyes lit up as she sifted through each one, getting more and more excited.

'These are so good, Yvy! I love them!'

'I've got another idea too. I was thinking of printing off all the different Pride flags and sticking them up with a description of what each flag means.'

'Love it!'

Katie took the posters and I walked to my desk that was situated in the middle of the long row of pods. Chloe and Fiona were already at their desks as they greeted me.

'Morning!' Chloe said, turning in her chair.

'Morning. How are you?'

'I'm alright.' she said, slightly slumping in her seat.

'What's up?'

'Oh nothing, I just want it to be the weekend!'

'The struggle is real!'

Fiona was still on a call so I gave her a smile and sat at my desk to log onto my computer. It didn't take long before Chloe rolled her chair over to me.

'Would you like a croissant?' She offered, knowing exactly what my answer was going to be.

'YES PLEASE!' I wasted no time grabbing a buttery pastry to go with the hot cuppa I was about to make.

'Morning Yvy,' Fiona said as she finished her call.

'Morning. Ooh, I'm loving the outfit, Fiona!' She turned in her chair, revealing her rainbow striped top, covered by a black dungaree dress that fit her feminine emo style. The soft, natural curls of her dark hair waved around her face as she flashed me a cheeky smile that said *I know I look good*!

'You get up to much last night, Chloe?' I asked.

'Not really. Just did a bit of reading. You?'

'I was making the posters for today.'

'I know, I totally forgot that we were supposed to wear rainbow colours today.' She looked down at her ensemble which was a complementary range of warm berry tones. Colours that suited her sweet, English rose demeanour.

'Well, I think I'm dressed up enough for the both of us. Besides, you can always wear my boa if you want!'

'What did you get up to last night, Fi?' Chloe asked before turning back to her desk to see who just messaged her on her phone.

'Oh, not much. Still trying to eat better and cooking from scratch.'

'Nice, what did you make?'

'I made a gorgeous broccoli Bolognese with a bit of sausage I bought from Aldi. It was fucking lovely! I brought some for lunch today too.'

'Oh, that does sound good! Think I'll probably go to the food market today for lunch. I fancy a burger or something.'

'A burger and some halloumi fries sounds real good right about now.'

Suddenly, Chloe spun in her chair, her brown hair spinning through the air and landing on her shoulders as she slammed her fist on the armrest.

'I *LOVE* HALLOUMI FRIES!'

Fiona and I burst into laughter at Chloe's emphatic response. Chloe, Fiona and I saw each other as more than just work friends. The three of us had very individual styles. Chloe had a classic charm. Although she was ten years younger than I was, we got on as if we'd known each other for years. She wasn't like most girls I knew who were in their twenties. Instead of partying and getting pissed every weekend, Chloe was much more content curling up with a good book at home and taking care of her rabbits.

Fiona was edgy and had the incredible ability of coordinating a black ensemble together that looked effortlessly stylish. Fiona was around the same age as Chloe, however the parallels between us were astonishingly accurate. From our taste in movies and our ability to quote *The Simpsons* accurately, to our similar partner relationships and mutual love of our cats. Fiona often said that when she looked at me and Jack, it was as if she was looking into her future in ten years.

I rummaged in my bag and pulled out a polystyrene block that had Chloe and Fiona slightly perplexed.

'What's that, Yvy?'

'It's a brick!'

'A brick?' Chloe asked.

'Yeah, it's to symbolise the brick that was thrown at Stonewall. It's said to have been thrown by Marsha P Johnson who was a trans woman of colour. If it wasn't for her, we wouldn't even have a Pride.'

'I love that you've written *PROTEST* on it too!' Fiona said.

'Where's Jack? Is he in today?'

'He on the late shift,' I replied to Chloe.

'Is he dressing up?'

'Can you imagine Jack dressing up in rainbow colours?' I said jokingly.

Just then, Katie came around to my desk and asked if I wanted to put the posters up with her. We walked down to each cabinet and started sticking the posters on. As each one was placed on the cabinet doors, staff walking by couldn't help but notice. Each one was colourful, sporting a powerful message.

PRIDE IS A
PROTEST

TRANS
LIVES
MATTER

RESPECT MY
EXISTENCE
OR
EXPECT MY
RESISTANCE

All ten posters were up and before long, people from other teams came around to check them all out. Some stopped to read my Stonewall poster, which had a brief history of how Pride began. It was heart-warming to see some of my queer colleagues feeling genuine emotion when looking at the posters, recalling the many struggles they experienced just by being a part of the LGBTQ community.

I knew there and then that it was the right thing to do instead of simply sticking a few rainbows and unicorns around the office. The more people came round, the more they took notice of the protest posters and the Pride flag explanations. It got the floor talking about queer history and about the vast gender spectrum that most of them had no clue about. I was pleasantly surprised by how receptive everyone was when learning a little about queer history.

By the afternoon, the day was beginning to drag and I was looking forward to finishing and having a relaxing evening at home. Jack and I had already planned on making a nice hot plate of cheesy nachos and watching *The Silence of the Lambs* for the 100th time. I sat at my desk, getting on with my work when my mobile started to ring. Usually, I didn't answer my phone at work, but the number was one I didn't recognise and I wasn't sure if it was from someone important. I answered the phone and quickly excused myself to the meeting room across from my desk. I was only in there for a few minutes, but I could see Fiona and Chloe looking at me through the glass, wondering if I was okay. After a few more minutes, I hung up the phone and returned to my desk.

'Is everything okay?' Chloe asked.

'You won't fucking believe what I've just found out.'

* * *

The shade of the trees cooled my skin. I could feel my head clear and the dizziness began to fade. Already a few of my colleagues that I recognised had noticed my approach. One in particular saw me and I could see he was feeling slightly uneasy. I couldn't blame him though. The last time we spoke was on the phone when he told me that someone on the office floor had complained that one of my posters was offensive. When I asked which poster it was, I was told it was my *NO TERFS ON OUR TURF* poster.

Apparently, the person complaining didn't want to reveal themselves, but described themselves as an 'outspoken feminist' and felt that my poster was not appropriate in the workplace. The moment I heard this; my blood boiled. I couldn't believe that I was being told that someone who classed themselves as a feminist actually thought that my poster was offensive. It was clear that whoever it was who complained was most likely the very type of person that my poster was calling out. A Trans Exclusionary Radical Feminist, or TERF as they're commonly known, refers to a person who does not believe that trans women are women and that they should not be included or recognised as women. This includes the belief that trans women should not be allowed in women's spaces, such as restrooms.

In a nutshell, a TERF believes that if you weren't born with a pussy, you are not a woman. *Fuck off!* It's so frustrating when people hide behind calling themselves a feminist and yet feel that I am not a woman. Being a feminist is about the equality of the sexes and not choosing who you think is a woman just because you were born with the privilege of being cisgender and not understanding what it means to be trans. *NO TERFS ON OUR TURF* means exactly that. TERF was not coined as a slur against people who believe in its ideology. Trans women have had to fight against people like this for decades, and for a TERF to call themselves a feminist is a fucking joke.

When I found out that someone was unhappy with my poster, I knew exactly why that was. I was surprised that whoever it was that complained didn't want to reveal themselves to me. What upset me the most was that I was asked if it was okay to take my poster down. Although I wasn't directly told to do it, it was heavily implied that I should, and I gave in to their request and took my poster down. The moment that happened, word spread within my team and my colleagues were outraged by this blatant act of transphobia. Rightly so. I was happy to see my colleagues rallying with me, understanding my anger, but my celebratory feeling for Pride quickly dissolved and all I wanted was to go home.

I exchanged a few pleasantries with the person I spoke to on the phone and made my way back to my group across the grass. I understood that he was just the messenger for someone else who seemed to have a problem with me, but it didn't take the sting out of his actions. It didn't make me feel any less discriminated against. Too many emotions stirred when that happened. For too long I have had to adapt to please others, with nobody giving my thoughts and feelings any consideration.

In fact, I was tired of having to take everyone else's feelings into consideration. Nobody gave a fuck about how I was affected, only that the poster was taken down and that I didn't cause a fuss. I was sick of this. My head felt heavy and I could feel my dizziness creeping back. *Stop it, Yvy. Don't do that to yourself.* I found my way back to my group and we were ready to make our way to the parade route and begin the Pride celebrations.

As the parade began, the thoughts of everything that was bothering me melted away and I worked the crowd as I moved in ways that made my skirt dance. Countless faces smiled and cheered as we walked along the streets of Manchester, the music pumping loudly. The sun was growing even hotter, but I didn't care. I felt free, walking beside an Asian drag queen who was dressed beautifully in a rainbow-colored lehenga and dazzling jewellery that caught the light.

As we reached the end of the parade route, something felt a little off. The group congregated and I watched as they all embraced in celebration. Sitting on the brick wall, the searing heat was catching up with me and I could feel my skin warming up. Kenneth had already helped to take the skirt off, but even with feeling a little lighter, I still felt shaky. *It's okay, Yvy. You just need some water.* I remained by the wall and watched everyone else go about their celebrations and taking pictures. It suddenly dawned on me that nobody was really bothering with me. *It doesn't matter, Yvy. Just drink some water.* I looked around and couldn't find anything to drink.

'You okay, Yvy?' A voice said from behind me. I turned and saw it was one of the people from the group that I had befriended at the last meet up. He was such a sweetheart to me and took the time to sit with me when I had nobody to talk to.

'Yeah, I'm okay. Did you enjoy the parade?'

'Yeah, I did! I loved it! I'm so buzzed!'

'Aww fab! You sticking around or—'

'Actually, I have to head off so I'm going to walk into town.'

'Can I come with you? I have to get to the Foundation to do my volunteering.'

As I walked past Piccadilly Station and into town, I felt safer knowing that I was with someone. I was concerned that maybe my blood pressure was dropping or something kidney-related was going on again, and I didn't want to be by myself. At the same time, I was in no mood to announce that I was feeling awful and took the opportunity when it came up to not try walking around town by myself.

When I reached the LGBT Foundation, I downed what felt like ten litres of water and cooled myself off. The heat outside was becoming intolerable, and wearing my witchy ensemble went from being a stylish statement to just plain fucking annoying. If I could, I would have happily done my volunteering in my underwear. However, given that my volunteering consisted of going into the Village and handing out safe-sex packs, I didn't think having my breasts on show would be the best thing to do.

I walked in and saw that a few volunteers were already hard at work, filling their trays with safe-sex packs and heading out the door. Even with the air conditioners on full blast, the heat was growing more intense and I was *this* close to going with my original plan of working in my knickers. I didn't even care that I wasn't wearing matching underwear and I hadn't shaved my armpits.

'Hi Yvy, how was the parade?' The coordinator asked.

'It was great!'

'Fab! Well, we have some t-shirts over there to wear so when you're ready we'll start getting these packs out to people. We want to try and get as many out there as we can.'

I looked over at the pile of navy blue t-shirts on the table and sifted through to find my size. I managed to find a medium, when I looked over and saw a larger size and suddenly had a thought. Grabbing the larger size, I excused myself to the restroom and peeled out of my clothes. I was sweating like a greased hog and spent the best part of ten minutes taking tissue paper and dabbing every crevice that had become increasingly uncomfortable.

Thankfully, my thighs hadn't expanded or started rubbing together yet. *Thank fuck!* The last thing I wanted to experience right now was bloody thigh chafing. After cooling myself down, my hair went into a high ponytail and I put on the large t-shirt and found that it was just long enough so that Missy wasn't showing. *This is all I'm going to wear.*

We headed out onto Richmond Street and already the streets were absolutely packed with people. I felt so much better after tying my hair back and losing the skirt. As I navigated through the crowds, a sense of urgency was upon me to give away as many sex packs as I could and head back to the Foundation to pick up some more. As time went on, the crowds were becoming increasingly rowdy. It didn't feel nice to be there.

The feeling of what Pride meant was lost in all the drunken faces and petty bullshit I kept bumping into every time I tried to say hello to someone or give them a pack. This wasn't the first time I had volunteered for Pride, and this certainly wasn't the first time I felt this way. A few years ago, when I first volunteered, I did the same job of handing out these packs. It was a busy Pride, but I hadn't noticed the messiness straight away, given that I was so excited to be working my first Pride weekend.

I looked so cute with my red Foundation t-shirt on and coordinating floral leggings. I was given the task of wearing the tray that held all the goodies that we were to give out to the crowds. As the day went by, so did people's consideration for social decency. Before long, I watched as the drunken fuckery took over, and when I almost stood in a puddle of 'water' that turned out to be a stream of piss coming from someone squatting behind a Vauxhall Corsa, I was fucking done.

The crowds were thick and full of shirtless men who noticed me trying to move through them. My buddy who I was partnered with for volunteering had already managed to get himself through the crowd, however when I made my attempt, I suddenly found myself backed up near the alley way that led to G-A-Y, surrounded by a bunch of men.

'Y'alright love, what we got 'ere?' One of them said.

'Fancy some free stuff?' I asked, feeling slightly intimidated.

The men immediately started grabbing for the condoms and lube.

'Only if I can use this on you, love!' One said in a way that made Missy cringe.

'Sorry boys, but you'd have a better chance using them on each other.'

'Oh c'mon, I haven't tasted a brown girl before.'

I was done. Officially. All I wanted was to get out of there, but my back was against a wall and I couldn't push past them with my tray. As one of the men started to feel my hair, I felt violated. I couldn't take it anymore and pushed harshly past them. As they yelled at me, I no longer cared about being courteous and continued to push through the crowds, not caring if I was inconveniencing anyone.

So why did I volunteer again, you ask? Well, it's pretty simple. I knew that what happened wasn't right and put me in a dangerous situation. But at the same time, I wasn't about to be scared away from a space that is just as much mine as anyone else who goes to the Village to feel safe. I wasn't going to become a victim to their bullshit and be scared away. From that moment on, I was ready for anyone who even attempted that shit with me. As I walked around the Village once again, giving out sex packs and wearing my t-shirt and boots, my guard was firmly up to anybody who tried anything with me.

The Village wasn't unknown territory to me. Ellis and I practically lived in the Village at one point, and even though nobody knew that I was trans at that time, it still felt like a safe space. As time went by, that feeling became a memory and the Village evolved into a new playground for a younger generation. Is that a bad thing? Absolutely not. Am I disappointed? In a way.

It wasn't until I spoke out about being trans that I started to see things differently. I saw the lack of trans spaces in the Village. I saw the divisiveness when it came to certain clubs. What I wanted more than anything was to connect with other queer people of colour. I hated that beside Ellis, I didn't have any trans friends to confide in. I had no community around me to reach out to. I tried to take part with organisations that were there for queer people of colour, but a part of me still felt alienated.

I needed to find somewhere that I could call my safe space. Somewhere that I could connect with other South Asian people and share my experiences.

Spending so many years focused on my transition had derailed me from connecting with my Indian heritage. I never went to mosque, I never learnt to speak Urdu fluently, I was an outcast in Blackburn. Everything about my childhood pushed me away from connecting with being Indian because of being trans. As a result, I lost touch with such an important part of me. So what to do? Brighton was such an amazing experience. I got the chance to be with people that embraced me in a way I hadn't felt since meeting Gillian, Isabel, Leanne and Kayleigh in college. Meeting those girls changed my life as they showed me that it was possible to see me for who I was, even when I wasn't able to be that person.

Being in Brighton, spending time with Ellis made me see just how he could connect with every facet of my queer identity and understand it without question. He embraced me before he knew I was trans, just like I did with him before he started his transition.

It was only a couple of months later when the incident at Tribeca occurred and I called Ellis for solace. It was then that I realised that I had evolved into a place that was beyond worrying whether I could party in the Village or find a community. At the end of the day, the people closest to me created the safe space I so longed for. I didn't need to worry about being on my own, I was an expert at it!

For so long, I took care of myself and although I hadn't paid much attention to my Indian culture, it was always a part of me. Suddenly, a force had awakened inside me. I wanted to explore being queer and Indian. So much of what I had gone through relating to my ethnicity was so negative. It was time to turn that on its fucking head and create some magick.

A BollyWitch Tale

Chapter Eighteen
Deansgate,
Manchester, 2019

The tram pulled up to Deansgate-Castlefield and I stepped onto the platform once the doors opened. The rain was pleading to fall from the sky, the air feeling dense. I never usually bothered going back into town after I finished work, mostly because I had already spent all day in town and once work was done, I craved nothing more than to get out of the city centre and back home to my quiet comforts.

Tonight was different though. There was a very special reason for me to be travelling back in town on such a cold December evening. I held my backpack in place, grasping the straps that pulled on each shoulder. The faux fur lining of my hood pressed against my ears and drooped slightly from the top, covering almost half my face. I didn't mind though, in fact, that was my intention. For the entire tram ride, I kept to looking out the window, leaving my hood up. I couldn't be bothered with anyone throwing me a judgemental stare.

Then again, who cares what they think. I may have painted my face to look like a gothic death witch and wore white contact lenses that were something out of a zombie movie, but I still looked fucking hot. Or at least that's what I told myself. I rushed my make-up so much that I knew it was rough around the edges, and knowing that I was about to stand in front of a room full of people, I was beginning to dread what was about to happen.

Lock 91 was not far from the tram stop, but each step felt so heavy as I made my way down the stairs and around the corner. The streets were pretty quiet, but then again it was 07:00 pm on a weekday and Lock 91 was a little bit out of the usual busy areas of city centre. Walking across the cobbled stones, I was almost at the entrance when I felt my gut rumble.

A sudden feeling of anxiety warmed my insides like a shot of whisky working its way through my veins. *Are you making a mistake?* No, I wasn't. I knew I wanted to do this. Hell, I've been wanting to do this for so long, and after what happened to me in Tribeca, I had to believe that I was doing the right thing. I pushed the door open and walked in. The bar looked lovely with its rustic furnishings and wooden pillars. I walked past the bar area and towards the narrow staircase that led upstairs. Standing at the foot of the stairs, I heard people chatting above, causing my anxiety to build again.

Oh, shit! I walked up and before I knew it, I was looking at rows of empty chairs facing the stage, which was set towards the back. The ceiling curved on each side, coming to a point in the centre like a church. Along the side walls were Christmas garlands lit up with warm, white fairy lights. It was a beautiful scene that somehow calmed my nerves. The stage already had some chairs and a microphone stand set up, and in the far corner was the DJ booth. I stood still, thinking about what was about to unfold here and whether I was ready to take this step. I mean, it was one thing to contemplate performing in front of a crowd, but to actually go through with it was something else entirely.

'Hello beautiful!' A voice sounded behind me that was warm and welcoming. I turned and saw a witch, dressed in black and wearing a pointed hat. Her skin was painted green and her eyes were a beautifully haunting vision of black and silver. I instantly knew who she was.

'Hey Misty!'

'How are you, lovely?'

'I'm good, thanks! A bit nervous.'

'Oh, don't worry. You're going to be fantastic,' she reassured.

'I hope so! Is there somewhere I can—'

'Oh yeah. Of course. You can get ready back there behind the curtain. It's pretty cramped but just get in there and take some space.'

'Thanks.'

I pushed my way through the curtain and saw a closed bar. In front were the drag artists, all getting ready for the show. I only recognised one of them, who turned around to greet me.

'Y'alright, Yvy love?' Glitter King said as they turned from applying their own brand of glitters to finish off their drag look for the show.

'Hiya!'

'Find yourself a spot, love, just squeeze in, you'll be fine.'

I moved through the artists who were all getting ready and chatting about people I didn't know. I wasn't too sure how to inject myself into the conversation, or if I even should do. I smiled as I stepped around bags and coats and finally propped myself by the corner of the bar near the window. Placing my bag on the table, I unzipped it and took out my outfit that I was going to wear for my performance. *My performance.*

I pulled out a cerise-coloured lehenga with matching cape that went all the way around my bust. Although I did my make-up at home, I didn't want to wear my outfit on the tram. Instead, I decided to wear a t-shirt and my black, cotton leggings as I knew I could easily get changed at the venue. My dress lay on the table and it suddenly dawned on me that I left my sandals in my bedroom. *Fuck!* I had no shoes to wear and there was nowhere near enough time to go back home and get them. I looked around and saw Misty applying more green paint to her arms as she chatted with the other artists who all seemed to be spilling tea.

I would have loved to participate in the conversation if I wasn't too busy panicking about my shoes, or actually knew any of the people they were discussing. All I had with me were the shoes I wore to get here, which were my chunky, 90s' style black shoes that didn't remotely go with the outfit. *What the hell am I going to do?* I didn't want to do the performance barefoot, so the only other choice I had was to just do it in my black shoes. *Great start, Yvy.*

***

Ellis was listening intently as I poured my heart out to him, explaining what had just transpired at Tribeca. I was too angry to cry or let my voice break. All I wanted to do was talk to the one person that fully understood the level of anger I was feeling.

'That sounds so awful,' Ellis said. 'Are you sure you're okay, Yvy?'

'Yeah, I'll be alright. Thanks dude, I really needed to get that off my chest.'

'Dude, always. You know I'm always here for you.'

I knew that was true. In that moment, I missed being with him. It's funny, Ellis and I had such a closeness for almost as long as I had known him. Most people thought that we had a thing going, given how close we were, but that wasn't the case. Our closeness came from a bond that we both understood completely, even before we knew it was there. When I was around Ellis, I was around family. It was as if we grew up together and became so tight that we could almost finish each other's sentences. After seeing him in Brighton, it was so enlightening to see how we had both somehow stayed connected, despite being so far away from one another. Our spiritual journey was so harmoniously in sync that it made being around him even sweeter.

After we finished talking, I ended the video call and watched his face disappear. The bedroom was silent and I could hear Jack in the living room watching television. He was concerned about me, but he knew I needed a bit of time to myself and respected my wishes. My head was spinning. I felt my thoughts spiralling, playing out every different scenario I could think of that resulted in me fucking up all of those racist cunts. Everything I wished I said and done. *Don't do this to yourself, Yvy, just go to bed.*

The next morning, I felt better, but still a little bruised from what happened. I hated that feeling when you wish you'd done more in a situation, but now you can't do fuck all about it except play it over and over again in your head. What was it about my skin colour that made people think it was okay to treat me in such a demeaning way? Are we that determined to hold onto a racist ideology that has plagued our society for literally hundreds of years? Is it easier to be racist than not to be? Why is society so fucked up that it refuses to evolve past the hurt it has inflicted on us?

I started to spin again, but this time it wasn't about what happened, but about my own perception when it came to my skin colour. I knew that I was Indian, but I seldom celebrated it, and yet time and time again I have been targeted and brought down because of it. *No more.* I was tired of feeling the knife that was twisted into me too many times. I wanted it out. I didn't know where to start though. I wanted to do something to celebrate who I was as a queer, Indian woman, but I couldn't find anywhere to channel that energy.

I had already spent time with other people of colour, hoping to find a place for myself where I felt comfortable enough to express the things that longed to come out and play, but nothing seemed to fit right. I wound up in the same place again, alone. Jack saw what this was doing to me for months and knew he couldn't do anything to help, as it was difficult for him to fully understand what I was looking for. A connection to a part of me that lay dormant for so long. Being in Blackburn, I was surrounded by people of my own ethnicity. However, being a queer person automatically bought me an express ticket to eternal damnation with no chance of anything that resembled being authentically me.

No wonder I had such a fucking disconnect from being Indian, I barely had the opportunity to connect with it in the first place. I felt so lost.

I looked down and saw my phone light up from an Instagram notification. As I opened up the message, it was from one of the artists I saw at Tribeca.

> **Hey Beautiful. I'm sorry
> and sickened to hear what
> happened last night after the
> show. Absolutely disgusting.
> I hope it doesn't put you off
> coming out and being yourself
> and supporting local artists.
> I saw on your insta you class
> yourself as a queer witch! If
> you like things on the spooky
> side I'd love to guest list you to
> my next show on October 1st
> if you can make it!**

It was from Glitter King. I was touched by their willingness to actually reach out to see if I was okay and even invite me to one of their shows. I didn't want what happened at Tribeca to discourage me from going to see other shows, and the thought of a spooky drag night sounded like a lot of fun. Since coming back from Brighton, I spent so much of my time searching for something that I couldn't put my finger on, and I was exhausted. I was tired of feeling so shit and made the decision to go to the show.

It was the first time I had been to Lock 91, and to *Glitterfye*. It was named that after the creators of the show, Glitter King and Misty Fye. I hadn't ever heard of either of them before, nor did I know that there were drag shows outside of the Village. I saw plenty of drag around the Village on my many nights out with Ellis, but they usually consisted of old school performances or contemporary pop numbers that were entertaining but a bit overdone by this point.

I hadn't experienced a drag show like this before, so I knew it was going to be an interesting evening. Although I was a 90s R&B kid growing up, I definitely saw myself as more eclectic now. From my early teens, I grew to love music from artists like *Evanescence, Björk* and *Rob Zombie*. Something about their unconventional sound and powerful lyrics resonated with me. Don't get me wrong, I always had time for *All Saints* and *Billie Piper* growing up too (still do, by the way), but a side of me felt compelled to explore a darker genre of music and discovered such beauty in it.

I didn't know many people who would enjoy a show like this, and although Jack would've said yes if I asked him to come because he's that fucking wonderful, I didn't want to bring my husband as I knew it wasn't his scene. If I was planning a night out that consisted of sitting in The Salisbury Pub for hours drinking beer and listening to *Motörhead* on full blast, he'd have been more than happy to join me. There was only one person that I knew would love to come with me. *Chelsie.*

I knew Chelsie from work and we instantly bonded. Chelsie was one of the funniest and most charming people I had ever met, and being that she was a witch too, I saw a lot of myself in her. It didn't take long to establish a friendship with her that went beyond the standard workplace acquaintance and developed quickly into a close bond that consisted of talking about spells and sharing our mutual love for *Rock of Love with Brett Michaels* and other trashy reality shows from the early 2000s.

Already there were people taking their seats, waiting for the show to start. I arrived before Chelsie and made my way to the front and found us some seats in the second row. I expected it to be a standing show, sort of like a club setting, but this was different and I loved it. As more people started to arrive, I waited for Chelsie to show and saw Glitter near the back, talking to some of the other performers. I was too nervous to go over and introduce myself.

They all looked so amazing and I hadn't actually met Glitter before, so I wasn't sure how to approach a bunch of drag artists without coming across like I was fangirling. *Just stay put, Yvy. You'll get a chance to say hi later.* The show was a few minutes away from starting when Chelsie arrived and saw me signalling her to come and join me.

'Sorry, I'm late. Bloody bus was taking ages.'

'No worries! How are you?'

'I'm alright, bit excited to see how tonight goes!'

'I know!'

I got into position with my phone, making sure to get some good footage of all the performances. As the show started, Chelsie and I watched as Glitter King performed a spellbinding number while handing out wisdom cards to the audience. The coloured lights beamed onto their face, lighting them up in deep shades of green, pink and blue. Draped over their shoulders was a mesh cape, covered in delicate stars.

As the music played, Glitter moved through the audience and back on to the stage. Their lip-sync to *Olivia Newton John* was so on point, pulling us all into a glittery nightmare. Misty, dressed as a gothic marionette, commanded the stage in a black and white ensemble and marionette strings hanging from her hair. The music started to play that sounded like a children's music box, the audience completely silent against its eerie sweetness.

Misty approached the stage, one heavy foot at a time, until she reached the centre, her limbs stiff as if she was made of porcelain. As she turned, so did the music and *Dead Inside* by *Muse* began to play. My heart skipped as she moved around the stage with sharp precision, taking us all on her intended journey of macabre beauty. I couldn't believe what I was watching. The level of uniqueness and artistry was something I had never seen. As more artists took the stage, Chelsie and I watched as Eva Serration, dressed as the Grim Reaper, performed a haunting rendition of *Zombie* by *The Cranberries*.

Another ripped the audience in half the moment they stepped onto the stage and raged into a powerful *Rammstein* number that attacked my senses with full force. By the time Chelsie and I had to leave to get the last bus and tram home, something started to awaken inside me. For so long I wanted to perform, act, sing, something that I could put out into the world as art. I never acted on it because I had too much to focus on when I was younger, and by the time I reached my thirties, I didn't see much point of entertaining the notion of becoming a performer. But as I stared out of the tram window, my thoughts wandered back to an idea that made me so excited.

***

I stood by the doorway of the bar where all the acts were getting ready for their second numbers. I was all dressed for my performance, wearing a pair of long, black PVC gloves with elongated fingers for added creepiness. The show was going well, as all the main acts had done their first performances and we were at intermission before the Creature Features opened up the second half. The Glitterfye Creature Feature was open to anyone who wanted to perform who were new to drag or just wanted an opportunity to perform somewhere. After watching a drag king perform during October's show, I felt like this could be an amazing opportunity to take a chance. Glitter was more than happy to take a chance on me.

GK: Aww I'm so glad! If you do happen to put those drag skills to use you could do our creature feature slot sometime! In November we've got Vanta doing it who was at the Pride show. I'm really proud to have this queer space out of the gay village. People come and be who they want. Last night we had gender bending artists just living their art!

Y:That would be amazing! I'd love to do a Bollywood Death Witch performance!

GK: Yessssss! That's what we want! Versatility! We just love the diversity of people's art! We would loveeee to see a Bollywood dance! I think our December show is currently vacant for the creature feature.

Y: I'll do it! x

Intermission was almost over, and I waited nervously at the back for Glitter to announce me. I draped myself in an Indian scarf to cover my dress, sort of acting as a low budget reveal for my performance. Holding onto it with my gloves was proving difficult, as the material of the scarf kept slipping through the smooth PVC. My nerves were building to an uncontrollable level.
Just calm down, Yvy!

What if I go on that stage and they fucking hate it?

They won't. They're going to love it.

They won't get it. Ugh, this was a mistake.
You're going to blow them away with this. They've never experienced something like this before and you're going to be amazing at it. Just have fun and do what you know you can do. You're so amazing!

Usually, the thoughts in my head were my own, but this time they weren't. All I could hear was my wonderful Jack, speaking to me as if he was right next me with his arms wrapped around my waist. I heard his words. Words he said to me when I was plagued with the very same doubts the moment I agreed to be

December's Creature Feature. His calming voice soothed my nerves, just as it always did when I found myself spinning. I closed my eyes slowly and in one slow blink, I pictured my husband's smile.

One thing about Jack that I adored was that he never tried to hide his feelings when it came to his love for me. Whenever he saw me falling, he never hesitated to remind me of how strong and capable I was. He never took anything from me. That was one of the many reasons why I loved who he was as a person. Suddenly, I felt so much better and was ready for the stage.

'Okay, Yvy, darlin',' Glitter said as they emerged in their second look of the evening from behind the bar curtain. 'I'm about to introduce you!'

At the very last second, I decided to ditch the fucking gloves. They were just getting in the way and the last thing I wanted was to look clumsy. I pulled off the gloves and tucked them away against the back table. *That's better!* Glitter took to the stage, holding the microphone in one hand and an energy drink in the other, dressed as Dorothy from *The Wizard of Oz*.

'Hello everyone! We've got a right special treat for you for our first Creature Feature! So, this artist is called Yvy. She's all the way from…Salford.'

The crowd gave out a cheer that made me laugh as I stood at the back, waiting to take the stage.

'She did take the tram to get here you know, no expense spared! She's just like you, she'll be on the tram home. But I think I'll let her speak for herself with this next beautiful performance. Please give it up for Yvy!'

The crowd cheered once more and the music began to play. *This is it!* The gentle chiming of Indian jewellery played through the speakers as I walked down the aisle, past the seated crowd. I knew that Chelsie and her roommate Bethan had come to see me perform, catching a quick glimpse of them recording me from the corner of my eye. Soon, the intro ended and the song began to play.

By the intro, I had made it to the front of the stage, wrapped in my scarf and giving the audience a little shoulder shimmy. I knew the music to *Maar Dala* was about to kick in, so I turned slowly until I was facing the crowd, my head to the floor. The music kicked in and I flung my scarf open, revealing my cerise lehenga. The crowd cheered as I hoped they would. The nerves melted away and I became the character. I became Chandramukhi, the character from the movie, *Devdas*. Chandramukhi was a courtesan who was devoted to Devdas, a man who visited her in a brothel after he was rejected by the woman he had been in love with since he was young. This was one of my all-time favourite Bollywood movies. It was beautiful, yet heart-breaking.

I imagined what it would've been like to be Chandramukhi, who was played in the 2002 movie by Madhuri Dixit. I imagined her pain and longing for a man who she wanted to love and be loved by, yet never truly could. I imagined her pain, her undying devotion, her sincerity. In this song, she performed for Devdas as he sat back, a drink in hand, and watched her dance. My energy shifted and I could feel something flow through me like a powerful force. My body woke up and I let the music enter me. The melody continued, and I moved to every wave of sound that flowed through me. I was more than Yvy in that moment. I let something out that took over the stage. The crowd screamed and cheered as I continued my performance.

As the song grew to a close, I knew what was about to happen. I felt it in my veins. Towards the end of the song, Chandramukhi bursts into a frenzied dance to please her beloved, unbeknownst to her that Devdas was spiralling out of control the more he drank. He begins to panic as his emotions take over, when the loss of the woman he loves becomes too intense. As he continues to drink, Chandramukhi continues her dance.

That part of the song was fast approaching. I walked slowly to centre stage, basking in the beaming spotlight above me. As the music quietened for a second, I stood still. Suddenly the booming rhythm of the tablas blasted through every cell of my being. My body began to writhe uncontrollably, as if I had no will of my own. My back arched deeply and my arms flailed in the air.

The crowd screamed in excitement as they watched me go from performing an elegant dance to being a woman screaming to escape her inner demons. The last few seconds of the song played and I span as hard as I could, dropped to the floor and leant back so that my head touched the wood. All I could hear was the people in their seats going crazy, completely mesmerised by what they just witnessed. I picked myself up off the ground and turned to the audience, every single one was cheering for me.

'Oh, my goodness me! Give it up for Yvy!' Misty said as she approached the stage. The crowd went wild once more. 'Thank you so much for bringing your art to our stage, that was absolutely incredible.'

Once the show came to a close, I found myself dancing to Christmas music with performers that most people would class as weirdos and misfits. Yet here I was, feeling more at home than I had ever felt in a long while. *You did it, Yvy.* I knew I found something special. A truly horrific experience led me to this place with these wonderful artists, something that may never have happened if the incident at Tribeca never transpired.

I looked at myself in the mirror as I danced around, realising that I unleashed something that I always knew was there, but never expressed. I wanted so badly to embrace my Indian culture, and being a witch gave me the balance I needed in a life that felt anything but balanced. I combined those two things that gave me so much happiness, and expressed it on a fucking stage. That December night, in a room full of queer monsters, The BollyWitch was born.

Chapter Nineteen

The air was thick as the sun beamed down, warming the sand beneath my feet. I had no idea where I was or how I got here, yet everything felt strangely familiar. I guess that was always the case when one was dreaming. I knew this wasn't real, but it felt real to me. The sky was beginning to change as the sun made its inevitable descent, causing streaks of pink and orange to bleed like water colours on a blank canvas. I looked out over the rocky stones and saw open land, stretching beyond my eye's reach. The ground was golden with grains of sand and delicate flowers that pushed their way through the dry cracks of the earth. The quiet was like music, easing my mind and ridding me of any thoughts that once plagued me.

As the breeze ran over my body, I felt a comforting feeling rise inside, something I hadn't felt in this twelve-year-old body for a long time. In this place, I didn't feel like Saleem. I felt the person that I was inside, whoever that may be. *I can't wait to meet you.*

I stood at the top of a sloping path, shielding my eyes to see where it led. My eyes struggled to focus as the sky shimmered brightly, the way a film of black oil reflects a rainbow on the ground. I saw something in the distance, but couldn't quite make out what it was. The rustling of wildflowers that ran all the way down the rocky path echoed in the wind, releasing a sweet scent that was soft yet distinctive. The smell of incense. I took a step forward, then another, and then another.

Carefully positioning my feet on the hot ground, I walked down the open path towards the unknown image before me. With each step, it became more in focus. It was tall and dark, almost intimidating. I wasn't scared though, almost as though something told me not to be. My heart was surprisingly calm, not racing. My approach quickened as the blurry vision began to take form. I grew nearer and saw a building made of old stone.

The door stood before me, tall and made of some sort of dark wood. It was beautifully carved and etched with patterns that looked as though they were moving. I studied the carvings for a moment, noticing how the people depicted all resembled someone I felt that I knew, but couldn't quite put my finger on who they were. Embedded in the carvings were shimmering flecks of gold that came to life with the sun's rays. The cast iron door knob was within reach and I took hold to push as hard as I could. The door resisted against the sand, making it difficult to swing open.

A gust of cool air hit my face as I managed to open it enough to enter the stone house. The echo of the hinges rattled through my bones and into the room I was about to enter. I took one last look behind me, at the vast desert, covered in colourful wildflowers. I saw myself, stood in the very spot I was once standing in at the top of the long path, looking back at me and smiling. I turned and entered the house.

Walking with calm caution, the room was dark and spacious. It felt old and full of memory. The dust that sat gently on the floor was undisturbed, nobody had entered this room in a long while. I looked up and saw a dome that had almost fallen to pieces, exposing the orange sky that since deepened so much it was as if the sun had burnt the clouds. In the middle of the circular floor stood a pillar, dusty and worn. The walls were made of the same stone as I saw outside, the mortar looking as though it would crumble at the lightest touch. It was hard to see much else, other than the lights that flickered in the distance.

In this room, nothing felt in place. Although it was empty, I felt uneasy being here. A moment of uncertainty washed over me as I looked at the ground. The cracks along the stone flickered as though something lay beneath, something that was about to burst through and fill the room. I walked gently to the other side of the room, past the pillar and noticed that it was covered in words that were etched into the stone. Unlike those on the door, these etchings were rough and fierce. They must've been done with a blunt tool, as the words appeared to have been carved angrily into the old stone. The words themselves were angry too. I brushed some of the dust off and saw that the words were telling a familiar story, one I knew intimately.

Today I saw a boy at school. I don't know why but I can't stop thinking about him. When I go to bed, all I can think about is getting to know him. But I can't. Not the way I want to. I'm not supposed to feel this way. That's what everybody tells me. I'm sick of being so alone. I hate being in a room full of people and never being noticed, except for when they want to laugh at me. Am I that big a joke? There's no escaping this. I wish I wasn't here.

My hand reached out and I saw that every word was one I had written elsewhere, in diaries that I kept. I saw my whole life, written on the cold, hard, solitary column that had no choice but to stand in the middle of this dark room, alone. I walked around the thick pillar, reading the words out loud.

I couldn't do it. I couldn't bring myself to go into the changing room. I was with the rest of the class and as soon as he said we were playing football for the lesson, I wanted to cry. I can't do this anymore. I already know that I'm a failure at being a boy, I don't need humiliation to remind me of that. It was terrible. I tried to hurt myself on the pitch to get out of playing. I wanted so badly so twist my ankle or even break my own arm, but I couldn't do it. I wasn't strong enough.

The words bounced off the walls, but the voice wasn't my own. I heard a woman's voice speaking the very words I said out loud. I looked down and saw more etchings around the pillar.

I ran away today. I can't stay at home anymore. Nobody understands what this feels like. How can I be so lost inside? Is this body even mine? It doesn't feel like it is, but I can't be anywhere else. Fareed and I aren't getting along. It's too hard to be his brother. I don't know how to be a brother. I'm better off on my own.

A tear ran down my face, reading all the truths engraved onto the pillar. This was my tomb. Here lay everything about me that I wanted to forget. I wanted all of this to die. How is it that I've only just started high school, yet I have already gone through so much? Isn't youth supposed to be enjoyed? Or is turmoil simply something every youth has to suffer through? I didn't know, I couldn't know. There was no way for me to understand any of this when I couldn't even find a place in the world that felt like mine. This tomb was mine, but I didn't want it.

I looked down and saw my tears falling on the rubble collected on the stone floor. The rocks were thick and sharp, some painted on one side with beautiful colours that had long since faded. I looked up and saw the hole in the dome and knew that these had fallen from there, causing the beautiful mural of what looked like an ethereal goddess to look incomplete. The sun had almost gone down and the sky was a deep purple.

I noticed the large rock amongst the rubble had a face painted on, the part of the mural now missing from the dome. I wiped the dust away and saw a face looking back at me. Her eyes were warm, her lips pursed gently and smiling. Her features were soft, yet striking. I knew her face, but couldn't place her. She looked like a distant relative, maybe a cousin. She seemed so familiar, yet it was as if I was seeing her for the first time.

Laughter could be heard in the distance and I saw a glowing light coming from the narrow hallway across the room. The tomb was getting colder as the sun sank into slumber. The moonlight was taking over the sky as it became an ink stain of darkest blue. I willed myself off the floor and looked at her face one last time before turning to the hallway. My hand brushed against the pillar as I walked by, feeling the hard ridges so much it almost felt like it broke the skin.

My eyes twinkled at the amber lights before me, walking through the narrow corridor that was lit by rows and rows of soft candles. The warm flames flickered as the wicks crackled gently. The floor was warm, unlike in the tomb. As I walked into the next room, my heart filled with wonder. I stood inside another round room, only this one felt nothing like a tomb. The walls were made of the same dark cherry wood as the door, but were smooth and polished. They were beautifully carved with what looked like a story.

I stepped closer and examined the carvings. Etched flawlessly into the wood were faces, children and animals, stories of magical lands and adventures that looked like a paradise. Something I wish I could experience. Throughout the walls were small ledges that housed candles and trinkets, I wanted to badly to look in each and every one to see what they all were. One had a small incense burner, made of Indian gold, letting out a gentle smoke that smelt like sweet jasmine. One had a glass jar, filled with fireflies. Another had glowing crystals, releasing gentle vapours.

I couldn't help but wonder what they all meant, looking at the hundreds of ledges that ran all the way up to the top of the walls. I looked up and noticed that there was no roof, just the open air and the stars shining down.

This place felt so familiar, like somewhere I visited before but couldn't recall. I noticed a carousel in the middle of the room. It was dark and motionless, barely registering to the naked eye. Little glimmers of its vintage frame came into view as the light from the candles in the walls flickered gently. I stepped towards the giant carousel, compelled by its beauty. A pale horse was in my sight, motionless with its legs frozen in position as though it had been running for an eternity. I reached out my hand to see if it was real.

'Hello.'

I turned suddenly, completely caught off guard and I thrust my hands behind my back as quickly as I could. I saw a girl standing before me. She was my age, dressed in a green sari, decorated with elegant gold jewellery.

'Hello,' I said.

'What are you doing here?'

'I don't know. I-I don't-don't know how I got here.'

'You don't remember being here?'

'No, I've never been here before.'

She smiled and started walking towards me. She stopped in front of me and flashed a smile as she manoeuvred her head around my shoulders, as if to be looking for something.

'What have you got there?' She asked.

'What?'

'Behind your back. You look like you're hiding something.'

'No, I'm, I'm just—'

'I'm just teasing!' She said with laughter.

I smiled bashfully, feeling a little embarrassed by the way I reacted when she saw me. I felt like I was caught stealing and was trying my best to conceal what I took.

'I don't know why I'm here.'

'Does it matter? If you feel at home then that's all that matters.'

'I guess I do. It all seems so familiar. That other room, the cold one, I just came from there.'

'What other room?' She asked.

'The one down that corridor.' I turned and saw that it had disappeared. I was confused. 'It was there, I swear!'

'I believe you,' the girl said, 'but it's not there now.'

'How? Why?'

'Why keep it if it's not needed anymore?'

I didn't understand, but I was somewhat comforted by what she was saying. This place felt like a sanctuary, even the parts I found difficult, because regardless of whether it was good or bad, it all felt like it belonged to me.

'It does,' the girl said, answering a question I had left unspoken.

***

The summer of '96 was a sweltering one. I managed to get through primary school and I had six weeks of freedom to spend however I wanted. After finishing school, I thought I would've felt a sense of accomplishment for doing so, but instead it felt like I survived primary school, not completed it. Nothing about the experience was particularly joyous, even the moments that I did enjoy, because the negative parts constantly overshadowed it.

I sat on my bunk bed, staring down at my diary that I kept for the last couple of years. I flipped through the pages, reading snippets from entries and feeling how unhappy every word was. The words of the girl I saw in the sanctuary were ringing in my head. *Why keep it if it's not needed anymore?* I grasped the diary in my hand and made a decision there and then. *Throw it away, Sal.*

'You ready to go?' Feroza said as she entered my room.

'Yes!'

Going to town with Feroza was one of my favourite things to do. She and I always spent time together, which I cherished more than anything. I loved the fact that I could be silly around my big sister and she never judged me. One thing about Feroza was that I always felt safe around her. Even though I couldn't talk to her or anyone else about how I was feeling inside, being with her made all those things fall away. I could be safe and loved and not have any worries. I loved that the most about my sister.

We walked down Shear Bank and into town. The sun was beating down on us, so we kept to the shade under the many trees down Shear Bank before we got to Preston New Road. Feroza wanted to go to Zodiac to buy a new ring for her eyebrow piercing, which was fine with me as it gave me the opportunity to go to my favourite shop in Blackburn. When we arrived, Feroza pushed the door open and I was instantly hit with the smell of candles and incense.

As we entered. I was greeted with an array of crystals, new age ornaments and dreamcatchers hanging from the ceiling. Feroza made her way to the back of the shop where they sold piercings and had a small tattoo studio. They also had a selection of beautiful gothic dresses that I wanted so badly to try on. *Maybe they'll let you if you just ask.* No way, I wasn't brave enough to ask. I didn't want them to laugh at me. I walked around to the other side of the shop as Feroza looked at the piercings showcased inside the glass display boxes.

I walked slowly past the shelves, taking in all the trinkets on display. Wooden trays held a range of crystals and stones, all glistening with mystical beauty. I picked up an amethyst stone and stared at it intently. It was light and smooth, with a purple hue that caught the light when I moved it around in my palm. Placing the stone back in the wooden holder, I saw that there were a few books in the back corner near to where Feroza was. Books on candle magick, tarot card readings and Wicca were displayed, filling me with such intrigue and excitement.

As I sifted through each book, I came across one that I knew I had to buy. The purple cover had a witch with flowing hair flying through the air on a broomstick. It was called *To Ride a Silver Broomstick* by Silver RavenWolf. I had never heard of this person before, but flipping through the book I saw so much information that I really wanted to sink my teeth into. I had no real knowledge of Witchcraft, other than watching *The Craft*, and although I was completely obsessed with that movie, I was very much aware that I wasn't going to be walking across water or receiving a dead shark as a gift from Manon any time soon.

I bought the book and some candles and we went to El Greco's which wasn't far from Zodiac. Going for lunch at El Greco's was a ritual for me and Feroza whenever we came into town. We walked in and made our way downstairs, grabbing a tray before heading to the food area. The restaurant was very much set up like it was a school canteen; you grabbed a tray and went along the line, picking whatever it is you wanted and paid when you got to the end. Feroza got her usual, a buttered scone and a cup of tea, followed by a cigarette.

I went for my favourite dish at El Greco's, spicy curry and chips with a can of Coke. One thing I loved about this place was that it wasn't pretentious at all. You can always tell when you're in a down to earth, meat and potato pie eating, plastic seat nailed to the floor seating, chain smoking near the toilets type of restaurant. El Greco's was exactly that. I loved it.

Feroza and I got our food and made our way to our seats near the back. Once we finished eating, Feroza lit up a cigarette and took another sip of her tea. I knew we were almost done with our trip to town, and all I wanted to do was go home and read my new book.

I sat on the carpet by the heater in the front room as soon as we got home. I placed the long candles to one side and opened my book, reading what it said about being a witch. I read about the special days of celebration, deities, altars, sacred spaces, and candle magick. I was stunned at what went into being a witch, but it was all so comforting. My mind was filled with perfect clarity. I knew this was the direction I wanted to go down.

Mum did so well to teach me the ways of Islam, and I never faulted her for doing so. It was such a huge part of my heritage, however she never pressured me to follow religion and I was so tired of my own community condemning me. All I seemed to get was Asian classmates talking shit and relatives ridiculing me. Suddenly, the memory of what happened to me in the playground at school filled my head. I recalled standing at the top of the concrete steps that led to the bottom playground where all the boys played football on the gravel. My arms were tucked into my coat and I didn't see the boy behind me getting ready to push me down the stairs.

I was too late to get both of my arms through my coat sleeves when the sheer force of his push hurled me down the stairs and I crashed into each step until my head smashed against the gravel, the rest of the boys all laughing. My mind skipped to another memory, of being in Sheffield visiting my older cousin whom I adored. She was older than I was, but we got on so well and I always enjoyed her company. When staying at my aunty's house on one occasion, they all went to a relative's home for dinner and since I was staying with them, I was invited too.

It was a traditional household, filled with religious plaques and a wall tapestry in the living room that depicted a scene from Mecca. We all gathered on the floor to eat, the food set out beautifully on a large, floral mat. As everyone started serving their food, I had my eye on the lamb biryani, which was my favourite dish. As I reached over to grab the spoon, one of the elderly women said something to me in Urdu. I was confused, as I wasn't fluent and felt as though what she said to me was important. She waited for a response, but I didn't know what to say.

The old woman looked straight at me, her eyes burning with disapproval. I felt my cheeks flush with embarrassment and I didn't know what to do. She said something again, only this time she was much more forceful and gesturing in my direction. Everyone looked at me, waiting for a response. I didn't know what else to do, other than sit back and stare at my empty plate.

'She asked if you speak Urdu and if you understand her,' my cousin said.

'Why do you have to explain it to him?' One of the men asked. 'Doesn't he understand?'

I felt invisible. I was in a room filled with my uncle's family so I didn't know any of them. I felt so vulnerable, surrounded by people whose attention was currently fixated on me.

'You a Muslim, Son, and you can't speak Urdu?' The man said before chuckling.

I sat quietly as my cousin served me my food. She knew I was beyond embarrassed. I hated being judged on the basis of a religion I didn't even want to follow. I had nothing against the ways of Islam, except for how certain people used it to judge me. From speaking Urdu, to being feminine, every fibre of my being could be summed up in one gut wrenching question that plagued me. *Are you Muslim?* No, I'm not.

Being Muslim is fine, but it shouldn't wholly define a person. I learnt all about different religions, yet I felt no connection to the idea of religious faith. The reason I struggled with the concept of faith was because that was never taught to me. As loving as she was, Mum taught me the ways of Islam through text books and exercises to read Arabic, but I never actually learnt anything about faith. It wasn't until much later that I educated myself on faith, but by then I had already experienced so much negativity about how I wasn't acting like a proper Muslim, that I lost all interest in living a life of religion.

I sat in front of the fire, thinking about what it was that drew me to Witchcraft. I was a spiritual person, and I always felt an energy that I believed could be channelled into anything I set my mind to. I was comforted with the idea of everything being connected somehow, not by a religion or an all-encompassing being, but by an endless wave of energy that makes all things operate.

I liked the thought of being a witch as I felt as though I could tap into that energy to create positivity and healing, something I knew would be a huge help right now. I flipped through the pages of the book and came to a clear realisation that this was what I wanted to do. I had no idea if this was real or if being a witch was a complete waste of time, but all I could think was that I had nothing to lose from going down this path. What made the decision even clearer was that I was making this decision, it wasn't made for me. I wanted to open myself up to something new and I already felt so much more positive. I had no real concept of what being a witch really meant, but I was excited to find out.

Chapter Twenty
Manchester, 2020

Almost four months into lockdown and I was beginning to lose my mind. I was no stranger to being forced to stay at home, especially after spending many months with a nephrostomy tube coming out of me when I almost went into renal failure, but this was very different. It wasn't too long ago that I performed for the first time as *The BollyWitch*, which led to another opportunity to perform a month later.

Then everything changed. Not just for me, but for the whole world. A massive shift in how we functioned in life forced so many people to adapt to a difficult and different way of living. But a pandemic is nothing to be fucked with, so I was more than willing to stay home and be safe. I sat at my altar, ready to start my midsummer ritual to celebrate Litha.

This particular Sabbat was one of my favourites. Litha celebrates the Summer Solstice, or the longest day of the year. The sun is at its peak and from that point on, the days gradually shorten towards the end of the year. Litha also celebrates the abundance that comes from planting what you want to grow, and seeing it flourish. Like most crops, they are then harvested to provide a form of sustenance, but before that, the Summer Solstice provides a moment to celebrate what we have manifested earlier in the year.

Yes, I am aware that can sound like a lot of gibberish, which was exactly what I thought when I started learning about the Sabbats. But as I grew older, I came to appreciate what each Sabbat meant and how they all symbolise so many things that we can apply to our own lives. The Sabbats celebrate the constant cycle of energy that fuels our very existence, without any discrimination. All the natural beauty in the world can be seen through this cycle, from the moon all the way down to the smallest creature. Everything has its purpose and takes its energy from the constant cycle that is around us every day.

I liked the thought of everything in life having its purpose, it provides an equilibrium that I appreciated. Nothing about being a witch made me feel as though I was better or worse than anybody else, I was simply paying attention to the energy around me and channelling it in positive ways. My version of religion I guess, except that I wasn't subscribing myself to the writings of a singular book, but instead opening myself up to an acceptance that I was a spiritual being who was capable of seeing the world in a way that many choose not to. Being a witch and being queer flow together so beautifully.

For as long as I could remember, I saw the world differently from everyone else around me. Even as a child, I knew instinctively that my body, my thoughts, my everything was meant for more. The problem I struggled with as I grew older was the constant negativity from a society who attempted to stifle any attempt at flourishing. Religion played a big part in that, when I had to endure preachings from family relatives, neighbours and friends who saw my attempts to be myself and wanted to put a stop to it because their religion told them to.

Looking back, it pissed me off that I had to endure that, as I soon came to realise that it wasn't the religion, it was the people. I studied the history of Witchcraft and was disgusted that the blood of witches was spilled in order for modern Christianity to dominate and erase them, turning witches into blasphemous beings that deserved to be tortured and killed. The more I read about it, the more I understood why witches were persecuted, and it made my blood boil. Witches were a threat to a religion that wanted more than anything to be the only faith, and they couldn't have a faith that was already in existence threaten that. It was easier to just wipe them out.

Being trans felt very much the same. We too are persecuted by those who want to be the only ones, the standalone, the cookie-cut perfect stereotype of what a human being should be. A witch can see how the world is more than what society is fed to believe, and trans people are exactly the same. We see how the gender galaxy spans vastly and isn't restricted to a binary that has been force-fed to us all since birth.

I mean, did anybody else think it was weird when you were little that there was always that one creepy relative that asked you if you had a girlfriend, despite the fact that you were a fucking five-year-old? Well, I did! It's crazy that even at such a young age, I was made to believe that I had to have a girlfriend because that's what boys do. *Fuck off!* I was sick of playing by rules to a game I didn't even want to play. When it comes to being a witch, my beliefs are exactly that, mine. If I believe in it, that's all that matters.

I don't expect others to follow me or think that I am judging them because they don't live life in the same way I do. People that use religion to preach their beliefs are forgetting that a religion is what you subscribe your life to, therefore you choose to believe whatever you want, because it's your religion. I am a witch, but I'm not going to start knocking on people's doors trying to convert them. I am trans, but I'm not going to stand outside TK Maxx with a microphone and shout at people for not being trans. I was through with people trying to control me. I wanted to strip that all away and listen to the energies around me. I wanted to be able to focus on my own abilities and the power of magick when you tap into what the world is made of and take what you need, then giving something back.

Witchcraft and Wicca are two different things. Although Witchcraft does embody a lot of the same things, Wicca is a nature-based religion. For so long, I have had a predisposed view when it came to religion, which I most definitely blame on my experiences growing up. Through the years, I saw how being a Muslim can be such a wonderful thing, but by that point I had become so alienated from anything that resembled my culture that I had no interest in religion. One thing that always stayed with me since I was a child was being a witch. I always felt connected to something that felt so much bigger, yet never intimidating. An energy that told me that my place in this world was needed and that I would somehow find my way through all the turmoil I was experiencing.

Being a practicing witch can be clumsy and uncomfortable when you start out. Although, watching every episode of *Charmed* in the 90s made rhyming couplets so much cooler when I sat at my makeshift altar in the front room. When I began my transition, being a practicing witch took a back seat and I focused all my energy elsewhere. As a result, I lost touch with my spiritual side and spent all my time facing the reality of being trans and having to cope with all the obstacles life threw at me.

With that said, I never let go of my belief that I was meant for greater things and that I was capable of so much. My energy, my vibration, could make real change. In some ways, I traded in my altar and instead used my transition as a way of focusing my energy on a singular goal. I never realised it at the time, but that was in itself magick. It was my magick to manifest and to allow it to grow into something I could then take forward. Such a process takes time and does not come easily, and like anything you plant, you don't know exactly how and when it will grow. All you can do is give it the necessary attention and energy, then watch what happens.

My transition was a magickal experience for me, as I manifested my intentions and gave myself time to grow into the person that I knew I was. Litha very much encapsulates the essence of my transition, which is why it's one of my favourite Sabbats.

The incense was flowing delicately through the air and I gathered all the dried flowers I saved from the bouquet Jack bought me for our fifth-year wedding anniversary. A stunning range of pink roses, sea lavenders and Peruvian lilies. Placing them in the centre of my altar, I picked up the orange spell candle and lightly coated it in intention oil, then sprinkled my special midsummer herb blend so that it caught on and held in place by the oil.

My phone was to the right of me, playing my favourite playlist of Italian classical music. I adored Maria Callas, who was singing her wonderful rendition of *Ave Maria*. Listening to her voice took me to a completely different realm. I could only imagine what it must have been like to experience her exquisite voice in person. As her serenade filled my head, I lit the candle and prepared to cast my circle. Picking up my athame, I dipped the tip of the blade into the small bowl of salt, drawing a faint pentagram.

I consecrate this salt and ground it
for this magickal working.
So, mote it be.

Taking the athame and placing the blade in the goblet of fresh water, I closed my eyes and continued.

I bless this water for this magickal
working, expelling all negativity.
So, mote it be.

I added a pinch of salt to the water and sprinkled it around me until I made a full circle. Salt is often used to purify and cleanse, ridding negative energy and creating a boundary of protection. Water is a powerful conduit, so ensuring that no negative energy runs through it during a ritual is important. I looked ahead at the small, cast iron cauldron that sat on top of a wooden chest of drawers and pulled out one of my sage smudge sticks and a long black feather.

Lighting the smudge, I moved around the circle, using the feather to waft the smoke all around, cleansing the sacred space. I picked up my athame again and pointed it to the North. I stopped for a moment, giving myself a pause to feel the energy around me and channel it into the blade. I envisioned it to be a bright energy with flecks of purple, like an amethyst. I began to see the light so vividly, surrounding me until it found its way to the blade. Moving in a deosil motion, I cast the circle.

I call the North, the Spirit of Earth
I call the East, the Spirit of Air
I call the South, the Spirit of Fire
I call the West, the Spirit of Water
The Circle is cast.

I sat quietly, listening to Maria Callas sing *Casta Diva*, causing every nerve in my body to jump with excitement. Behind my eyelids, I saw myself sitting in the Teatro alla Scala. I sat in the centre of the floor seats, completely alone. On either side of me were rows and rows of vacant opera boxes. The decadence and history could be seen in every single detail of the room. The gas lamps warmed the walls with their soft glow, casting faint shadows against the red cushions. The gold balconies spanned the entire room.

I tilted my head up to the chandelier hanging from the ceiling. The stage was set beautifully and a woman stood before me, dressed in an elegant, boat-necked ivory dress. Her veil was pinned to the back of her hair that was pulled into a tight bun, decorated with delicate flowers. Her dress was synched at the waist, giving a dramatic flair as it reached the floor. She brought her arms to her chest, her eyes looking down as she waited for the music to play.

The orchestra began, and although I was alone in the room, I felt the presence of every person who had ever been in these seats, waiting with bated breath for this magnificent woman to cast her spell upon us with her enchanting soprano. She opened her mouth and a voice like no other filled the room.

Casta Diva
Casta Diva che inargenti

Queste sacre
Queste sacre, queste sacre antiche piante

I leant forward, unable to stay still in my seat. I couldn't believe that such a voice was coming out of her so effortlessly. She seemed so poised, beautifully regal and making only the slightest of gestures as she sang.

A noi volgi il bel sembiante
Senza nube e senza vel

As she reached the note that caused my heart to swell, I watched as her dress began to dye into a shade so dark it resembled the night sky. In that moment, pink rose petals began to fall, gently at first, then more started to float down.

Tempra, o Diva
Tempra tu de cori ardenti
Tempra ancora
Tempra ancora, tempra ancora lo zelo audace
Spargi in terra quella pace
Spargi in terra, Spargi in terra
Che regnar tu fai nel ciel

I looked up to see the chandelier suspended in the same place, yet the celling had completely disappeared. I gazed at the petals falling from a dark sky, filled with stars. I held out my hand, and as each petal fell into my palms, they dissolved in an instant.

MEEEOOOOOOWWW!

I opened my eyes at the strange note that I wasn't expecting to come next. I looked down at a black and white cat with a pair of glassy yellow eyes looking back at me, her wet nose wanting to boop with mine. *Nyssa, you little menace!*

***

When I first became interested in Witchcraft, it was around the same time that I frequently went to visit relatives who lived in Harrow whenever I could. I'd hop on the National Express and take the long five-hour journey to London Victoria and spend some time in Harrow with my younger cousin and my aunt. It was so freeing to go for a visit, as it was the furthest I had ever been from Blackburn, which felt like all the issues I was dealing with were completely gone.

My trips to Sheffield became less frequent, because as I grew older, the more I had to interact with people that I didn't like who kept on at me for not being the right type of Asian. I didn't get any of that in London. Close to where I was staying was an indoor market that I loved to visit. It wasn't big, it was one of those small local markets that only had a few little stores selling essentials at rock-bottom prices. Inside was a store that I came across by chance, *The Midnight Moon*.

I had no idea it was there at first, wandering around the market stalls looking for some cheap tea light candles to buy. I turned a corner and saw the sign for the shop, painted in black with a white moon and stars decorated around it. It didn't seem like a shop that sold proper witch supplies, more like one of those new age stalls that sold incense and an abundance of religious figurines, but as I got closer, I soon came to realise that it wasn't the case with this shop.

I approached and saw that it was only a tiny store, but housed so much. To the left of the entrance was a glass cabinet, containing athames, chalices, pendants and expensive tarot card decks. In front of me was a long desk, filled with crystals and books. To the right was another table that had obscure items that I didn't recognise, except for the small bottles that contained rose water and magickal oils.

'Hello, there!' A booming voice said from the right-hand corner.

'Hello,' I said, slightly thrown. I hadn't noticed the till area tucked away so neatly that it almost resembled a phone booth.

'Haven't seen you here before.'

'No, I don't live here. I'm from Blackburn.'

'Blackburn? Where's that, then?'

'Lancashire.'

'Ah, no wonder I never heard of it, I haven't been up there.'

'You're not missing much. This shop is amazing!'

'Thanks. It's a bit tough these days, not many people coming around here.'

'Have you been here long?' I asked.

'A few years. I also do Reiki for a lot of people too as my job.'

'What's Reiki?'

'It's an old form of energy healing.'

'Oh, wow, that's amazing. I've only just started getting into Witchcraft. I'm still learning.'

'You never stop learning. There's always something new to discover. That's the best part. So, what brought you to the craft?'

I wasn't sure how to answer, not because I didn't want to, but because I didn't know how to put it into words. I decided to give it a stab and see if it made any sense once I said it.

'Well, I was searching for something, you know, inside. I wanted to feel...connected.'

'That makes sense.'

'It does?'

'Of course. Many people find spirituality a great way of connecting with so many parts of themselves and the world beyond what we can see. Once you connect yourself to it, so much opens up to you.'

'Yeah, that's how I feel. I'm trying to understand it more. Bit difficult though for me, I only have one shop I can go to and it's really good, but nothing like this!'

'Well, I'm always here if you need any help.'

'Actually, I'd love some advice on any spell books you think are good.'

'Yeah definitely. What's your name, by the way?'

'Sal.'

'Nice to meet you. I'm Barry.'

I stood and spoke to Barry for the best part of an hour. He recommended a few books and I was on my way back to my cousin's house with a bag full of things to get me started.

The next time I went down to stay, I couldn't wait to go back to *The Midnight Moon*. It had been a few months since I visited my cousin, so I was a little worried as to whether the shop would still be there. Barry did say that he didn't get many customers. I went to the market and gladness filled me when I saw the sign still there and the door still open.

'Hiya there, Sal!'

'Hi! I thought you wouldn't remember me!' I said surprisingly.

'Of course. You here for a while?'

'Yeah, I'm staying for two weeks.'

'How are you getting on with your craft?'

'A bit better. I did my initiation, which went well. Felt a bit weird though. My altar is just a piece of wood made out of a desk my uncle built for my brother. I have to keep my altar a secret at home.'

'Plenty of people don't have the luxury to display their witch tools at home. You don't need a fancy altar anyway. Just make do with what you have. So have you done much spell work?'

'Only one so far. I did a protection spell. I'm having a hard time at the moment.'

'With what?'

I paused. Not knowing if I should actually tell Barry what was on my mind. Strangely, I felt at ease around him. He was one of the only people who actually asked how I was, and it helped that he wasn't a part of Blackburn in any way.

'I get picked on at school. I-I keep being called a girl. I thought things would be better once I started secondary school, but it's much worse. I did a protection spell because I don't want to get hurt.'

'Have you spoken to anyone back home about how you're feeling?'

'No, I can't. I-I don't want to.'

'Why not?'

'Because I don't know how I should feel inside. People call me names, but I don't know what anyone can do. I'd rather just be quiet.'

'Listen, you're just starting out in life. You've got plenty of time to figure things out, and kids at school who pick on you are just as confused about their own lives as you are about yours. You just don't have to let them into yours. Remember, how you feel inside, nobody can touch that.'

I looked at Barry, amazed at how he was able to get right to the core of how I was feeling within seconds. In that moment, he healed a little part of the hurt. It never crossed my mind that what Barry said was true. Nobody could take away how I felt inside. I didn't know when the time would come when I figured out how to be the person I felt that I was, but my journey to finding that out was all mine.

***

Nyssa jumped onto the futon beside me, curling up in a ball with her head still up to watch the candle light dance. I stroked her head, feeling her brush against my palm and purr. I turned to my altar and saw the orange Litha candle was burning, melting its way onto the dry petals and twigs surrounding it. I completed all of my Litha celebration spells and was almost done with my evening of magick. I sat quietly, listening to Becthoven's *Für Elise* play softly, the melodic sounds swirling around the room like sage smoke.

I closed my eyes once more, listening to the music and the crackling of the flame as the Litha candle was close to completing its expectancy and distinguishing. I saw myself back at *The Midnight Moon*. Barry was there, sitting by the till like he usually did. I smiled and watched as he extended me the same courtesy. I looked around the shop, which seemed bigger than I remembered, and saw something there that I had never seen before. A thick curtain of deepest red velvet hung from the ceiling all the way down to the floor. I felt a warm draft expel from the small slivers of space as the curtain moved ever so gently.

I walked towards the curtain, uncertain of whether I should proceed to end my curiosity. Before I knew it, my hands were on the gold tassels that were loosely tied. I turned to Barry, who didn't seem to be paying much attention to me, which made me feel slightly alone and scared. I decided to pull the knot free and enter. The moment the knot came undone, a bright light engulfed me, blinding me to a point where my eyes began to sting. Sitting at my altar, I felt my eyes burn behind my lids as a tear rolled down my cheek. I didn't want to stop meditating. I needed to know where I was being led. The light shone for what felt like an eternity. Suddenly, it faded and I slowly regained my focus. I stood at the top of a hill, the sand beneath my feet and the smell of wildflowers filling the air. *I know this place.*

Ahead was the same door I was all too familiar with. I pushed it open and saw that the tomb was no longer there. The pillar lay in ruins, broken and crumbled against the ground. The words that once were etched roughly into its stone had faded, leaving nothing left to read. The lights for the room ahead called to me. As I walked through the candlelit hallway, there stood the carousel in the middle of the room, only this time, she wasn't sleeping. The lights were beaming from the roof of the carousel, illuminating the horses that galloped in circles, their legs moving with speed. Music played softly from a music box on one of the small ledges in the wall that housed endless amounts of trinkets.

'Hello again.'

I turned quickly and saw a little girl. The same little girl I had seen here years before. She hadn't aged at all; she was still the same twelve-year-old girl. Only now, I knew exactly who she was.

'Hello Yvy,' I said.

'You came back. I knew you would.'

'Did you?'

'Yes, I wanted to thank you.'

'Thank me for what?'

'For taking care of him. He needed you to keep him safe and that's exactly what you did. You keep him safe.'

I looked over at the carousel and saw him there. *Saleem*. I watched as he sat on a carousel horse, going round and round, smiling. I looked over at the little girl I wished I could've been when I was young, and held her hand. The music played until I opened my eyes.

The spell candle burnt out, leaving a sudden smouldering scent. I wasn't sure what I had just experienced, but I knew that it was real, the memory of a subconscious destination that only I could travel to. I never imagined that I would have revisited the carousel sanctuary, a place I vividly remembered for so long and then let go of. I wasn't sure if it meant something or if I would ever return, but upon seeing my younger self again looking so happy, my heart grew bigger inside my chest. I never thought seeing him again would make me feel so much more in tune with who I was.

Knowing that I came face-to-face with the person I wanted to be as a child, I understood why she never told Sal the reason he was feeling so lost. It was just like what Barry said to me all those years ago. What I felt inside, nobody could touch. It was up to me to figure things out, even if it meant having to go through pain and turmoil, as it made it even clearer that who I am and what I'm capable of was beautiful. I could take all those negative experiences and still become the woman that every single person who tried to bring me down failed to destroy.

Despite all their efforts, they still didn't stop me from becoming the force of nature I inevitably became. I smiled at the thought of that. I smiled at Sal, who remained inside me safe and sound, the same way he protected me when I wasn't ready to face the world.

I was ready to release the circle and end my evening of celebration. I picked up my athame, ready to move in an anti-clockwise direction. I felt the energy wash over me again, its brilliance running through my arms, to my fingertips and into the blade as I pointed to the North.

I call the North, the Spirit of Earth
I call the West, the Spirit of Water
I call the South, the Spirit of Fire
I call the East, the Spirit of Air
The Circle is open, but never broken
May we meet, may we part
And may we meet again.

Chapter Twenty-One

'Is the camera angle right, Jack?'

I stood in the living room, the sofas pushed to either side to free up the back wall, ready for my performance. I was in front of the tripod that held the beaming ring light, with my phone secured in the centre and ready to film. Jack was my camera operative, making sure that everything was in place and the way I wanted it. I stood in front of the camera wearing my black sheer body suit, the flower embroidery just about covering my nipples. Red ropes were tied around my waist and arms, and some wrapped around my chest to give the illusion of a harness. My hair was a fiery orange, and considering I bought the wig off eBay for a tenner, I looked pretty good in my opinion.

I was ready to record my next BollyWitch performance, something I was really getting the hang of doing since lockdown. I won't lie, I was fucking gutted when lockdown hit, as I only got the chance to perform on stage twice beforehand and finding any gigs with venues that were willing to take a chance on me was hard enough to begin with. Something about being an Indian, trans witch that doesn't perform in English and wants to freak people out just didn't appeal to many of the places I contacted.

It was a safe bet that most clubs were after performers who did the usual pop numbers that got the basic gays and uninvited straights cheering for joy. There wasn't much room for a queer performer like me, or was it that they didn't want to make room? Either way, I managed to book a couple of gigs outside of Manchester that I was so excited for, but when Madame Rona came along with her riding crop of infection, bitch slapping as many people as possible, the pandemic took over and anything that resembled a live gig was out the window.

I was so disheartened at the thought of not being able to perform, especially when I was an unknown and finding places to establish myself were few and far between. The digital age of performing began to grow, giving artists the opportunity to do more, which was something I wanted to take full advantage of.

Being a witch is, and has always been, something I seldom promoted. I always felt that people either a) didn't really want to know, b) thought that I was delusional or c) thought that I was trying to convert them. I never felt the need to preach my beliefs onto anybody, mostly because I knew exactly how that felt and I never wanted to subject that type of bullshit pressure onto someone. I was a witch, very much so, because I wanted to live my life that way and not tell others how they should live theirs.

So, what is it that draws me to being a witch? Well, I'm a much more spiritual person than I am a religious one. It's not like I was really into religion to begin with. Don't get me wrong, I loved learning about religions in school, as it was fascinating to learn about different cultures and how religion was interpreted and applied to people's lives.

One of my favourite things to do when I go on holiday is to visit religious sites, because often they are stunningly beautiful and although I don't follow it, it doesn't mean I have an ignorant view on people who happen to be religious. For me though, I saw myself as spiritual, which didn't require a religious conduit to access. When it came to God or Heaven and Hell, I couldn't say that I didn't believe, but I couldn't say that I could either. I had no idea if there was an all-seeing, all-powerful God that was responsible for all life. I had no idea if people went to Heaven and Hell depending on their sins.

But one thing I did know was that this religious construct had such control and power, which was afforded to men who used it in ways that I simply couldn't get on board with. We hear it all the time. *God moves in mysterious ways. God has all the answers. It's God's will.* I never felt comfortable with this because my whole life I was told this, but the moment I came out as gay and then later on as trans, the tune quickly changed. *God will punish you. You are an abomination in God's eyes. You must repent.* So, which one is it then? Is God moving in mysterious ways or is there fuck all mystery and God basically wants to punish all queers? The more I saw this, the more my mind was opening up to a truth that I felt was being twisted.

The truth being that nobody knows what the fuck happens when you die or if God really is responsible for chocolate-covered pretzels, subatomic particles and Cher. At the end of the day, I can totally understand why people believe in God. Who knows, maybe I will too someday. But until that day comes, I will never tell someone that believing in God is wrong, but I will never condone the actions of those who prey on a person's beliefs and use religion as a way of control.

Being a witch is a conduit to my spirituality. Witchcraft does have an element of worship when it comes to deities and higher beings, something I struggled to find comfort in. Worship is such a foreign concept to me, as I find it difficult to devote myself to a higher power. Instead, I respect and revere nature and the energy that makes up everything around me.

The Horned God symbolises the dark half of the year and the Goddess symbolises the light half. Even though it is seen as the God and Goddess, I can see it as a way of referring to that particular energy. That's probably as close to worship as I'm ever going to get. Being queer gives me a view on Witchcraft that isn't afforded to other witches.

My whole life, I have seen the world differently. I looked inside myself and saw that my mind and spirit was capable of things nobody could comprehend or believe should even exist. For so long, I thought that I was beneath the idealistic cis, straight white people who were seen as a perfect specimen of what a person should be. What I came to realise is that I was not restrained by a forced binary, or the control of a white machine that wanted to keep me in check. When it comes to being Muslim, I didn't allow the community I grew up in to use the small-minded depiction of what a child should be so to not shame the family. I was free from all of that. As a result, I could see just what I was capable of when I refused to let my life be dictated by something I never chose to follow in the first place. I was my own world, my own universe.

I grew up believing that I had an entire world inside of me that was mine and only mine. I grew up seeing the world in a way that I hoped one day would see me in the same way. I saw beauty and power. I saw endless possibilities, even when I felt trapped and lost. It was that very belief that made me see myself the way I did. I never questioned who I was as a child. I knew how I felt inside and who I wanted to be. I felt that magick. My journey started there.

***

I sat outside HOME, waiting for Chelsie to come and meet me. I was so excited to go and watch *Midsommar* with her. I had already seen it, but the fact that it was a full-on Pagan horror that was reminiscent of *The Wicker Man*, I knew that she was going to absolutely love it. When Chelsie and I started working together, it was around the same time that Chloe started working with me too. I was their trainer and I instantly took a shine to them. It's not that often that I discovered real friends at work, but Chloe and Chelsie were exactly that. It wasn't long after they started that we began a tradition of going out for meals when we got paid.

Jack, Chloe, Chelsie and I became really close and our love of food was mutual. Every time we booked a restaurant, all we thought about was stuffing ourselves and having a laugh. Chelsie had a witchy style that I adored. Her fiery hair and subtle make-up of deep colours gave off such a mystical vibe. To top it off, her personality couldn't have been more inviting. I loved her sense of humour, her wit and her vulnerability. She and I had so much in common, which made opening up about our lives even easier. Being a witch, she too was in the same boat as me, meaning that we both wanted to get back to being more practical with our craft, and so we decided to create our own little coven. It was only us two, but it was a safe space for the both of us to talk spells and rituals, and about how we were feeling. After a while, it was almost as if we had known each other our whole lives.

When we went to our first Glitterfye show, we made our way downstairs after the first half as the performers took a thirty-minute intermission. Given that this was our first time at the show, Chelsie and I were incredibly impressed, but we knew we were going to miss the second half if we wanted to get home. We went to the bar for a drink and found some seats near the balcony area.

'Some of them acts were fucking amazing! It's so good to see different styles of drag,' I said.

'That's it, isn't it? You get bored of seeing the same thing all the time.'

'It's crazy what led us here though. To think I never would've even heard of this if it wasn't for what happened at Tribeca.'

'I know!'

'It kinda pisses me off in a way.' Chelsie looked at me, puzzled. 'I mean, I've never heard of any of these performers, I didn't even know that drag shows happened outside of the Village. I'd love to see more shows like this down Canal Street getting its props. In a way, I feel like I'm caught in the middle of belonging and not belonging.'

'What do you mean?'

'I've always wanted to perform but I've never done it. I never knew how to get started or if I even could!'

'You should definitely do it!'

'Oh, believe me, I know I can do it! It's more about whether or not I'd be accepted or if people would even give a shit. Makes me feel a little bit directionless.'

'Yeah, I get that.'

'I've been thinking about that, you know. I was looking at creating a spell that helps with my direction. I've been so unfocused lately and I can't seem to get any balance.'

'I know how you feel. You just want things to level out and it refuses to, and you end up lying in bed watching *Rock of Love*!'

'Not a bad way to spend an evening, to be fair. Although Jack is starting to get sick of me showing him clips from it!'

'Jack doesn't like watching Bret put his glossy lips all over a bunch of half-naked strippers? What's wrong with the man?' Chelsie said with a sarcastic smile on her face.

'I have no idea! He'd rather watch some serious crime drama while I'm in the bedroom watching Frenchy rub chocolate mousse on her tits in a peep show booth for Bret. We're just two very different people!'

'I'm shocked at his taste levels,' Chelsie replied with a cheeky grin. 'Have you put anything together for a spell to help you?'

'I have actually. I'm going to give it a try this weekend. I'll send it to you if you want?' I offered.

'Yeah definitely! It'll be good to get back to doing more spell work. I've just not had the energy lately. But I've been doing some reading and I found something that I really liked. It said you don't need all these fancy bits and bobs to do spells. All you need is your intent and whatever you have around that will help put your spells together.'

'Totally agree. I had a look online and it's fucking expensive to get supplies. I couldn't bring myself to spend that much money on stuff. I wish there were still shops around that sold witch supplies. They pretty much all bloody disappeared after the nineties.'

'Well, that's it, we have no choice now but to shop online and everything is so overpriced. It makes it hard to get started, but at the end of the day, magick is all around us. We can channel it in our own way. Makes it more personal, I think.'

'Totally. I see that in you, you know. Before we met, I was contemplating getting back into being a practical witch, but I wasn't sure if I could. And then you started at work. You literally came into my life at the exact time when I was basically starting over as a witch. I definitely saw that as a sign.'

Chelsie approached as I sat across from HOME. I loved going to see movies here. It felt less like a huge cinema full of young kids that get on your nerves. It was geared more towards the trendy generation that you usually see hanging around the bars in Northern Quarter, which if I'm honest are just as annoying in a more pretentious way. Still, HOME was more artsy than your standard cinema as it even had a theatre and often held small art exhibitions. Definitely more my kind of thing.

'Hello, you!' Chelsie said.

'Hey! How've you been?'

'Alright, the usual, really. Looking forward to *Midsommar* though! This is the highlight of my week!'

We sat in the cinema, waiting for the movie to start. Watching it the first time with Jack, I was blown away by it. To watch what was essentially a break-up movie in a way that incorporated a Swedish Pagan cult that turned horrifically violent was right up my street. By the end of the film, Chelsie was just as obsessed as I was.

'That's it,' Chelsie said. 'We're moving to Hälsingland.'

***

I was getting really good at putting together a digital performance after giving it a go a few times. Seeing that digital drag was blowing up online, I felt compelled to step my game up and be as creative as possible. This performance was my favourite so far. A surreal, macabre BollyWitch number, inspired by one of my favourite horror movies, *Suspiria*. What's not to love? Filming was done and I spent the best part of four hours editing and putting it all together, but the end result was perfection. I felt inspired, wanting to do more but way too knackered to get off my arse.

The evening called for relaxation, and I wanted to sit at my altar. One thing that took me a long while to get used to was sitting at my altar. Often when using an altar, I felt uncomfortable and awkward, as if I was not permitted to sit there unless I was conducting a ritual or casting a spell. It was some time before I felt comfortable just sitting at my altar with no other intention than to simply focus on myself. My altar wasn't huge, I just used a cheap table I bought from Argos and threw a witchy table cloth from Afflecks over it. I arranged my altar a little differently recently.

As any witch would attest, having an altar is an exciting thing, as it's not uncommon for a witch to either not have much space to have a permanent altar or they may not want to promote being a witch so openly just yet. I never had a permanent altar growing up, instead using a small wooden board with pagan symbols drawn on with blue marker. I never felt comfortable having this stuff out in the open in Blackburn. Being a witch felt very much like how I was feeling on the inside as a child. I knew that it felt good and right, but I knew the world would tear me to shreds if they found out.

Things were very different now. These days, I couldn't give a fuck what anybody has to say about me being queer or being a witch. That mentality came from years of not feeling that way, which built me up to a point where I was no longer willing to carry the negative bullshit that other people forced onto me. In short, they can all go fuck themselves.

Meditating at my altar with no real purpose or intention was always a good feeling. I don't know about you, but trying to shut my brain off and not think of anything is a real bitch to do. I'll start off by listening to my breathing, maybe visualise a calm meadow, which then turns quickly to that scene in *Midsommar* when Dani watches her boyfriend burn to death after being sewn into a dead bear.

Then my mind goes to Jack, thinking about how cute he would look if he was sewn into a dead bear. Then I'll skip to that episode of *Buffy the Vampire Slayer* when she fights a bear on Thanksgiving and asks Giles for a ricer, not knowing that a ricer is a tool to make mash potatoes. Then I think that having mash potatoes with some delicious brambly apple sausages and thick gravy for tea would be fit!

By that point, I open my eyes and stare at the wall, totally confused. *You call that fucking meditating?* I'm so rubbish at meditating, which is weird since it's one of my favourite things to do. I know that there's a technique to meditating that requires steady breathing and relaxation, but I'm so fucking impatient that I can't be bothered with all that and just do it my own way. A lot of the time, my mind does wander off to weird places, and at first, I got so frustrated and down on myself that I wasn't doing it right. But as time went by, I stopped that and just let my mind go to those places, because once I've done that, it usually lands at a place that calms me. Trying to force myself to visualise a meadow or an ocean or whatever it is that feels calm just never works. The moment I try and tell myself to relax, it's game over!

My altar was decorated plainly of late. For so long I thought that I needed to have everything on my altar. A cauldron, a chalice, my athame, candles, incense, crystals, potions etc. If I had a bigger space, I probably would have everything on it, but as I was using a table that wasn't much bigger than those wooden desks from primary school that you could put stuff in, I didn't want it to be too cluttered. I had my small wooden three-drawer box at the centre of the table, pushed back to the wall. On either side were two brown beer bottles, covered in melted wax that dripped from the long tapered candles. I wanted a clear space, so all I had was my incense, clear quartz crystals, dried flowers and my tarot card deck. I sat quietly, listening to some calming music and closed my eyes. Suddenly, my phone went off and I saw that I received a message.

C: Hey my love! How are you? xx

Y: Hey Chels! I'm okay, just about to do some meditating, or at least trying to!

C: Nice! Just wanted to check in to see if we're still on for tomoz? Am I ok to stop at yours? x x

Y: Of course! Looking forward to having you over! Pizza and Midsommar on Blu-Ray! Jack is even dressing up as a bear for the occasion…he doesn't know it yet ;-)

C: That man will do as his wife tells him! We'll wear flower headdresses and everything!

Y: Done! Lol! See you tomorrow! x x

C: See you tomoz. Love you! x x

I set my phone down, closed my eyes and let my thoughts drift across all sorts of random things. Thoughts of Helen Mirren as DCI Jane Tennison in *Prime Suspect*. Jack and I had just started re-watching the entire series. *I fucking love Helen Mirren.* I soon drifted to other shows that I loved to watch. I stopped at *American Horror Story.* My favourite to watch was Asylum. *So, twisted.* A part of me was always drawn to dark things. I can't tell you how many times I've sat watching serial killer documentaries on YouTube. *Too dark, Yvy. Too dark.*

I opened my eyes quickly, realising that it probably wasn't the best avenue to go down when trying to relax. *Start again.* I closed my eyes and saw something unexpected. I saw Florence, the city that is, not *and the Machine.* I visited Florence with Jack for my birthday in 2018. So many memories that I hadn't thought about in so long materialised. The music played from my phone as I sat calmly with a smile on my face, the warmth from the candles touching my cheeks. Soon my thoughts took me to a place I was very familiar with.

I was inside The Sanctuary, a place I had been to before. The room was still the same, with its wooden wall carvings and small ledges that held hundreds of different trinkets and candles. The carousel, large and illuminated, turning slowly as the horses galloped. Seeing this place always felt more like a memory to me than a dream or vision. It was as if I was returning, and although the surroundings were recognisable, it was always slightly different. I looked over at the carousel and saw Sal, someone I seldom thought about these days. I saw him on the horse, just as I did the last time I was here. He was still smiling and laughing, the happiest I had ever seen him.

I stood watching, thinking about how much I had evolved and who I was. A sudden realisation came to me that rang so true. Happiness wouldn't have been achievable for me if Sal had never found his happiness. When I was young, I experienced happiness just as all children did, but it wasn't enough. I spent so many years in turmoil after having my gender surgery. I found it so hard to connect with who I was or find the happiness I so desperately wanted to experience to compensate for all the good times I never got the chance to have as a child. Then it dawned on me, my joy was directly linked to that child. Without his joy, I couldn't have mine.

As soon as I realised that we were one and the same and my life wasn't one of transition but of evolution, it opened my heart and mind up to a world where I was able to find my place. For so long, this Sanctuary was a place I had visited, and now I knew why. It was my way of understanding what it meant to be me and how I can respect my past and embrace my future. Sal was protected, secure and loved, because I didn't deny his experiences. I saw everything he went through and allowed him to be happy by giving him a voice. I opened my eyes, a tear running down my cheek. I looked down at the candles burning brightly and smiled.

Yvolved

Chapter Twenty-Two
Florence, Italy, 2018

I never wanted to visit a place more in my entire life. When Jack surprised me with a trip to Florence for my birthday, I was overjoyed. Ever since I first stepped onto a plane, I was obsessed with travel. You'd think I had been travelling my whole life, but I only got my very first passport in 2012. For so long, I had an aversion to getting a passport, which I guess is no surprise coming from a trans person. Anything that can be seen as an official form of identification for a trans person can fill them with dread.

The main issue is usually how your name and gender is plastered all over it, and a passport is no exception. I looked outside the plane window, the wing cutting through the clouds, and felt a sense of accomplishment. Having a passport with my chosen name on it meant everything to me. It may sound trivial, but to a trans person it is anything but.

Ever since getting my passport, Jack and I travelled to so many amazing places. Barcelona, Thailand, Prague, Bruges, Amsterdam. I've never been on holiday without Jack, but our tastes were so similar that it never crossed my mind that I might want to try going on holiday with someone else. The one thing about Jack and I was that we had hardly anything in common, except each other. I loved the fact that we were so different, as it kept our relationship interesting. However, our vision of the ideal holiday was very similar. We weren't the type to go on a two-week vacation and sit by the pool all day. We were adventurers, wanting to explore everything about the places we were visiting. Lying on the beach sounds lovely, but after an hour or so, I'd be bored out of my mind.

Florence was going to be such an adventure, but I wasn't as pumped up as I thought I would be. Not because I wasn't looking forward to it, but because of something else. I sat on the plane, rooting through my bag until I found my passport. Jack sat beside me, reading his book with his earphones in, noticing what I was doing.

I sank into my seat, opening my passport and looking at the woman in the photograph. She looked scary, like a prison mugshot under bad lighting. Why is it that no matter how hard you try, a passport photo seldom comes out nice? I scanned all the information beside the photo. Name, passport number, sex. I stopped, staring at the beautiful *F* that was solidified on the sheet of paper. All the anxiety and struggle just for a letter.

'You okay?' Jack asked, taking his earphones out.

'Yeah. Just thinking.'

'About what?'

'What happened at the airport.'

'Don't think about it. It's over with. You've got such a beautiful holiday to look forward to now.'

'I know. I'm just sick of it though. Every fucking time.'

'I know.'

'Do you remember what happened when I applied for this?' I said, holding up my passport.

'I do.'

'When will it end? If it's not one thing, it's a-fucking-nother.'

'But you don't let things like this stop you.'

The flight to Florence was an early one, and Jack and I made sure to get to Manchester Airport with plenty of time to spare. I loved the anticipation of going away. The thought of getting on a plane and flying to a part of the world that I had never seen before, to experience new ways of life that the people who resided there saw as just a typical way of living. The airport was far from quiet when we arrived, so we got everything in order with our bags and made our way to security.

The standard protocols were followed, putting my lip balm and mini moisturiser in a clear bag and getting frustrated with idiots who tried to get their shit together at the last minute as they reached the front of the damn queue. I watched as they unpacked electronics from their bags and struggled to take off belts and jewellery, wondering why they hadn't done that before reaching the front of the queue. Still, I was excited that once this was done, I was a step closer to being in Florence. Something about Italy just sang to me. The only other place in Italy I had been to was Rome, which held a special place in my heart for a very big reason. I yearned to return to Italy someday, even if it wasn't Rome.

We inched further and further to the front of the queue and I was ready. I never wore much when travelling somewhere. I couldn't be bothered fussing about with jewellery and belts and opted instead to wear a maxi dress and some slip-on shoes. The quicker I was done, the quicker I could get through and have myself a nice hot chocolate and a sausage barm before take-off. The attendant called me forward first, and then Jack. I put my few belongings in a grey tray. My shoulder bag, the clear bag with liquids and my phone.

I looked over at Jack, putting his keys, wallet and phone into his tray. He barely carried anything, mostly because half his stuff was in my bag. We both stepped forward, side-by-side, waiting to be called through the scanning machine that resembled that weird entrance tube in *Spooks*. I knew what was about to happen, but a huge part of me hoped to be proven wrong. I wanted so badly to see a different outcome to what I already knew was about to happen.

'Can you step through the machine please?' The man said, motioning me forward. Jack did the same on the other side and we both stepped into our tubes. Within seconds, I saw Jack walk through, the attendants smiling and pointing to the tray area to pick up his belongings. The machine spun round, scanning my body as I held my hands up. Something about this process felt so intrusive. The scan ended and I stepped out. Nobody said anything to me for a few seconds and a sudden rush of exhilaration filled me. *Yes! It didn't happen this time!*

'Miss?'

I turned around to see another gentleman staring at me, his hand signalling me to approach.

'Take your shoes off.'

He didn't even ask. It was an order. It was then that I knew that this was going to be like every other time Jack and I had travelled together. Without exception, every single time I stepped foot in an airport, I was never told to keep walking at security. I took my shoes off and let the man scan them.

'Now put your hands up, please.'

'I already did that in the booth though,' I replied.

'Put your hands up, please.' His eyes pierced through me.

I looked over at Jack, who was waiting for me at the other side, knowing what was happening. I could tell he was angry that he couldn't do anything. I lifted my arms and cringed as I felt the security staff's hands on me, working his fingers along my body with my dress being the only thing separating his touch from my skin. As his hands continued to roam, I felt him under my breasts, gently running his little finger against them. I flinched, looking away from him in disgust.

As the lady beside me sat by a monitor that scanned the baggage, the man finished by running his hands up my legs and looking at me with an accomplished glint in his eyes. A look that said he got to do that and there was nothing I could do about it.

'You can pick your shoes up over there,' he said, pointing over at the trays. I walked over and picked up my belongings, quickly grabbing a hold of Jack's hand as he took me to get my hot chocolate.

***

The sun was shining gloriously as we made our way to the Leaning Tower. We figured that since we had to travel via Pisa to get to Florence, we may as well add a little stop to our trip and visit one of the most iconic Italian landmarks. The moment we stepped on to the warm Italian streets, a feeling came over me that was very recognisable. I don't know what it was about Italy, but I felt so connected here.

We walked down street after street, following the signs for the Leaning Tower, until we soon saw it in our sight. The streets were busy, filled with tourists and locals, small stalls selling souvenirs and groups of people trying their best to get the perfect selfie stick shot with the tower. Jack and I walked up to the tower and relaxed in the gorgeous weather. Suddenly, it dawned on me that I was forgetting to include a very special addition to our travels.

'Sweet Constancy!' I said, surprising Jack.

'What about her?'

'I left her in the suitcase!'

'That's okay, we can go back to the station and get the suitcase.'

'No, it'll take too long to walk all the way back again. Damn.'

'Don't you usually put her in your bag? I'm sure I saw you do that before we left.'

I think Jack was right. Why would I put Sweet Constancy in the suitcase? I always liked to keep her close by. I took my backpack off my shoulders and unbuckled the flap, flipping it open. I rummaged and eventually felt something soft right at the bottom. As I pulled it out of my bag, I saw her cute face staring up at me.

'There she is!' I said.

'I knew she'd be in your bag. You going to get some pictures of her in front of the tower?' Jack asked.

'It's only right that she gets the first picture!'

I looked around for a cute spot to set her down, knowing it had to be somewhere scenic, and eventually settled with a patch of grass that nobody was bothering with. Before you wonder any further, no, Sweet Constancy was not a pet that I smuggled in my bag all the way to Italy. I'm not that crazy! No, Sweet Constancy was a plush giraffe that went on holiday with us. Okay, maybe I need to re-evaluate that whole *not being that crazy* thing.

Sweet Constancy was very special. She was a gift from an amazing friend of Jack's that I soon came to love. Her name is Hannah. Jack grew up with Hannah and I got to know her more and more over the years. She was a gorgeous human with long red hair and a love for *The Rocky Horror Picture Show* and all things *Buffy*. On top of that, she was an amazingly stunning woman, inside and out. I didn't get the chance to see her often, but when I did, it was such a joy to be around her. We just clicked from the first moment we met.

When I became ill with my kidney problems, she bought me tickets to go see *The Rocky Horror Show* Live and we had such a wonderful time. I was still living with a nephrostomy tube and petrified to leave the house, but being at the theatre with Hannah and Jack was so much fun. It was Hannah who bought me the giraffe when I was subsequently admitted to hospital for my surgery.

When I was alone in my room, in pain and trying desperately to stay positive, the only company I had was this miniature giraffe who sat on the table with her cute face looking back at me. I loved that ever since then, I started a little tradition and took Sweet Constancy on holiday with us as my way of remembering not to take life too seriously. Whenever I took a picture of me and Sweet Constancy, regardless of whether people around me were staring, it gave me such a sense of fun and light-heartedness that I feel a lot of us need to hold on to. Taking life too seriously all the fucking time is so exhausting.

After spending a bit of time around the tower, we made our way back to the station. As beautiful as the Leaning Tower of Pisa was, there wasn't much else to do around there and we didn't want to cut into our time in Florence too much. We made our way back through the crowds, my hand firmly in Jack's as we enjoyed the hot sunshine. As we came to the crossroad, I pulled Jack's hand, signalling to stop. I noticed something on the wall of a building that looked like a block of old flats. Everything in Pisa looked so historic and untouched by anything resembling the sterile, modern look that comes with newly built buildings. The wall was a wash of yellow paint, the wear over the years chipping away to reveal the white stone underneath. Something was spray painted on the wall in purple. A symbol that I knew all too well and was compelled to take a picture.

It was the transgender symbol, with a fist in the middle representing the fight for trans rights. I didn't expect to see this here. I was incredibly moved. I pulled my phone out of my bag and took a picture. When I was done, we caught the train and made our way to Florence.

Hannibal Lecter holds a very special place in my heart, so the thought of actually seeing places where Dr Lecter murdered and ate his victims was too much to handle. I was so giddy. I imagined this was the same feeling a *Star Trek* fan gets when they go to a convention to meet their favourite stars from the show and become starstruck. That's what it felt like as I stood in front of the Palazzo Vecchio, staring at the balcony where Dr Lecter disembowelled Inspector Pazzi and pushed him over the ledge, hanging him and watching his intestines splatter on the ground below. I couldn't help but smile at the thought of actually being there. Yes, it sounds weird, but I can't express just how much I love horror movies, and Dr Lecter is one of the most horrifying and seductive characters I've ever encountered.

The courtyard was packed with tourists, but I couldn't help but notice that they were all scurrying around, trying to get as many pictures as possible and quickly moving from one spot to another. I stood still and saw everything slow down. I wanted to take in every second. I looked around at the beautiful statues, the stone floors, the Palazzo Vecchio standing so firmly with such greatness. *I could stay here forever.* Throughout the day, we visited the Palazzo Vecchio, the Museo Casa di Dante (where Dante Alighieri himself once resided), and the International Centre for Performing Arts. I didn't know much about Italian theatrical art, so walking through the exhibitions, seeing picture after picture of beautiful Italian sets of productions and shows was fascinating. Seeing them all set up so beautifully, I imagined what it must have been like to be in attendance at such wonderful performances.

I heard the faint sound of singing in the distance, and it immediately caught my attention. The voice was so smooth and powerful, full of raw emotion that pulled my heart in her direction. Jack was looking at some props as I drifted towards the woman's voice. I turned the corner and saw a beautiful set costume dressed on a mannequin. On the walls were concert posters and photographs of a woman dressed elegantly. She was stunning. I studied the concert posters and saw that her name was Maria Callas. As the TV screen replayed clips of her on stage, I watched with amazement, listening to her voice. As Jack approached, he could see just how enthralled I was, staring at the TV screen and listening to her sing.

'She's incredible,' he said.

'Yeah, she's amazing. How have I never heard of her?'

'I guess it's not something you'd usually listen to.'

'Well, that needs to change immediately.'

A day of exploring and taking in so much beauty took a lot of energy, and a nice rest before going back out for dinner was very much needed. We arrived back at the hotel, which was more like an old Italian block of flats. The entrance to the building was on the street, its oversized doors opening to the foyer. The lift stood in the centre, with a stone staircase wrapped around it like a coiled snake. The lift was very old-fashioned, with a metal shutter you had to pull open with some force in order to get in.

I adored how everything in this building remained as it would have been when it was first built. Our room was equally traditional, with its high ceiling and wide windows that let the sunshine illuminate the lemon coloured walls beautifully. As soon as we lay down on the bed, we fell asleep. Before I knew it, my eyes opened and I felt Jack's arm around me, holding me close as he slept. I curled up, sinking my body into his, feeling his breath gently against my neck. Without waking, he felt my presence and kissed me behind my ear. I smiled as my sleepy haze slowly started to fade.

The window was open, the fresh air slowly cooling as the sun was setting. I knew that we needed to get up and find somewhere to eat before the restaurants started getting busy. My head was heavy, refusing to lift up from the pillow. Outside, I could hear the sounds of the streets, wanting so badly to walk amongst the people and the places once more, but something was stopping me. Jack began to turn slightly, pulling me closer to him. It suddenly dawned on me, as brightly as the sun that caught the reflection in the window as it set, making my eyes sting.

It had been a few years since I told Jack that I was trans, shortly before we got married. That was one of the scariest conversations I ever had with him, given that we'd been together for some time by that point and he had no idea that I was trans. When he proposed to me in Rome, I realised that I was ready to tell him, and chose to do so when we began preparing for the wedding. He was so open and understanding when I told him, which was a response I was convinced I wouldn't get. Since then, our relationship grew stronger.

However, I still had a nagging feeling. Something inside felt unfinished, like a conversation cut short or even never begun. I knew that I had so many things to talk about with Jack that hadn't been discussed on the night when I told him. Things that I only realised as time went by, that plagued me in some way. Jack was the first man I had ever been with that found out I was trans after getting into a relationship. People I've dated in the past either knew from the beginning, weren't in a relationship with me or had absolutely no idea.

No matter what relationship I was in, whether it was casual or not, I always had to hold something back. I could never fully give myself to someone because of the possible consequences. One of, if not the most difficult challenges a trans person faces is trying to find someone with whom they can be fully open with. A lot of the time, a queer person may find another queer person to form a relationship with. It can be easier to be yourself if you're with someone who has shared a similar experience.

When a trans person dates someone who is straight and cisgender, that's where complications can lie. Jack and I got together initially as a casual fling. I was fresh out of my break-up with Benjamin, a man who didn't know that I was trans, and I kept so much from him to hide my secret. After we broke up, I didn't want to get close to anybody else. I figured that if I kept people at a distance, there was no need for explanations. But after a while, not talking about what really matters to you becomes even more tiring than keeping secrets.

However, when you are trans and navigating through relationships, often one has no choice but to keep the very thing that makes you so strong a secret. Not everybody sees being trans as a strength. I wanted to talk to Jack about how I was feeling, about things that plagued my mind way before I was even in a relationship with him. Now was my chance to have this conversation with a straight, cisgender man, knowing that I was safe to do so.

The sun had set, and we walked around looking for a nice restaurant to dine in. As it was a warm night in Florence, we had plenty of choice, but we didn't want to go anywhere too busy or touristy, so we walked a little further out to less populated areas in the hopes of coming across a quiet place to relax. We eventually settled with a quaint restaurant that had white tables and chairs lined under a gazebo covered with fairy lights. The air had cooled as the moon shone brightly. We took our seats, ordered some food and relaxed.

'I'm absolutely starving!' Jack said.

'Me too, we did a lot today though.'

'Yeah.'

For the first time in a very long while, I felt awkward around my husband. I didn't know how to act or what to say. All I knew was that I had something on my mind and had no idea how to bring it up. I had so many things I wanted to talk about with Jack, maybe I should just blurt them out. Jack looked over after taking a sip of his cold beer, noticing the expression on my face.

'You okay?' he asked.

'Yeah, I'm just, I don't know.'

'Is something wrong?'

'No, I've just got a lot on my mind.'

'Like what?'

I paused. This was as good a time as any to talk about my feelings. I looked over at Jack, and he returned my gaze intently.

'Do you remember that night, before we got married?'

'Of course.' I didn't even have to tell him which night.

'I wanted to talk to you about that night. It was such an intense moment in our relationship and I had to find that hard balance between respecting you and whatever your decision was going to be after I told you I was trans, but at the same time not letting my story become all about you and how it affected you. Does that make sense?'

'Yeah, it does,' he replied.

'It's a difficult thing to do as well because I didn't want to make it out like I didn't care what you thought about me, but it was also important to not turn it into that when I was trying to explain what I've gone through in my life.'

'Yeah, I mean, when I was sat there with you, I just wanted to be as supportive as possible.'

'Was it a shock when I told you?'

'If I'm being completely honest, the possibility of it had crossed my mind in the past.'

I was stunned. I didn't want to react to his words, but inside, I felt every nerve pinch my skin. I kept my composure and responded, 'Really?'

'Yeah, and the reason why I didn't say anything when you were telling me was because part of what was so important was for *you* to tell me. The last thing I wanted to do was butt in and tell you that I thought you might be. I also didn't want you worrying, I hope that you're not worrying now, that there was something about you that gave it away or made you feel that something was wrong with you.'

'I get that.'

'It wasn't anything specific, it was a lot of small things that cropped up over our relationship. I was pretty sure that there was something from your past that you were keeping from me. I got a feeling that something was up because, and I have no issue with this, but the things you'd tell me about your past often changed. And I don't know if it was because you yourself changed your story in the past with different people and you got a bit confused. But it was never really about things that I thought were important, so I didn't say anything. I know some people would get really angry about stuff like that and call you out, but it didn't matter to me, because I didn't feel you were concealing something that I needed to know. It didn't change how I felt about you.'

'Totally, and I knew that when I talked about my past relationships or my family, my story sometimes changed. I had to hide so much of my past to build a new future, so I fabricated so many different things. It's so tiring, when all you want is some form of normality in a relationship, but you have to keep people at a distance to stop them discovering something that you're worried will make them hate you. But the closer you got to me, the more I had to reveal about myself. And I agree, my stories changed, but a part of me felt good on a subconscious level about it because I was just so tired of hiding something about myself that I wasn't ashamed of, and shouldn't have to hide.'

The waitress came over, breaking my concentration. My frustrations were quashed the moment I saw my delicious spaghetti bolognese. I was so ready to stuff my face, but I wanted to continue the conversation. I grabbed the chilli flakes and sprinkled them on my food as I continued to talk.

'When you proposed to me, that's when everything changed. That's when I realised that what we had was really serious.'

'Probably because I'd been so adamant that I never wanted to get married!' Jack said, a wry smile on his face.

'Yeah, and I was totally fine with that when we first got together. But when you proposed, it was such a magical moment and you did it in a way that was so you! I mean, we were in Rome and I love that you tried to find a romantic spot to propose and ended up doing it at the hotel, just you and me. You didn't do any of that soppy shit or tried something elaborate like getting a fucking dove to place the ring on my finger!'

Jack laughed as he ate a slice of his pizza. I finished adding the chilli flakes and swirled my fork around, coiling the spaghetti and tomato sauce around it.

'Do you remember how I was when we were planning the wedding?' I asked, putting the fork in my mouth.

'Yeah, I noticed how you weren't that excited about it at the beginning.'

'I wasn't. I had so much that I—'

I stopped talking, my mouth frozen in place mid-chew. Jack was surprised that I had gone quiet.

'Fuck me!' I said at the side of my mouth.

'You okay?'

'Those chilli flakes are fucking burning my gob! What the fuck is this? Are these chilli flakes or Satan's fucking dandruff?'

Jack started laughing as he watched me attempt to swallow my food. Back home, I was always generous with the chilli flakes, but I made a big mistake in thinking the ones here were just as mild. I felt like I lost a few Desi points for not being able to handle how hot these flakes were, but fuck me, they were scalding my mouth like Hell opened an off-license on my tongue. I took a few swigs of water and felt fine to carry on.

'Yeah, I wasn't excited about getting married to start with, and I tried to make it out that it was because I was working a lot and we had to save so much money to pay for it ourselves, but I knew it was because I didn't want to stand in front of you on the day, knowing I was keeping something from you. A part of me thought that it was too late to tell you because you had already proposed. It felt too late in the relationship. Maybe I should've told you before, but then I had no idea you were going to propose in the first place. It was so confusing.'

'I can't imagine what that must have been like for you,' Jack said, 'because even though we were doing well, there must have been something in the back of your head saying if I tell him, would that be it?'

271

'I did, and that's because I've been around people who were so nice to me and the moment they found out, they switched and saw me as something disgusting. I've gone from being Yvy to a creature that crawled under their skin and defiled them. I couldn't bare that happening with you because you were so unexpected. I wasn't planning a long-term relationship and I was very clear about that at the start, but we developed so organically and turned into something. I hated the thought of risking that.'

'That makes sense,' Jack said. He took another bite of his pizza and I tried to work around the chilli flakes to find some spaghetti that wasn't covered in little shards of Satan's breath. I failed to do so after putting another forkful in my mouth and finding that the off-license was once again open for business. *Give it up, Yvy, you ruined it!*

'Another thing I was so scared of, and I feel so stupid for saying this, but I was petrified of you finding out in case you rejected my body. That would have destroyed me because I worked so hard to achieve the person that I am inside and out, and the moment I told you, I instantly thought that you were never going to touch me again.'

Jack put down his food and looked at me, straight in the eye. He could tell that I had been holding that in all this time. He knew that I wanted to talk to him about this.

'I can completely understand that,' he said, 'and that's pretty much why the first thing I did after you told me was take you through to the bedroom.'

My face went red, and not because of the fucking chilli flakes. My mind went back to that moment when he showed me just how much he loved me, making my whole body feel good.

'I wanted to show you straight away that I had no reservations and I wasn't going to be weird about it. The last thing I wanted was to have you thinking that.'

'And that's another reason why I felt on some level that you may have known, because for me as a trans person, it's difficult for me to be fully spontaneous when it comes to sex. It was difficult to accept that Missy wasn't able to just go from zero to full-on fucking at the drop of a hat, which I hated so much because one thing I always wanted to experience was that thrill of having sex at any given moment. I had to learn so much about my body and I learnt that I needed a bit of time to feel fully prepared before having sex. But being an incredibly sexual person, it's frustrating when your body doesn't react the way you want it to. You were so understanding from the very beginning and we've had some amazing experiences with each other. But I still worried about whether it was an issue that I needed a certain amount of warming up.'

'I mean, when I started thinking about whether you were trans, all these things crossed my mind. But none of it has ever been an issue.'

'How is that?' I asked, astounded by his response.

'One thing I always do is run through hypothetical situations in my head, constantly. It drives me fucking mad sometimes, to be honest. Every day, like totally random shit that just pops into my head about any situation. What if this happened? What if that happened? And the first time I consciously thought about the subject of trans people was when all the shite shows like Jerry Springer were on back in the 90s and it was always showing stuff like *His Wife Used to Be a Man*. I used to think it was fucking vile that they'd speak about people like that, but it would cross my mind and I'd think about how I would feel if I met the perfect woman who I loved and was happy with, and then found out she was trans. Would it change my feelings? No, why would it? I don't understand how that would ever change my relationship.'

'I think it speaks to how secure you are with your sexuality and being who you are as a person. A lot of men feel that it puts their sexuality or their masculinity into question because their attraction to a trans woman somehow taints their identity as a cisgender, heterosexual male. You don't seem to do that.'

'For me, I don't understand why someone would question their sexuality because at the end of the day, you're attracted to them as a woman because she is a woman. Finding out later on doesn't change that. You never changed in my eyes. You've always been my Yvy.'

I looked at his face and smiled. I knew that he was being sincere. Never once had he made me feel like he was lying or telling me what I wanted to hear. He was completely in love with me and showed it to me every day. For so long I had wanted to talk to him about his true feelings about me. I needed to pick the right time, when I was ready. We finished dinner and walked around for a little while before heading back to the hotel.

The Duomo was lit up with spotlights, making it look even more striking against the night sky. By midnight, we were back at the hotel and I undressed to go to bed. I unzipped my dress from behind and felt Jack take my hand and unzip the rest, letting it fall to the floor. I turned slowly and saw his warm eyes looking back at me. He smiled and gave me a kiss. I leant back and felt his arms warm against my skin as he lowered me to the bed. He lay on top of me, his kisses deepening as I raised one leg across his broad back. He moved his head and buried his lips into my neck. I leant into him, knowing full well where this was going and wanting him so badly. I turned my head, looking at the wall and noticed something that took me out of the moment.

'Fucking hell!' I said out loud.

'I've only just started!' Jack replied.

'No, look at the wall!' I pushed Jack's bearded chin in the direction of the wall, showing him the huge puddle of water that had grown across the floor.

'Bloody hell!' Jack said as he got up and looked in the bathroom which was on the other side of the wall

'What's happened?' I asked.

'The fucking toilet is leaking! There's water everywhere!'

The rest of the night was spent waiting for the emergency plumber to come to the room to try and fix the issue. By 02:00 am, our tender moment had long passed and we called it a night.

Chapter Twenty-Three

I stood silently, listening to the people around me move around in a discreet and respectful manner. We woke up early to visit the Il Grande Museo Del Duomo. For the past few days, we had only seen its spectacular exterior, and I couldn't wait to see inside.

Just the day before, Jack and I walked further away from the centre of Florence and towards Fort Belvedere, another spot that was engrained in my mind after watching Clarice Starling ask Dr Lecter about his drawings and him describing the Duomo, seen from the Belvedere. I couldn't come all the way to Florence and not stand in the very spot that Hannibal spoke of. The air was gusty that day, causing my hair to fly around like I was Medusa with a head full of snakes. I didn't care though; I needed to see the Fort and explore. I wasn't surprised to find I was blown away by it, even though there wasn't much in the way of touristy things to do there.

Although it was nothing more than an empty fort, I felt a sense of solace there. I stood at the top, looking out over Florence, the Duomo right in the middle, and felt my heart fluttering. I took off my rainbow pashmina and held it up by my shoulders, letting it dance frantically in the windy air. I knew that I belonged here.

It was our last full day in Florence, so visiting the Duomo was a must. More importantly, it was my birthday. Since having gender surgery, I had a somewhat turbulent battle with whether I should continue to claim this day anymore. I know it sounds strange; it was a strange idea to me too. But when you've lived a life that never felt like your own and then worked towards claiming that life back, I felt as though the real birth of Yvy was the day I woke up in Charing Cross Hospital after surgery. On that day, I was born.

But did that mean the date that I was brought into this world was no longer valid? Or does it now mean I have two birthdays? It took a while for me to figure that out, as I didn't want to live in the past, but I also didn't want to disregard a special day that I had celebrated for most of my life. In the end, I figured that I didn't need to do anything. My birthday was mine, regardless of how I came into this world. The day I was born, I was given my gender by some doctor and brought up as a little boy because society hadn't grappled the concept of letting a child understand their own gender. The tools simply weren't there.

It didn't make my mum a bad parent; quite the contrary. Despite the traditions of being Muslim and a society that lived a binary law, Zohra still rebelled against it and allowed me to be the feminine little wonder with a jumper on my head. She allowed my gender to flourish, even when she had no idea how I would turn out. I didn't have to change my birthday, because without my first birthday in 1984, nothing I had accomplished would have happened. I couldn't throw all that away just because it was a hard road to get to where I was today. My strength, the very core of who I was came into this world on that day, and that was something that I was so fucking willing to celebrate.

The dome of the cathedral loomed above me, grandiose and magnificent, painted beautifully with angelic images. I looked up at it, studying the murals when Jack came over to me.

'You okay?' he asked.

'Yeah, it's so beautiful in here.'

'I know. It's incredible.'

'Shall we get going to the gardens?' I asked.

We made our way to Villa Bardini to walk the grounds. It was a little further out of the centre of Florence, but I loved the quiet. It's funny how the tourists refused to walk that far, but it made walking around the villa gardens even better as they weren't cluttered with idiots trying to take photos with iPads and screaming kids running about. The gardens were full of beautiful flowers and stunning statues, filling me with inspiration.

Being in Florence cleared my mind and body in ways I hadn't experienced before. I had a special yet annoying ability of holding on to energy I didn't need any more. Being a witch meant I was very in tune with my own energy and I knew that holding onto bad energy was not good, but I found it so difficult to let go. Florence was helping me filter it all out. I sat in the shade with Sweet Constancy as Jack looked out over the stone walls at the vast gardens. I looked at him, smiling. I often wondered what was going through his head when he was silent.

One thing about Jack was he could never sit in a silent room. When we're at home, I'm more than happy sitting quietly with my own thoughts, but the moment Jack enters, he has to be watching something or listening to something. In the end we usually end up either listening to *Dio* or spending over 20 hours watching all six extended editions of *The Hobbit* and *The Lord of the Rings*. To be fair, I had absolutely no problem with either scenario. Seeing him so relaxed in such quiet surroundings was an odd sight. I wondered if he was thinking about the conversation we had at dinner the other night. I wondered if he was pondering any unanswered questions.

I still had more to say, but maybe now wasn't the time. Suddenly, a feeling of dread washed over me. *Shit! Did I say too much the other night?* I didn't want to overwhelm Jack with my feelings, but then again, he's never made me feel like I was an inconvenience. Jack was so open and understanding about everything I had to say to him, but I still didn't know if he had any burning questions for me. I picked up Sweet Constancy and we walked over to Jack.

'Hey,' I said, as if I was a stranger.

'You okay?'

'Yeah. You?'

'Yeah. It's just so relaxing here.'

I placed Sweet Constancy on a statue of a dog that Jack was stood next to and took a picture, before putting her in my bag. Looking at Jack, I held my phone up again.

'Let me take a picture of you and the dog!' I said.

I took the photo and couldn't stop laughing at Jack's expression. I loved that he felt comfortable being so carefree and silly around me. When I first met Jack, he wasn't like this at all. I could tell that he had a carefree spirit but he never fully let go, even with someone he felt at ease with. I loved that he felt so comfortable around me now. It made our relationship so much more fun. The last thing I wanted was to have a husband who felt he needed to be serious around me all the time. We made our way down the stone steps to the lower area of the gardens and walked along the pathway that led back to the entrance.

'I've been thinking a lot about what we talked about last night.'

'Yeah?' Jack enquired.

'Yeah, I was going over the time before I told you I was trans and how I was so torn about whether I should.'

'Yeah? I can't imagine how hard it must have been to make the decision.'

'It was. Mum has been with me through my entire journey, but she was reluctant for me to tell you. She was so worried about what would happen. I told her that I needed to tell you and one of the reasons she was so reluctant was because of how people in your life might react. It made me quite torn because I didn't want to not think about your feelings but at the same time, I couldn't help but feel like nobody thought about my feelings or how it would affect me. I know Mum didn't mean it that way, and to be honest, even I had the same concerns. But it still felt like I was being selfish and I wanted you to think my way, which wasn't the case. All I wanted was to be myself around you, without having to worry about other people. How did that sit with you after I told you? Were you concerned about what people in your life were going to think?'

'At first you were more comfortable just keeping it between you and me, which I wanted to respect so I didn't tell a single person. I knew that it wasn't my secret to tell and I wanted to make sure you knew you could trust me with this. But when you then decided that you wanted to talk about it so publicly with your blogs and your social media, you weren't just telling a few people, you were telling everyone of your friends and mine. I was prepared that some people might have a problem, but there wasn't a single person in my life that I wasn't willing to completely cut off if they had a problem with you being trans.'

'Were there any?' I asked.

'Not a single one. But even with my closest friends, people I would have been devastated to lose, if any of them had a problem with you, I was ready to say goodbye to them.'

'It's interesting that you say that because I know what you're like. You're not the type to be massively open about how you're feeling, which is fine because not everybody wants to be so open. But after I told you, I was constantly worried that you were telling me what you thought I wanted to hear, but you secretly resented me.'

'I can understand that,' Jack said softly.

'And it took a long time for me to get over that feeling of *what if he turns around one day and fucks off with a 'real' woman.*'

'That must've been so hard for you.'

'I had nightmares about it. Seriously. Whenever I told you that I had a bad dream, it was always something like that. Seeing you with another woman and feeling so incomplete. Like I wasn't a real woman in your eyes. Those feelings were so hard to shake. For a while I had no clue why it was happening. I've never told you that before.'

'No.'

'I've had so many dreams like that. I never knew how to deal with those feelings, but then I realised that it all came from me not letting myself believe that you were a sincere person who wasn't going to hurt me. I had to believe that I was ready for a loving relationship that I didn't need to be afraid of. I couldn't live in fear any more. I went through so many years with a fear of intimacy. I couldn't get close to anybody growing up because no matter who it was, there was always something I had to hold back. All that went away the moment I told you I was trans and in all honesty, it scared the shit out of me!'

'That's understandable,' Jack said, his tone lifting. 'The main thing that changed for me after you told me was how my level of respect for you went up. You know I already had so much love and respect for you to begin with, just because of the type of person you are. You're caring, friendly, incredibly generous and confident. But it made me realise that behind that there was so much strength that you used to overcome everything you've gone through. I've gone through my own struggles in the past, but I've always been able to talk about it. I could go to the pub and talk to my mates about what might be troubling me. There was nothing I had to hide. I can't imagine what it was like, feeling how low I have been in my life, having to keep it all to myself. It couldn't have been easy for you.'

'Yeah,' I replied. 'That's one of the reasons why I am so strong-willed when it comes to dealing with problems, because I'm so used to dealing with everything on my own.'

'It was noticeable. I could tell that you didn't want to share certain problems with me at times, but I never quite understood why because you've never been afraid to talk about your feelings and it was confusing to me. I wasn't sure if it was something you felt you needed to hide.'

'I'm not used to asking for help. It's not something I like to do because I always said to myself that nobody can fix my problems so there's no point talking about them. That's a big reason why I went down such a dark road in 2011/2012 when I was drinking and doing drugs. It was an escapism for me because whenever I felt like I couldn't deal with my feelings, it took it all away and saved me from thinking about things when I was living on my own. I'm just glad that we were able to be so honest with each other. From our first holiday in

Barcelona, we really started opening up to each other, but a part of me still had to hold back. It's one thing to be open about your ex's and another to say you're trans. I tested those waters in my last relationship and I didn't get a good response. I was scared to test it with you, because I was afraid you'd have the same reaction and then—'

'And then you'd have to break up with me?' He asked.

'Exactly. It's such a complex issue to come out as trans to someone, but the moment I told you was the right moment. Enough time had passed for you to know who I was as Yvy, and I was telling you because it was my choice to do so, not because I felt pressured. And you know what, it made our wedding day that much more special.'

'I would've hated if you kept that secret on our wedding day. It would've always been there every time we looked back at the wedding. It was so much better that we both knew everything.'

'And there's a picture of us during the ceremony when we were about to kiss and I'm smiling at you. It's such a tender moment and I remember looking at you and knowing that I had done the right thing for myself by telling you before I walked down the aisle. The fact that you were with me, it just showed me that you could see every side of who I was and you were so happy and proud to be with me. I can't tell you how that made me feel.'

Jack smiled as we walked in the shade, planting a kiss on my cheek. We found a bench and had a quick rest and took in the scenery.

'It's really heart-breaking to think of what trans people have to go through, you know,' I said. 'I hate that we have to deal with so many issues just to be ourselves.'

'I agree. I remember when I was out one night with friends and I got talking about us and there were three trans women there too who were friends with some of the people I was out with, and they were so gobsmacked that I found out *after* I got with you. They were like *plenty of guys will get with us, knowing that we're trans in advance, but it's so unheard of to find out after being with someone for a while.* And it made me feel so bad that trans people have to deal with things like this. To me, our relationship is so great and it was upsetting that it made them so happy to see it. It shouldn't be that unusual a thing. People need to wake up and stop treating trans people like this. When they told me that hearing about us gave them hope, it was honestly heart-breaking.'

'There are so many people out there who deserve love and want to give love and yet they're judged, for what exactly?' I said. 'A trans person shouldn't fear letting people know who they are. It makes me so angry that people can be that judgemental to a point where it scares a person from living outwardly. So much is to blame for that. You look at TV and news and all the bullshit we've been fed over the years to make us look like disgusting creatures. It's fucking infuriating. That's why I spoke out about who I am. I'm not going to stay quiet anymore.'

I was ready for a lovely evening birthday celebration, and I had already picked out a quaint Indian restaurant I spotted on our travels during the day. My birthday was a day I never wanted to miss celebrating. I totally get that the novelty of celebrating can often wear off as the years go by, but ever since having my surgery, it made my birthday even more special.

No matter what I was going through, the struggles, the pain, all the bullshit I had to endure, my birthday was the one day of the year that I could claim as my own and celebrate everything about me. This was my day and nobody could take it away. This was a significant moment in time when the world changed as I entered it. That was definitely something to celebrate, regardless of what I was going through at any given time. Jack had already treated me so well today.

After our trip to the Duomo and the Villa Gardens, we visited the Da Vinci Museum where he bought me a beautiful, handmade journal, embossed with three beautiful women dressed in flowing chiffon. They looked like ethereal beings in an open garden. The moment I saw it, a sudden thought came to mind.

'I need that book!' I said to Jack as we stood in the gift shop.

'What book?'

'This!' I picked it up and felt its weight. It was thick and heavy. I opened it and touched the lined parchment paper inside, noticing its high quality.

'This is it. This is my Book of Shadows.'

A Book of Shadows is a witch's most personal possession. It's a place to write spells, rituals, thoughts and anything that relates to your magickal practice. It's more than a diary, it is the tool that shapes you as a witch and a place to pour all your knowledge and feelings into. After a while, it feels as though it takes a life of its own, given that every page has something that relates to a moment in your life when you felt compelled to write a spell or ritual that you know you wanted to implement into your magickal practice.

As such, choosing a Book of Shadows is a very personal and spiritual process. I remember when I was younger, and obsessed with watching *The Craft* and *Charmed*, I was desperate to start my own Book of Shadows and went through countless books, trying to force myself to fit the mould of the perfect witch. But none of them lasted. I only got a few pages in and I already knew that it didn't feel right. I just couldn't get comfortable with the idea of writing in them, which was frustrating given that I kept a diary for so many years.

Then it hit me; the reason I loved my diary was because it was my way to find solace with all the heartaches I was dealing with as a child. I poured my soul out through pen and paper and let it flow naturally. When I started a Book of Shadows in my early teens, it never felt natural as I thought it needed to look and be a certain way. *Wrong!* As a result, I never used a Book of Shadows for nearly twenty years. I never felt a connection to starting one and didn't feel inspired enough.

I hadn't practiced Witchcraft for most of my twenties and it was only when I reached my thirties that I wanted to connect to it again in a more practical sense. I thought I would have the same struggles as I did as a child with the practical side of being a witch, but it came back to me so naturally, like I had been doing it my whole life. Still, I had nowhere to put my thoughts and write my spells and rituals.

I stared at the beautiful book in my hands and I knew I had to have it. It was already mine.

'That's beautiful,' Jack said.

'Isn't it! I absolutely love it. This would be perfect.'

'You're right.' I loved that even though Jack was not a believer of Witchcraft or anything spiritual, he never took away from my beliefs, nor did I with him.

'How much is it?' he asked.

I flipped the book over and saw the price tag, almost choking on the high price for a handcrafted, embossed book from the Da Vinci Museum! 'Yeah, I can't afford that much. Damn!' I exclaimed.

'Do you want it for your birthday?' Jack asked.

I was so moved. I knew that he wanted to treat me to something for my birthday in Florence, but this was truly touching.

'Yes! Thank you so much!'

That evening, the toilet was still leaking and the bathroom was flooded with water. The wall was getting increasingly damp as I watched the water stain travel slowly, growing like a terrible infection across the pale wallpaper. It was almost time for us to be at the restaurant and I was ready to go. I chose to wear a beautiful mustard-coloured anarkali that Mum had given to me, paired with a delicate necklace I bought from Monsoon.

We were ready to make our way to the restaurant when a knock came at the door. I walked over, trying to avoid the slight spillage that puddled from the bathroom. Opening the door, I saw a short woman, dressed in a white blouse and pencil skirt, her hair tied in a messy bun that pissed me off because she made it look so effortless. Whenever I tried to do the same, I always aimed to look elegant and wound up looking like Ms Trunchbull.

'Hello,' she said. 'I'm from the hotel, I need to talk to you about the bathroom.'

'Okay.'

'We need to get someone to come look at it again tonight.'

'Okay, that's fine.'

She paused. I could tell she had more to say but wasn't spitting it out.

'I need to ask if you have put anything in the toilet that you shouldn't be.'

'No, we haven't. We read the signs in the bathroom and we've followed the instructions.

'Yes, because sanitary towels will clog.'

'Yes, I know. But I haven't done that.'

'Are you sure?' She asked.

'Yes, I'm very sure.'

I really didn't want to get into the reason why I had no need to use or flush sanitary towels down the damn toilet. Furthermore, I didn't want this conversation to go where I thought it was heading.

'It's just that if we do find anything like that, you will have to pay the repairs.'

Yep, exactly where I thought this was going.

'Well, trust me, it's not us that's done this.'

'Please wait here,' she said as she walked off.

I looked over at Jack, wondering if this was going to take much longer as I was eager to continue my birthday celebrations and head over to the restaurant. Not long after, the manager turned up with a repair man who came to check the bathroom. He was standoffish, eyeing up me and Jack like we were the prime suspects in the mystery of the overflowing toilet.

'We need to check the toilet,' the manager said.

'How long is this going to take?' Jack asked.

'Why?'

'Because we have plans. We're supposed to be at a restaurant ten minutes ago.'

'Well, we cannot fix the toilet without you here,' he replied.

'If you knew that, why couldn't you let us know you were coming to fix the bathroom sooner?' I asked. I was so pissed. I got no response and we had no choice but to wait.

Over an hour later, the toilet was eventually fixed and we were able to leave the room. Our dinner reservation at the Indian restaurant was long gone and I was still all dressed up, ready to celebrate my birthday but with nowhere to go.

'I'm so sorry,' Jack said. 'This is so shit.'

'It's okay, but we definitely need to find somewhere to eat.'

It was creeping towards 10:00 pm and we had no idea if we were going to find somewhere that would seat us for dinner. We walked along the street our hotel was on and came across the tiniest restaurant that was harshly lit and completely empty. We weren't sure if it was empty because it was closing or because the food was shit and nobody ate there. Nonetheless, we gave it a go and walked in.

The man at the bar bounced over to us, happy to see two customers and seated us near the back wall. He stumbled slightly as he walked towards our table and judging from the state of the bar, he was already on the shots. He had a cheery disposition so I wasn't too bothered that he was pretty much legless. We sat down, ordered some food and got a couple of drinks.

'Sorry you have to spend your birthday like this,' Jack said.

'It's not your fault. Besides, I've had a great day!'

'Me too.' Jack reached out his hand to mine. 'I'm glad that you talked to me about what's been on your mind all this time.'

'Me too. I've been wanting to get that stuff off my chest for a while. I'm so happy with us and I needed to let go of the insecurities that have been with me for so long.'

'I get that. Can I ask you something?' Jack asked.

''Course you can.'

'How do you feel about opening up to me about your past?'

'Honestly, I feel liberated. I have no shame in who I am, and keeping secrets implies that I want to hide something from you and that's something I never want to do. You know me, I don't get jealous or suspicious of you because I know that you are your own person and I have to trust that you are here for me. I never wanted to change who you were because that's the person I fell for in the first place. I mean, look at how many people at the start of our relationship had their doubts about us lasting!'

'I know,' Jack replied.

'It's crazy that friends of ours thought that we would never last. I know that you're so different to me, but I love that. It doesn't bother me when you go out with your friends or go to gigs. I don't want to change you. And when it comes to your past, I never meddled because what happened before me doesn't concern me. I've never judged you for choices you made in the past because I have no need to. I know first-hand how it feels to want to move forward in life and not be judged for what I went through.'

'Totally.' He said. 'I was so worried about making a mistake early on. I liked you so much and I didn't want to do anything that might jeopardise what we had.'

'And I fully understood that. I was exactly the same. I didn't want to reveal too much about myself and ruin something that had the potential to grow. But after a while, I felt like I went from letting the relationship breathe to keeping secrets. We got to a point where our relationship had blossomed and after about a year, I knew that we were pretty much solidified but I still hadn't told you about me. By then, I figured it wasn't going to ever be an issue and continued to not say anything, but then like you said before, I had to keep fabricating my past and it got so fucking tiring.'

The food came and I didn't realise until the waitress put a plate of rare steak, chips and shaved parmesan cheese in front of me that I was absolutely famished. I wasted no time stuffing myself and once my hunger was satisfied, I continued my conversation.

'I feel so much better in myself now. I'm at a place in my life where I am so in tune with myself that I experience life so differently. I don't want to waste time worrying about us or having to keep secrets. I know that we are strong and a big part of that is because of you. You are one of the strongest people I have ever met. You've given me so much and I love that we are equals. You never try and stop me from being me and I love you so much for that.'

Jack smiled and put his hand on mine again.

'I'm just so proud of everything you've done. I know that you've gone through so much that I'll never be able to fully understand, but I'm so proud of you and I'll always support you.'

***

Being trans is a journey that most people will never experience. It's a journey of self-discovery and self-acceptance, which is then intercepted by people in power who tell us that we must fit a certain criterion that they set out. We have to jump through so many hoops and basically convince some cis, white men that we are who we say we are and hope that they don't think we're delusional.

To say this process is demeaning is an understatement. I speak from experience. For so long I had to face situations where I was having to explain my very existence, or even worse, debate it. I fucking hate that trans lives are still being debated. Why? Why are trans people asked to explain the validity of their existence? Why is being trans still a debate for some?

My journey taught me so much about myself that I would have never found out had I been born cisgender. I found an inner strength that built me up and showed me what I was capable of. I never realised it at the time, but I was continuously evolving so that I could finally lift the veil and see the world and its many truths for what they really were. I am valid. I refuse to hear otherwise.

When I see the many people in power who threaten the lives of trans people, we cannot ignore it. We see the hardships that trans people have faced throughout history, and more often than not those hardships are a result of an oppressive system led by cisgender people who want to eradicate our rights and ultimately us. You know what I say to that? *Fuck you.*

It took so long for me to realise it, but being trans is incredibly powerful. So many trans people, including myself, have had that moment when we wished we could have been brought into this world in the right body. In short, we wished that we were cisgender. It's completely understandable that a trans person may think this, given the amount of hatred one person can receive from a society that targets us. But the older I got, the more I evolved and understood the power of being trans, of being queer. We see the gender galaxy in all its vastness, which enables us to see the beauty in so many people.

I see non-binary humans, I see gay men, I see lesbians, trans people, trans lesbians, gender non-conforming individuals, I see you all and find you incredible. I see the power in us because we see past the veil. We are unfiltered and undiluted. The energy around us flows freely, without being hindered by the idea that we must conform to a social construct that we never subscribed to.

My journey started when I was brought into this world and my mum saw my potential, allowing me to grow. Yes, I went through the tough times as well as the good. I explored my sexual urges and had some interesting encounters along the way. I delved into the darkness when I felt lost and derailed. I found my spiritual gateway and became a witch. Being a witch gave me a profound connection with my queer power and the energy I possess. What I love about being a witch is that there is no right way to do it, just like being queer. There's no right way to be when it comes to your gender identity.

No matter where you are on the gender spectrum, nobody can tell you that how you feel and who you are is wrong. I learned so much about being the type of witch that fits my being, and also found that being trans is nothing to be ashamed of. In fact, I found that being trans gave me so much power. What I hold dear is my long road to reclaiming my Indian heritage and wearing it proudly. Being constantly told that you can't be queer and Indian almost cost me the very thing that forms my being. I have no shame in being queer and Indian. I wear it proudly.

The moment I reclaimed my heritage, true magick began to blossom. To see such energy flow through me and create The BollyWitch, I truly see how reclaiming what others attempted to strip away can grow into a force that cannot be reckoned with. That's what these people who try to stifle you are afraid of, and you know what? Good! Be afraid of me, because I'm not going anywhere. You will see me as the queer, Indian trans woman that I am and your approval is not needed. This realisation was a long time coming.

Was it a bumpy ride? Yes. Do I regret any of it? Absolutely fucking not. This is my story, and I wouldn't change a thing. What's exciting for me is that my story will continue and I will never stop Yvolving. I don't ever want to stop Yvolving. We are powerful beings and it's up to us what we do with that power. Start with accepting who you are and watch what happens…trust me, you won't regret it.

Epilogue

Dearest Yvy,

I want to start by telling you just how proud I am of you. You've come such a long way and although you may not have realised it at the time, I was always there with you.

You don't have to apologise for trying to forget me. I understand. I can't say it didn't hurt, but I understand that the memory of me was something that you wanted to escape. I was your constant reminder of where you came from. I was the secret you couldn't tell anybody. As a result, so much of who you are and what you said to other people had to be suppressed because of me. I get why that must've been so hard to deal with and it felt easier to try and forget.

We share the same energy. My life is your life, and my time came to an end. I wasn't intended to be in the world any longer than I was supposed to, and that's because we had a greater destiny to fulfil, which is exactly what you are doing right now. You are living proof that my life had purpose.

Because of that, I am at peace. I hold no resentment or hatred about the way things turned out, because on some level I always knew you would turn out this way. The key is to continue on and be the best version of Yvy you can be for yourself.

I will never be forgotten. You won't let that happen. It doesn't mean you can't move forward or that you have to hold onto the past. All it means is that you can find solace in the idea that my time was spent being the conduit for you to find your place in the world, and I couldn't be prouder to do that.

You know that Sanctuary you visit, the one with the carousel? That's exactly where I am. That's where you keep me safe. That's my happiness. I'm still that little boy who knew I was destined for so much more and I'm so happy that I was right. You saw to that.

Do me a favour, Yvy. Never stop shining. Don't doubt yourself. You will go forward with the knowledge that your path is endless and you have so many adventures ahead of you. Don't worry about me, I'm always with you.

I love you so much.

Love, Sal x

P.S. – If you ever need me, you know where I am.